# Journeys to Yesteryear

A Chronological History of the

## Rocky Mountain Railroad Club

*&*

## Rocky Mountain Railroad Historical Foundation

Denver, Colorado • 1938 – 2003

## David C. Goss

**EDITION LIMITED TO 1000 COPIES**

Front cover painting
"Photo Stop, 1947" by artist Philip A. Ronfor.
**COURTESY OF THE COLORADO RAILROAD MUSEUM**

◄ Inside front cover photo
Rocky Mountain Railroad Club's pride in preserving narrow gauge equipment is
former Rio Grande Southern locomotive 20 on display at the Colorado Railroad
Museum near Golden, Colorado. **J. L. EHERNBERGER PHOTO**

 For information, Rocky Mountain Railroad Club, PO Box 2391, Denver, CO 80201-2391. www.rockymtnrrclub.org

Book design and composition by Mary Sue Alexander, MSA Design, Denver, CO

David C. Goss

Journeys to Yesteryear: A Chronological History of the Rocky Mountain Railroad Club and Rocky Mountain Railroad Historical Foundation by David C. Goss. 1st Ed.

ISBN 0-9620707-1-8

FIRST EDITION

**Frequently Used Abbreviations:**

- Ed. – Editor
- Pres. – President
- Secy. – Secretary
- Treas. – Treasurer
- V-P. – Vice President

**Railroad & Other Abbreviations:**

- AT&SF – Atchison, Topeka & Santa Fe
- C&LC – Cadillac and Lake City
- C&S – Colorado and Southern
- CB&Q – Chicago, Burlington & Quincy
- D&IM - Denver & Intermountain
- D&RG – Denver & Rio Grande
- D&RGW – Denver & Rio Grande Western
- D&SL - Denver & Salt Lake
- D&SNGRR - Durango & Silverton Narrow Gauge Railroad
- DSP&P – Denver South Park & Pacific
- E. D. - Eastern Division (of the Rocky Mountain Railroad Club)
- GW - Great Western
- M&PP – Manitou & Pikes Peak
- NRHS - National Railway Historical Society
- PCC - Presidents' Conference Car
- RGS - Rio Grande Southern
- RMRRC - Rocky Mountain Railroad Club
- RTD - Regional Transportation District
- UP - Union Pacific

Unless otherwise noted, place names that do not include the state are located in Colorado.

Published in the United States by the Rocky Mountain Railroad Club and the
Rocky Mountain Railroad Historical Foundation
PO Box 2391
Denver, CO 80201-2391
Printed at Pioneer Printing & Stationery Co. Inc., Cheyenne, WY

# Table of Contents

# Introduction

The history of Colorado is forever tied to its railroads. When the first train of the Denver Pacific pulled into Denver from Cheyenne on June 21, 1870, amid much hoopla and speechmaking, it marked the beginning of the Queen City of the Plains regional prominence. No longer was the town merely a popular jumping-off place for miners and other Argonauts; it was an economic and social center.

Narrow-gauge rails webbed the state's canyons and mountains, making it possible to move to market the enormous mineral wealth that lay beneath the peaks and the farm products that blossomed on the once-barren plains. Railroads at last linked the region with "the States," meaning a journey of several weeks could be made in a matter of days, bringing a new wave of settlers.

When Carl Hewett called the first meeting of the Rocky Mountain Railroad Club for an intimate gathering of about twenty in the basement of the Union Pacific freight house at 19th and Wynkoop streets in downtown Denver on March 30, 1938, he could not have known what a far-reaching influence the Club would have.

It is thanks to the efforts of the members of the RMRRC, who now number nearly a thousand, that Colorado's rail heritage has survived. Through books and other publications, hours of volunteer effort, restoration of equipment and thousands of photographs and moving pictures, the Club has helped preserve the state's rail heritage for a new generation of Coloradans. From its first publication in 1949, M. C. Poor's now-classic and much sought-after *Denver South Park & Pacific*, rail enthusiasts have turned to RMRRC publications for colorful and accurate accounts of the state's rail history. It is thanks to the Club that Otto Perry's 20,000 railroad negatives wound up safely in the archives of the Denver Public Library.

It hasn't always been easy. In 1940, for example, the Club's coffers were running so low that member Dick Kindig pleaded for someone, anyone, to pay his dues so the Club could offer to do a mailing. In its sixty-five year history, the Club has attracted noteworthy members, including Robert Athearn, Lucius Beebe, Robert Richardson and Jackson Thode, but it is thanks to hundreds of lesser-known members that equipment and, just as important, the memories of the men and women who built the railroads have survived.

In these pages are preserved the year-by-year activities of the Club. Excursions, which at the time were enjoyable outings for participants, have become a record of the state's vanished railroads. The Colorado Midland, Rio Grande Southern, Denver & Salt Lake, Colorado & Southern and others have disappeared into the mists of history but their existence and history lives on.

Today, there is a renaissance of rail travel. Despite its financial struggles, the public will not let Amtrak die; commuter rail along the Front Range is gaining political support, and light-rail service is expanding rapidly in the metro Denver area.

It is thanks, in no small part, to the continuing efforts of the Rocky Mountain Railroad Club's members and others like them that we can look back and recall the rail glory that was Colorado's and look ahead to a day when rail travel once again becomes an integral part of the American transportation system.

—- Dick Kreck

*Dick Kreck is a columnist for **The Denver Post** and the author of three history books, **Colorado's Scenic Railroads**, **Denver in Flames** and **Murder at the Brown Palace**. He also was instrumental in the revival in 1992 of **The Post's** annual train to Cheyenne Frontier Days.*

# Acknowledgements

In 2001, the Officers and Board of Directors of the Rocky Mountain Railroad Club and the Trustees of the Rocky Mountain Railroad Historic Foundation voted to explore the possibility of merging the two organizations into a single tax-exempt, non-profit organization. During the evaluation of this idea, we met with an attorney who asked many questions. In trying to respond to his questions about the Club, its history and activities, it became apparent that we did not readily have the information he needed in an easily readable format.

Therefore, we began to assemble data that included history, activities, organizational structure, listing of Club assets, and significance of the Club's efforts in historical preservation and education. We have used original Club records, photographs, outside publications, memorabilia and the recollections of members to create what is essentially, a concrete, institutional memory of the Rocky Mountain Railroad Club and Foundation up to this point.

Putting together a book such as this volume cannot be done without the contributions of many people. First and foremost are the members of the Rocky Mountain Railroad Club, whose membership throughout sixty-five years enabled this Club to become a world class organization. The collective participation of each and every member, no matter how frequent or infrequent, contributed to the achievements, memories and history of this Club. In collecting details related to trips, excursions, field trips and other activities, a number of invaluable sources emerged. The Colorado Railroad Museum has acquired over the years, many Club items, from a complete set of newsletters, to papers, letters, tickets, brochures, flyers and announcements of Club activities. Through the assistance of Chuck Albi and the guidance of Kenton Forrest many missing pieces of Club memorabilia were located. Current members such as Jim Ehernberger, Herb Edwards, Darrel Arndt and E. R. Haley donated items from their personal collections (including photographs, memorabilia and papers collected by their fathers Walker Edwards and Ed Haley) to the Club. Darrell Arndt provided many photographs and information on trip activities from his vast collection, including the use of the Ane Clint's hand-tooled leather scrapbook. The Club is indebted to Jim Ehernberger for providing a large number of photographs from his massive 50-year collection. These images are credited to the photographers whose efforts really made this publication possible. We are thankful for each photographer's and collector's contribution.

Dick Kindig, Jackson Thode, Jim Ehernberger, Irv August, Neal Reich, Ed Gerlits, Herb Edwards and others spent many hours reviewing the text and giving candid insight of past events. In 1987, then President John Dillavou initiated a project of recording an oral history of five members of the Club. Jackson Thode, Lillian Stewart, Jack Morison, Ed Haley and Irv August participated in taped interviews. The transcripts of these interviews enriched the details contained in many of the events described herein.

Roger Sherman, Herb Edwards, Jim Ehernberger, Jimmy Blouch and Mary Sue Alexander spent many hours reading, proofreading and re-reading the corrected text. Jim caught many inconsistencies as the text was being revised, no matter how many times it had been reviewed. Roger created the extensive index, a tedious but invaluable task. Mary Sue is to be commended for her eye for balance and creative suggestions for the layout of the book. For their patience and enduring commitment I thank them.

I must not forget to thank my wife who has had to endure many hours sitting in rail yards as I scampered about taking photos and letting me take a "short detour" to some rail site. Countless times she hoped to hear me to say," Well I'm tired of waiting for another train, let's go." She and all rail fan widows deserve deep understanding of their abiding love for those afflicted with this hobby. I think she is glad the book has been published as many nights she heard me on the keyboard far past bedtime.

**Note**: Only a small number of those persons who have been Club members since 1938 are identified in this publication. It would be impossible and impractical to attempt to provide credit to each person who served on committees, as excursion or field trip leaders or who in some way contributed to the legacy of the Rocky Mountain Railroad Club. If your name does not appear, it is not because you are not appreciated, but rather because space limitations and incomplete records do not permit us to do so.

David C. Goss, November 2004

# Preface

The Rocky Mountain Railroad Club was formed in 1938 in Denver when a group of local railroad enthusiasts agreed to meet periodically to share stories, take trips and show photographs and films of Rocky Mountain region railroad activities. The early founders included men who would become famous writers and film historians. The Club began as the idea of Denver man, Carl Hewett who enlisted the aid of others including Jackson Thode, Otto Perry and Dick Kindig. Later men such as Ed Haley, Irv August, John Maxwell, Neal Miller, Mac Poor, Morris Cafky, Ross Grenard, Bob LeMassena and Jim Ehernberger would join many others to create an organization that would become known and honored for its books and the photographs taken by its members. During the earliest years, meetings were held at various locations and usually included a formal presentation or program by a member. At all times, the meetings were open to the general public.

The early members recognized that the era of narrow gauge railroading and steam locomotion was ending. The Club consciously attempted to include in their activities trips on railroads that were about to be abandoned. Trips on chartered trains were arranged with the express purpose of recording pictorially the equipment and operations of these railroads. As such they became important historical events in their own right. The Club's international reputation for promoting and conducting unique excursion trips was established in the 1940s and 1950s. Most of the early trips were on narrow gauge railroads of Colorado. In the 1950's the Club began organizing standard gauge trips on the Union Pacific Railroad, the Colorado and Southern, the Denver & Rio Grande Western, the Great Western and other lines in the Rocky Mountain region. For many years, volunteer Club members coordinated and conducted all aspects of these trips, promoting them to the public in local papers as well as national and international railroad publications.

Thousands of photographs taken during these trips have been preserved for future generations through the publication of books and videos. The Club established a reputation for scholarly and comprehensive railroad history when it began publishing books on Rocky Mountain region railroad subjects. In 1949, the Club published its first book, a definitive history of the Denver South Park & Pacific Railroad by M. C. Poor. In 1959, the Club published a *Pictorial Supplement to Denver South Park & Pacific* by R. H. Kindig, E. J. Haley and M. C. Poor. Using photographs, scholarly notes, memorabilia acquired by members and personal experiences of others, these two books recorded forever, the images of early railroading along this long abandoned narrow gauge line.

Club members took not only still photography but also movies of historic railroad operations. Beginning in 1982, the Club began producing historic movies and videotapes of films taken by Club members. Photographers such as Otto Perry, Irv August, Dave Gross and others have provided museum quality historical videography. In 1962, the Club acquired a portion of the collection of glass plates and negatives of Portland area photographer J. Foster Adams. Mr. Adams was a pioneer in early railroad photography, taking early action photographs of trains operating in the Pacific Northwest as well as across the United States. Upon receipt, the collection was catalogued and prints made from each fragile glass plate. It is anticipated that the Club will publish a book that will feature the western railroad images of Mr. Adams, taken early in the twentieth century.

The Club also has a collection of historic railroad equipment. Under a long-term contract with the Colorado Railroad Museum, a number of pieces of Club equipment reside at the museum and are on static display. In 1952, the Club

purchased Rio Grande Southern steam locomotive 20 for preservation. In 2000, the locomotive was listed in the National Register of Historic Places and the Colorado Register of Historic Properties. Two other pieces of the Club's equipment at the Colorado Railroad Museum are former Rio Grande Southern narrow gauge business car 021 the "Rico" and Denver and Rio Grande Western narrow gauge caboose 0578. The State Register of Historic Properties listed caboose 0578 on May 16, 2001. The Club also owns a rare Fort Collins Municipal Railway Birney car 22, which has been leased to the Pikes Peak Historical Street Railway Foundation in Colorado Springs. The Club has also leased to this same organization, a Los Angeles Railway PCC car 3101.

The most intensive project ever undertaken by the Club as the Rocky Mountain Railroad Historical Foundation has been the restoration of Denver & Intermountain Railroad car 25. Acquired in October 1950, the Club operated this car during the three remaining years of freight service on the Denver & Intermountain Railroad. In 1958 the car was placed on static display at the Colorado Railroad Museum. In 1988 the Club committed itself to restoring the car to its original condition as built in 1911. Volunteers have worked many years meticulously restoring this car which is now located in a leased building at the Denver Federal Center.

Membership in the Club has always been diverse. Members include men, women and children ranging in age from five years to over ninety. Past and current members of the Club are well known authors of railroad books. A partial listing of these individuals is lengthy and reads like a Who's Who of railroad historians including Dan Abbott, Morris Abbott, Robert Athearn, Lucius Beebe, Morris Cafky, Margaret Coel, Forest Crossen, David Digerness, Donald Duke, Jim Ehernberger, Howard Fogg, Ross Grenard, Bob Griswold, Ed Haley, Cornelius Hauck, Nils Huxtable, Kenneth Jessen, Dick Kindig, Thomas Lee, Robert A. LeMassena, Richard Loveman, Mel McFarland, Joe McMillan, David P. Morgan, Doris Osterwald, Richard Overton, Ernest Peyton, Jack Pfeifer, Mac Poor, Robert Richardson and Jackson Thode. It has been said that no other organization in America has among its members as many authors of railroad books whose works are known worldwide for their quality.

In addition to excursions, monthly meetings, a newsletter, publications and restoration of Club equipment, the Club performs service projects for historic and non-profit groups. Organizations such as the U. S. Forest Service, the Alpine Tunnel Historic District Association, the National Railway Historical Society (NRHS), the Colorado State Historical Society, the Colorado Railroad Museum, the Rollins Pass Restoration Association, the Forney Museum, The Ridgway Museum, the Cumbres & Toltec Scenic Railroad and the Durango & Silverton Narrow Gauge Railroad have all worked with the Club in a variety of activities.

The Club has been managed and staffed entirely by volunteers who serve specified terms as officers, directors and committee members. Many individuals have served on a variety of committees, including: the planning of excursions, field trips, programs, publications, videos and anniversaries; the restoration of equipment; the maintenance of financial, secretarial and membership records; and as archivists and historians.

The Club's vision was reaffirmed in 2000 when the Board created a Mission Statement and stated the goals of the Club as follows:

# Mission Statement

**Through our membership and public outreach, promote, educate and encourage interest in railroading by:**

- **Sponsoring excursions and field trips**

- **Hosting meetings for the membership and public**

- **Preserving and exhibiting historical artifacts**

- **Publishing videos, books and other printed material**

In conclusion, the enthusiastic and wide-ranging membership of the Rocky Mountain Railroad Club can best be summed up by a quote from Secretary Jackson Thode's letter of April 21, 1951:

Interestingly enough, the members come from non-railroad walks of life – farmer, postal employee, lawyers, doctor, businessmen, etc., with only one pensioned and one active railroad employee – bound together only by their intense fascination for trains. This preponderance of non-railroad people is still a major factor of the club's membership.

# Rocky Mountain Railroad Historical Foundation

The Rocky Mountain Railroad Historical Foundation was established in 1990 in response to Club Directors who saw the need to raise money to restore and preserve the Club's historic railroad equipment. On March 2, 1990, The Foundation was established and in June of that same year, was granted a 501(c) 3 exemption by the Internal Revenue Service. This allows donations to be tax deductible for the fundraising required to meet the mandate of preservation and restoration activities.

Since it was formed, the focal point of the Foundation has been the restoration of Denver & Intermountain car 25. This car, built in 1911 by the Woeber Car Company of Denver, served on the Denver & Intermountain Railroad Company until 1953. The Rocky Mountain Railroad Club actually obtained car 25 before it stopped operating for the D&IM. Throughout its years on static display at the Colorado Railroad Museum, Club volunteers made

various preservation efforts. When he was appointed Equipment Committee Chair, in 1980, Darrell Arndt became instrumental in the restoration of car 25. His vision and singleness of purpose began a lengthy process to restore the car to "as-built" conditions. Money has been raised by the Foundation through donations from Club members and outside interested parties. A large number of local businesses, craftsmen and friends have donated materials and time to the Foundation. Many members of the Club have made substantial donations, and through the skilled hands of many volunteers car 25 is equal to a museum artifact.

The Club continues to integrate the goals and activities of the Club and the Foundation to ensure a singleness of purpose and a coordinated vision. Directors of the Club serve as Directors of the Foundation and there is close coordination between the officers of both organizations.

*The Officers and Board of Directors hope that as you read this book you'll enjoy the story and recollections of more than sixty-five years of memories and adventures.*

# Rocky Mountain Railroad Club
## *Chronology of Major Events 1938 – 2003*

## Chapter 1: 1938 - 1949

1938-49

1950-59

1960-69

1970-79

1980-89

1990-99

2000-03

Color Extra

The reader will find that this narrative covers most all the activities of this organization. There may be some events that were overlooked, but that was not intentional. One will also see the evolution of the excursions. In the early years, events in remote parts of the state lacked amenities and sophistication that modern travelers take for granted.

**1938**    **Meetings at the Union Pacific Freight House at 19th & Wynkoop St. on the second Wednesday of each month, at 8:00 p.m. Pres. Carl Hewett; V-P. and Treas. R. H. Kindig (who was also Assistant Trainmaster); Secy. J. C. Thode (who was Chief Clerk). Forest Crossen served as Trainmaster. Dues were 50¢.**

March – the March issue of *Railroad Magazine* contains the following article:

> "I want to hear from persons interested in forming a rail fan group in Colorado, especially around Denver. Also, I'd like to organize a narrow gauge fan trip over the famous Georgetown Loop – Carl Hewett (ex rail), 1411 E. 33rd Ave., Denver, Colo."

March 30 – The first meeting of the Rocky Mountain Railroad Club was held in the basement of the Union Pacific Freight House with approximately 20 charter members present. As the years have passed, no accurate record of these members has been found. Based on the recollections of Jack Thode and others, they included: A.W. Ainsworth, Ed Calahan, Rollin Cordill, Forest Crossen, Arl Cuthbert, Walker Edwards, Roscoe Gordon, Jim Gywn, John Heatwole (a senior engineer for the Rio Grande, mainly on Trains 1 and 2), Carl Hewett, Harvey High, Dick Kindig, Les Logue, Ralph Metcalf, Otto Perry, Everett Rohrer, Joe Schick, Jack Thode and William Van Patten. Roscoe Gordon's son, Bill, then nine years old was too young to officially join, but he truly was a charter member himself. Several months after the Club was formed, Carl Hewett (who was instrumental in the formation of the Club) was offered card number 1, but he refused. Membership numbers were then assigned based on alphabetical order.

An undated, one-page typewritten letter, probably prepared by Carl Hewett announced two upcoming trips.

The first was a trip to Cheyenne to visit the Union Pacific Shops and terminal there. The Union Pacific granted Club members a round-trip fare of $3.25 on train 21 leaving Denver in the morning and returning at night on train 14. This trip did not go, for reasons unknown. The second was a proposed excursion on the Georgetown Loop. This trip was not operated either and the Colorado & Southern abandoned this route less than a year later removing the rails.

**1939**    **Meetings at the Union Pacific Freight House. Pres. Forest Crossen; V-P. and Treas. R. H. Kindig; Secy. J. C. Thode. *Rocky Mountain Railroader*, a newsletter, was published quarterly by Carl Hewett (June – Issue 1, September – Issue 2 and December – Issue 3).**

March 26 – Members toured the Union Pacific shops and roundhouse in Denver. *See photo on page 3.*

August 27, 1939 - The first Club excursion took place on the Manitou and Pikes Peak Railway. Engine 3 is shown near the top of Pikes Peak.
R. H. KINDIG PHOTO

May – Members toured the Burnham shops of the Denver and Rio Grande Western Railroad and the Pullman shops of the Union Pacific Railroad.

June – Carl Hewett published the first edition of the "Rocky Mountain Railroader" a newsletter that was subsequently published quarterly (June – Issue 1, September – Issue 2 and December – Issue 3). This evolved through the years to the newsletter now known as the *Rocky Mountain Rail Report* or simply the *Rail Report*. In the first issue, Carl states, "Our aims are to

December 31, 1939 - RMRRC at West 48th Ave. and Lipan St. (North end of route 72) on last day of rail service. **J. C. THODE PHOTO**

August 27, 1939 - Manitou and Pikes Peak 8 Diesel and train arriving at the top of Pikes Peak.
**JOSEPH SCHICK PHOTO**

August 4, 1940 - M&PP 6 0-4-2T and train in action on side of Pikes Peak. **JOSEPH SCHICK PHOTO**

impartially publicize all the railroads of the Rocky Mountains, and to assemble and preserve the history of the famous old abandoned mountain lines before they fade into oblivion."

June 11 – Members drove to Brush to observe the new Chicago, Burlington & Quincy Railroad Centralized Traffic Control system. A CTC panel from this system is displayed at the Colorado Railroad Museum.

June 25 – Members drove to East Portal of the Moffat Tunnel to observe train movements. The trip included a tour of the ventilating plant at East Portal. Had one wanted to take a roundtrip ride through the Tunnel the cost was 32¢.

July – At the Regular meeting Ms. Helen (Tatum) McGraw presented a program of movies of a trip over the South Park narrow gauge line to Leadville.

August 27 – Excursion on the Manitou and Pikes Peak cog railway (M&PP) to the top of Pikes Peak. This was the Club's first charter trip. M&PP steam engine 3 was used. The trip had been arranged by Carl Hewett and the fare was roughly $3.50. Approximately 20 members and guests rode.

December 13 – The D&RGW provided copies of two movies for viewing at this meeting. They were "Through the Rockies" and "Desert Empire."

December 31 – Excursion on the Denver Tramway Company Routes 66, 4 and 72. These lines were to be converted to bus the next day. Car 74 carried the group and the excursion was free.

**1940**  **Meetings at the Union Pacific Freight House. Pres. E. L. Rohrer; Secy. Otto Perry.**

Ed Haley, in an interview in 1988, recalled that the Club's finances were pretty thin this year. In fact at one meeting, Treasurer Dick Kindig stood up and said, "Will somebody please pay their dues – I don't have enough money to buy postal cards for Otto's mailing notices."

August 4 – Trip on the M&PP to the summit of Pikes Peak. Steam engine 6 was used.

October 27 – Tour of the Denver & Salt Lake shops and roundhouse at Utah Junction in Denver.

November – *Trains* magazine published the first of numerous photographs taken by R. H. "Dick" Kindig. Dick was well known to A. C. Kalmbach and later editors of *Trains* and other magazines. He was one of the most published photographers in the Club's history.

December 22 – Several members took the Denver to Cheyenne local to Cheyenne to photograph freight and passenger trains on the busy UP mainline.

## 1941 – 1945 Roll of Honor

The following are Club members that we know served in the Armed Forces during the Second World War:

Rollin A. Cordill, Forest Crossen, Harry A. Engleson (honorary lifetime member who was the traveling Passenger Agent for the Union Pacific Railroad), Richard H. Kindig, Lester Logue, John W. Maxwell, Ralph H. Metcalf, Everett L. Rohrer, Morrison A. Smith, Jackson C. Thode and William L. Van Patten.

**1941** **Meetings at the Union Pacific Freight House. Pres. R. A. Cordill; Secy. Otto Perry.**

March – *Trains* magazine features a number of Dick Kindig photographs in a article titled "Denver Railfan." Dick began his photography in 1934 using a 116 size Kodak camera with a top speed of 1/100-second. By 1937 he was using a postcard size camera with an f:4.5 lens and a top speed of 1/1000-second. He also had mounted a 35mm camera on top of his Graflex so he could take the same picture in black & white or color.

August 17 – Trip on the M&PP to the summit of Pikes Peak. Steam engine 5 operated on this trip. This was the final pre-war excursion.

September – *Trains* magazine published an article by Forest Crossen on the D&RGW's narrow gauge branch from Antonito to Santa Fe. Forest's colorful prose conveyed his passion and love of this area, a trait that was reflected in the many publications that he wrote.

**1942** **Periodic meetings at the Rio Grande Building (6th Floor Board Room) at 1531 Stout St. No dues collected from anyone in uniform. Pres. Preston George; Secy. Otto Perry; Treas. Joe Schick. Carl Hewett wrote Issue number 4 of *The Rocky Mountain Rail Fan*. This was simply a renaming of *The Rocky Mountain Railroader* of previous years.**

September – After a two-year hiatus, issue number 4 of the newsletter, now titled *The Rocky Mountain Rail Fan* was published, but the editor, Carl Hewett, does not identify himself.

It is interesting to note the building at 1531 Stout St. was an addition to the A.T. Lewis & Son Department Store at the corner of 16th and Stout St. In fact, the room on the sixth floor had been the nursery for children of patrons. This store and the Daniel's and Fisher's Department Store were Denver's two premier department stores. The Rio Grande had acquired the 1531 Stout St. building and refurbished the sixth floor into an Executive Board Room.

Ed Haley, who joined the Club in October, was assigned card number 42. This was the first year that membership cards were printed and distributed to members. As new members joined the Club, they were given the next sequential number. Over the years, as individuals dropped their membership, resigned or died, the remaining members moved lower in numerical order, indicating their longevity in the Club, a system still in effect in 2003.

**1943** **Periodic meetings at the Rio Grande Building at 1531 Stout St. Pres. Carl Hewett; Secy. Otto Perry; Treas. Joe Schick.**

September 3 – Carl Hewett sent out a letter to members offering them the opportunity to purchase for $1.00 (plus 10¢ for packing and mailing), a 5/16" scale drawing of D&RGW engine 3712 (4-6-6-4) that had been reproduced by Howard Ness, a draftsman for the U.S. Bureau of Reclamation. Mr. Ness took over 300 hours to create the drawing, which measured 16 x 38 inches in size and showed a full broadside of the left side of the locomotive.

**1944** **Periodic meetings at the Rio Grande Building at 1531 Stout St. Pres. R. A. Gordon; Secy. Otto Perry; Treas. Joe Schick.**

**1945** **Periodic meetings at the Rio Grande Building at 1531 Stout St. Pres. R. A. Gordon; Secy. Otto Perry; Treas. Joe Schick.**

June – A lengthy article by Carl Hewett on the Denver & Rio Grande Western appeared in the June issue of *Trains* magazine.

**1946** **Meetings at the Rio Grande Building at 1531 Stout St. Pres. J. W. Maxwell; Secy. Otto Perry; Treas. R. H. Kindig.**

July 13, 1946 - Club members inspect RGS goose 3 which had broken a pulley shaft. The trip was completed with everyone on board goose 4 waiting in the background. **J. C. THODE PHOTO**

Meetings in 1946 featured slides and sketchbooks of member's wartime experiences. Everett Rohrer, M. W. Swansick, W. L. Van Patten and John Maxwell all presented programs on Hawaii, Australia and the South Pacific.

May 5 – Members drove to Cheyenne to tour the Union Pacific shops and roundhouse.

June – Although the exact date is not known, the Club's now famous logo first appeared on stationery advertising the July 13-14 excursion on the Rio Grande Southern. Ed Haley was largely responsible for the design of the logo, showing three rails disappearing into a tunnel at the base of a mountain scene.

July – An article in *Trains* magazine titled "Denver Streamliner" included a photo taken by Joe Schick. What is interesting is the photo captures the D&SL train 1 disappearing into the East Portal of the Moffat Tunnel, and a group of Club members who are taking photos of trains at the tunnel.

July 13, 14 – Twenty members took Rio Grande Southern galloping goose excursion from Ridgway to Durango and return. Goose 3 started the trip from Ridgway, but a broken pulley shaft on the 3 forced everyone to shift to goose 4, which had been commandeered from the RGS's regular goose run. Goose 4 had just replaced goose 5 that had burned a connecting rod enroute to Telluride. Repaired overnight in Ridgway, the 5 ran to Dolores to meet the group returning from Durango the next morning in goose 4. Everyone boarded goose 5, but several miles outside Dolores, another connecting rod went bad and everyone had to shift back to the 4 to complete the trip. After descending Lizard Head Pass at top speed and meeting the regularly scheduled goose at Vance Junction, a wheel fell off goose 4 after its arrival at Ridgway.

August 4 – M&PP excursion to summit of Pikes Peak using engine 4. Fare was $4.60 and members had to drive to Manitou Springs.

August 15 – The D&RGW publication *Green Light* carried an article (written by Jack Thode) with photos of the Club's July excursion over the Rio Grande Southern.

December 29 – Tour of the D&RGW shops at Burnham, including the research laboratory. Members met at the foot of the stairs from the West 8th Avenue viaduct.

**1947**  **Meeting in the Rio Grande Building at 1531 Stout St. Pres. C. S. Ryland; Secy. Otto Perry; Treas. W. L. Van Patten.**

May 30, 1947 – The Club's train stands at the Ridgway Station, proudly diplaying the tail plate used for the first time. **FOREST CROSSEN PHOTO**

Club members Ed Haley and Charlie Ryland construct a tailplate (or drumhead) for mounting on Club trips. Ed designed the logo still in use today and using materials from around the house (including Ed's daughter's playpen) they made a 28 inch diameter wooden plate. Using an enlarger, they were able to reproduce the Club's logo and printed it on enlargement paper. For less than $10, these members built a drumhead that was placed on many excursions for more than twenty different railroads and one that is still maintained by the Club.

May 30, 31 – Excursion on the Rio Grande Southern from Ridgway to Dolores via Lizard Head Pass. RGS engine 20 was used between Ridgway and Dolores. However, due to leaky boiler flues, D&RGW engine 319 was used on the return. The four-car train included two coaches 320 and 306, a gondola on the end and caboose 0403 behind the locomotive. This was the first time the tailplate was used on an excursion. The fare for this trip was $13.50 for railroad tickets and a noon meal both days. Hotel accommodations in Dolores were an additional $1.50. The hotel menu boasted T-bone steak for $1.50, Roast Pork for 80¢ and breakfast for fifty or seventy-five cents. The *Ouray County Herald* reported that 55 members took the trip. The oldest person was 81 and the youngest, three and a half. Riders came from as far away as New Jersey, Michigan and California.

June 22 – Excursion on the Denver & Intermountain from Denver to Golden via the Morrison Branch, using car 23. Members were encouraged to take their own lunch, and the announcement stated, "A popular Golden product will be available at 5 cents per 11 oz. container." The price for the trip was 75¢ per ticket, provided at least 40 passengers rode. Tickets for this excursion carry the date of June 6, but the trip was actually run on June 22. The total cost to the Club for this trip was approximately $100.

September 6, 7 – As advertised in August issue of *Trains* magazine, the Club operated a D&RGW narrow gauge excursion from Salida to Cimarron through the

May 30, 1947 - RGS engine 20 at Lizard Head Pass between Ridgway and Dolores. **R. H. KINDIG PHOTO**

May 31, 1947 - D&RGW engine 319 was used on the return trip.

**R. H. KINDIG PHOTO**

September 6, 1947 - D&RGW engine 499 pulls the Club's excursion train on top of Marshall Pass. **OTTO C. PERRY PHOTO**

June 22, 1947 - Club excursion on Denver & Intermountain car 23 from Denver to Golden via the Morrison Branch. Passingers are boarding at the Interurban Loop at 15th and Curtis St. **C. S. RYLAND PHOTO**

Black Canyon and return via Gunnison and Marshall Pass. Fare was $5.00 and included overnight accommodations in Gunnison.

September 6 - The five-car train consisted of a baggage car, three coaches and the parlor car "Chama " on the rear. Engine 499 handled train from Salida to Gunnison.

September 7 – Trip to Cimarron through the Black Canyon using engine 361. Gondola 1115 was added to the head end of the five-car train for the segment to Cimarron and back. Engine 499 handled the train between Gunnison and Salida.

October 12 – D&IM narrow gauge excursion from Denver to Leyden and Golden. Cars .02 and .03 were used. Car .02 carried the Club's drumhead on the front above the cowcatcher.

1948    **Meetings at the City and County of Denver Municipal Courtroom 101. Pres. E. J. Haley; Secy. Otto Perry; Treas. Les Logue. At this time, there was no "Trip Chairman" and it fell upon the President to organize and arrange for all trips.**

The Club's logo appeared on membership cards for the first time this year and has appeared every year since.

1938-49
1950-59
1960-69
1970-79
1980-89
1990-99
2000-03
Color Extra

September 6, 1947 - D&RGW 499 emerges from the snowshed atop Marshall Pass. **R. H. KINDIG PHOTO**

April 25, 1948 – D&RGW train 10 stopped briefly at scenic Rock Creek Canyon on the former D&SL line so members could pose for a quick photo near the observation car "Royal Gorge." **E. J. HALEY PHOTO**

It is interesting to note that early Club excursion tickets were actually printed on photographic paper. Ed Haley would take a Club envelope with the logo on it and letter what needed to be placed on the ticket. Charlie Ryland would then shoot a reduced negative and print 60 or 70 tickets and use dyes to color them for half (children's) fare or full fare. These rare tickets are quite unusual. How much has changed with computers and desktop publishing. The ease has improved, but not necessarily the quality.

March – In an article in *Trains* magazine, Willard Anderson described a five-day excursion by California railfans on the Rio Grande Southern and D&RGW. Engine 20 is shown in several photos as are the interiors of the cars ridden. The article also humorously describes railfans in general and their different approaches to photography and train riding. Although not about the Club, the article gives

insights to typical Club trips when it describes, camaraderie, humor, misadventures and Colorado narrow gauge railroading.

April 14 – Tenth Anniversary Dinner was held in Golden at the La Ray Hotel, which included trip on D&IM standard gauge interurban car 25 from Denver to Golden and return. This special car departed the Loop in Denver at 6:00 p.m. and left Golden at 10:00 p.m. Grilled filet mignon was the featured entrée. Dick Kindig presented slides of early Club days. M. W. Swansick showed the color movie "Parade on Sherman Hill" and Charles Ryland presented the color movie "Route of the Silver San Juan."

April 24, 25 – Trip on the Denver & Salt Lake from Denver to Craig using D&SL engine 119 (a 2-8-0) in the chartered observation car "Royal Gorge" behind the regular coach and baggage car. Heavy snow fell throughout the day almost all the way to Craig. Near Crescent, 21 miles outside Denver, the locomotive hit a rock damaging a cylinder cock. Repairs took about an hour, but the crew had a spare part on board. George Trout, in a letter he wrote describing the trip, noted there was more rail traffic between Phippsburg and Craig on Saturday than on the mainline. The train arrived in Craig at 8:05 p.m., having been delayed by rockslides twice between Orestod and Toponas. George noted that the train orders stated "Look out for rocks where rocks are liable to fall." The next morning, the train left Craig at 6:30 a.m. and the return trip was without incident. Snow showers were encountered until reaching the Front Range. Several photo opportunities were provided. Twenty-seven members rode the train, including six children. George noted that on Sunday, April 25 they met a freight at Egeria with engine D&RGW 3612 on the head end and former D&SL mallet 200 (not yet renumbered as a D&RGW locomotive) cut in as helper.

June 6 – D&IM standard gauge excursion to Golden, departed Denver from 12th and River Drive (the South Barn) for Golden. Electric locomotives 1106 and 1107 were used along with two "900-series" heavyweight coaches rented from the D&RGW along with D&IM caboose 902.

August 1 – Thirty-two members participated in a field trip to Waldorf, to attend in the dedication of the Mt. Wilcox monument. Gov. John Vivian officiated (the monument is long gone).

September 18, 19 – Two-day D&RGW narrow gauge excursion from Salida to Gunnison and Cimarron with a Saturday afternoon round trip to Crested Butte. The fare was $12.00, which included overnight accommodations in Gunnison. This was the largest train that the Club ever operated over Marshall Pass. Travel from Denver to Salida was by private automobile. Riders could purchase sandwiches and beverages on the train.

September 18 – This day's consist included two baggage cars, seven coaches, the parlor car "Chama" and the glass-topped observation car "Silver Vista" on the rear. Passengers were asked to limit their time in the "Silver Vista" to an hour to allow all riders the chance to ride in this car. Engine 494 provided the motive power all day.

September 19 – Continuation of the previous day's trip from Gunnison to Cimarron via the Black Canyon of the Gunnison. The eleven-car train was powered by engine 361 from Gunnison to Cimarron. In Cimarron, the local Chamber of Commerce delivered baskets of tree-ripened peaches to the train for the riders. Just west of Sapinero, engine 361 slipped an eccentric, requiring rescue by engine 360, which was at Gunnison. The delay was several hours as the 360 was cold at the time of callout. On this portion of the trip, an unfortunate accident claimed the life of a passenger, Anna Love. During a photo stop, it is speculated that Anna, who had a history of heart trouble, may have suffered a heart attack and fallen into the Gunnison River. Her body was found later near the Gunnison Intake Tunnel. Soon after that, the Club began carrying liability insurance to cover passengers on trips.

After the return to Gunnison, the train continued to Salida via Marshall Pass. Engine 494 was the road engine and the 498 was added as helper at Sargent for the trip to the summit of Marshall Pass. At the summit, the helper engine was cut off and the train arrived in Salida at midnight. A full moon illuminated the trip over the pass to the delight of passengers in the tightly packed "Silver Vista." To top off the trip, upon arrival in Salida, the roof of one of the coaches caught fire because the interior lamp was turned up too high. It is interesting to note that Bob Richardson and Carl Helfin made their first Colorado narrow gauge excursion on this trip. Consequently, the next year they moved from Akron, OH, to Alamosa, where they became partners in the Narrow Gauge Motel.

Souvenir ticket for the September 18-19, 1948 D&RGW "Silver Vista" excursion through the Black Canyon of the Gunnison.

September 19, 1948 – Engine 361 slipped an eccentric just west of Sapinero. Members pose while waiting for another engine to come from Gunnison, Standing, left to right, back row: Jack Thode, Joe Schick, Bill Gordon, Gail Wilhelm, Morris Cafky, Margaret and Preston George, H.P. Thode, Morrison Smith, Ed Haley and Jack Riley. Front row: Charlie Ryland, Les Logue, Mac Poor and John Maxwell.

R. H. KINDIG PHOTO

1938-49
1950-59
1960-69
1970-79
1980-89
1990-99
2000-03
Color Extra

This trip was also the Club's first excursion using the "Silver Vista," a narrow gauge car with a glass observation roof. The car was built from former coach 313 by the Denver & Rio Grande Western in 1947 and offered riders a unique view of the spectacular terrain and scenery along the D&RGW right of way. The car held approximately 36 seated passengers although many times the car had more due to standing riders. It was approximately 44 feet long with steel sides and ends and a woodsteel reinforced underframe. Unfortunately, the car was destroyed in a fire in the Alamosa shops in 1953.

Club membership had reached 91. Associate members were those members out-of-state who could not regularly attend meetings. Twenty-one of the 91 members were associates.

February 6, 1949 – The Club's only trip on the Midland Terminal Railway. This R. W. Andrews photo of engine 59, a 2-8-0, was taken at Cascade. **TOM KLINGER COLLECTION**

**1949**     **Meetings at the City and County of Denver Municipal Courtroom 101. Pres. E. J. Haley; V-P. Irv August; Secy. Otto Perry; Treas. Les Logue; Trainmaster Morris Cafky and Dispatcher, J. C. Thode. No monthly newsletter.**

In her recollections, Lillian Stewart recalled (in 1987) that when she joined in 1949, there were only a few women as members. A count of the 1949 roster indicates that 39 women were members, most of whom were not spouses of male members. The total membership that year numbered nearly 220. She also recalls that there was an understanding that women listened, but did not actively participate or speak out. Lillian remembers that Carolyn Bancroft, Colorado historian and member of the Denver Women's Press Club, once objected to a Club meeting that would have conflicted with her attendance at a Press Club. The Club meeting was postponed and her outspoken opinions changed the role of women in the Club. To that end, many notable women served in leadership and volunteer roles within the Club throughout the years.

February 6 – The Club's only Midland Terminal Railway excursion train ran from Colorado Springs to Cripple Creek. On this last run, engine 59 and four cars

were used. The first baggage-coach was the former D&RGW self-propelled motor coach 592 that had been used on the Westcliff Branch and the second was a D&RGW baggage-coach used on the Aspen branch. The other two cars were an ex-Cripple Creek Short Line combine 20 and wooden observation car 29, which was formerly Colorado Midland car 111. One hundred and sixty-nine members and guests participated, including the famous newsman, Lowell Thomas. The fare was $7.00 and the temperature on this clear, sunny day was minus six degrees F. Members drove to the Midland Terminal Yard in Colorado Springs and furnished their own lunches. As reported by the Keenesburg, Colorado *Keene Valley Sun* as many as 37 automobiles were counted keeping pace with the train from Colorado Springs to Cripple Creek and return. Member Joe Schick lived in Keenesburg and the local paper carried a number of articles during these years about Club trips.

March 31 – Volume II, Issue 1 (untitled) of the newsletter was published. Several photos were included. Morris Cafky and Jack Thode acted as historian and dispatcher, respectively. The publication schedule was "…when the spirit moves us, at least for the present."

May 14, 15 – Club members, including Ed Haley, Irv August, Les Logue, Jack Thode, Dan Peterson, Ralph McClure, Bob Andrews and several others repainted RGS business car B20 "Edna" at Ridgway in preparation for the Memorial Day excursion.

May 28, 29, 30 – Combination RGS/D&RGW excursions from Ridgway to Telluride and Pandora Basin, returning to Telluride and then on D&RGW through the Black Canyon.

May 28, 1949 – Members enjoy the scenery at Pandora (near Telluride) on this Rio Grande Southern excursion train. Black Bear Pass is seen in the distance.
**R. H. KINDIG PHOTO**

May 28 – For the trip from Ridgway to Telluride and Pandora Basin, engine RGS 74 (ex-Colorado & Southern) was used. There were two passenger cars (coach 311 and business car "Edna"), two gondolas and caboose 0400 in this consist. The fare for this trip was $17.50 and included overnight accommodations in Telluride (but no single accommodations) as well as supper and breakfast. One could sleep on the train if they wanted. If members used their own sleeping bag, the fare was $16.00. Irv August recalled, in a interview in 1987, that Marie Heyden, a member of the Colorado Mountain Club, surprised the crew when she climbed down off the coal pile in the tender, covered with soot and began yodeling (she was originally from Switzerland) as the train crossed Leopard Creek Trestle on the descent from Dallas Divide.

May 29 – RGS excursion from Telluride to Lizard Head Pass and return to Ridgway, again with RGS engine 74. At Matterhorn, goose 4 handling train 372 between Dolores and Ridgway failed on the mainline and had to be pulled into the clear by the excursion train. Again, near Lizard Head Pass, the train was called to pull into the clear of the main track stalled work goose 6.

May 30 – Club's last D&RGW trip through the Black Canyon was also the last passenger train though the canyon. The trip originated and terminated in Gunnison and was operated as an extension of the RGS excursion on the 28th and 29th. Tickets could be purchased at the train Monday morning so no reservations were necessary. The train left Gunnison at 9:00 a.m. for Cimarron where it was turned. Locomotive 361 was used to pull the nine-car train. The train included baggage car 126, seven coaches (including 306, 280, 284, 312, 319 and two unidentified others) plus the "Silver Vista" on the rear. Roundtrip fare for adults was $3.25 and $1.75 for children.

July 17 – Trip on the M&PP to the summit of Pikes Peak. Locomotive 6 was used.

August 28 – D&IM excursion to Golden using electric locomotives 1106 and 1107. The train consisted of two D&RGW coaches 1000 and 1004 and D&IM caboose 903.

September 25 – D&RGW narrow gauge excursion from Salida to Monarch to Villa Grove via Poncha Pass and return. Engine 499 was used on this six-car train. The train consisted of baggage car 163, coaches 306, 284, 280 and 319, with the "Silver Vista" on the rear. This was the first passenger train to Monarch in over sixty years. Only the locomotive could be turned at Monarch. The train was pulled backward to Poncha Junction.

November – This month's issue of *Trains* magazine featured photos by Robert W. Andrews, John W. Maxwell and Herb O'Hanlon in an article "Mikados to Monarch." Like so many members of the Club at this time, photographers such as these men recorded the last narrow gauge and standard gauge steam operations in Colorado. Articles and photos by Club members appeared throughout the years in *Trains* magazine, *Railroad Magazine* and many other publications, giving rise to the quality reputation of the Club and its members.

December 30, January 2 – Several Club members took a trip from Denver to Alamosa on D&RGW train 15. Then they took train 115 to Chama and to Durango, returning on train 116 Durango to Alamosa on January 1. They returned on train 16, arriving in Denver on January 2, 1950.

1938-49
1950-59
1960-69
1970-79
1980-89
1990-99
2000-03
Color Extra

August 28, 1949 – Seen just north of the Denver Federal Center on the Remington Arms branch, this D&IM excursion was double-headed despite having ony two coaches and a caboose. **E. J. HALEY PHOTO**

August 28, 1949 - D&IM is westbound at Federal Boulevard. **HERB OHANLON PHOTO**

The Club published its first book, *Denver South Park & Pacific* by M. C. Poor. The approximate cost of publishing was $9,000. The original idea was submitted to the Railway & Locomotive Historical Society, which wanted to condense the story down to fit the size of one of their bulletins. Approximately ten members each signed a promissory note of $1000 to cover the initial costs of printing. Because World Press was a small company, the first portion of the book was printed, and then the lead type that was used was melted to be recast to print the remaining portion. Hence, no reprints were possible after the book sold out in the fall of 1950. Publication date shows 1948, but the manuscript was not back from the printer until after March 1949. The limited edition run (1,000 copies) of the book cost $10.00 if ordered prior to February 15, 1949 and $12.50 thereafter. For the first one hundred persons who sent their remittance with their order, they received a section of the original South Park rail from the Alpine Tunnel.

With the publication of this book, the Club began a long and beneficial relationship with World Press. Besides publication of five hardcover books, World Press printed countless tickets, excursion flyers, onboard handouts, rosters, membership cards and stationery items for the Club.

After a fund raising effort, which began in May, the Club donated money to the Colorado State Historical Society to assist them in obtaining and preserving the photographic works of pioneer Western photographer W. H. Jackson.

During 1949, Mr. Jack Pfeifer of Omaha rode several Club trips, including the RGS and D&RGW in May. He rode the M&PP in July, and the D&RGW Monarch-Villa Grove trip in September. By the end of the year, Jack was member number 250 and good friends with Dick Kindig. Based on the Club's format, Jack and a number of railfans from the Omaha and Lincoln area met on October 21, to form a rail enthusiasts group. Eighteen people turned out for the first meeting and by January 13, 1950, at the third meeting, officers were elected, dues established and meeting nights set up. In March, Jack proposed the club be called the Iowa-Nebraska Railroad Club. However, other members were less than enthusiastic and someone suggested the Camerail Club instead. Thus, the formation of the Camerail Club in many ways paralleled the formation of the Rocky Mountain Railroad Club. It too has become widely known and respected for its excursions, authoritative information on midwestern and western railroading, newsletters, and top quality meetings. In correspondence from Jack in 2001, he states, "Beyond a doubt the existence of the Camerail Club is the direct result of my chance encounter with Dick Kindig in the Cheyenne yards, September 27, 1947 and my positive experience on the Rocky Mountain Railroad Club's excursions during 1949." He praises Dick Kindig for his positive nature and good humor. "...he never spoke unkindly about anyone and rarely, if ever, did he turn down a request for assistance or photos." Jack also states, "During my first contacts with other Rocky Mountain Railroad Club members in 1949, I was impressed by their friendliness and the manner in which their activities were organized and operated. The club rolled along like a well oiled machine." Jack's membership number in August 2003 was 15.

1938-49
1950-59
1960-69
1970-79
1980-89
1990-99
2000-03
Color Extra

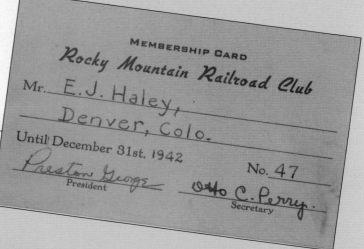

**ROCKY MOUNTAIN RAILROAD CLUB**

Invites all interested in locomotives and railroading in general to meet with them at the---

UNION PACIFIC FREIGHT HOUSE

Second Wednesday of Each Month at 8 P. M.

JACK THODE, SECY.
2251 FOREST STREET -- EAst 6048
DENVER, COLO.

LADIES INVIT

1939 – 1941 - Early meetings at the Union Pacific Freight House were announced on postcards like this.

MEMBERSHIP CARD

*Rocky Mountain Railroad Club*

Mr. E. J. Haley,
Denver, Colo.

Until December 31st. 1942

Preston George
President

No. 47

Otto C. Perry.
Secretary

1942 – The first membership cards were simple, hand-printed cards like this one that belonged to Ed Haley.

1942 – 1948 – Meetings were held in this room of the Rio Grande Building.

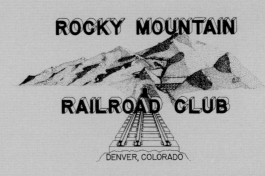

ROCKY MOUNTAIN

RAILROAD CLUB

DENVER, COLORADO

1946 – The Club's now famous logo first appeared on stationery.

---

**Railroad Interest in the Denver Area**

*In the city:* Union Station. Best hours are from 7 to 9:45 a. m. when streamliners of all railroads are represented among 23 arrivals and departures. D&RGW Burnham shops may be seen from the Eighth Avenue viaduct.

*One day railroad trips:* Lv. 9:50 a. m., D&SL station, ride to foot of mountains, along the escarpment, then into beautiful canyons to East Portal, Moffat Tunnel, 11:57. Detrain or continue through tunnel to Winter Park 12:12. Return to Denver from Winter Park at 12:38 or from East Portal 12:54. Arr. Denver 3 p. m.

To the Royal Gorge on D&RGW's *Scenic Limited.* Lv. Denver 8 a. m. Arr. Royal Gorge

12:45. Take cable railway to crest and back. Lv. Royal Gorge 3:49. Arr. Denver 8:45.

*Interurban:* Narrow gauge and standard gauge to Golden, fine trip. Frequent service.

*If you are driving:* You can spend weeks tracking down railroad interest in the area. Plan your trips to include: Boulder, Ward, East Portal, Central City (old C&S locomotive spotted here and another at Idaho Springs near by), Georgetown, Silver Plume (site of famous loop), South Platte Canyon, Como.

In any case you will find TRAINS map of Colorado railroads invaluable in making your visit more interesting. It shows all railroads and has historic notes about them as well. $1 postpaid.

1946 – Bordered table showing "Railroad Interest in the Denver Area" from the July 1946 issue of *Trains* magazine.

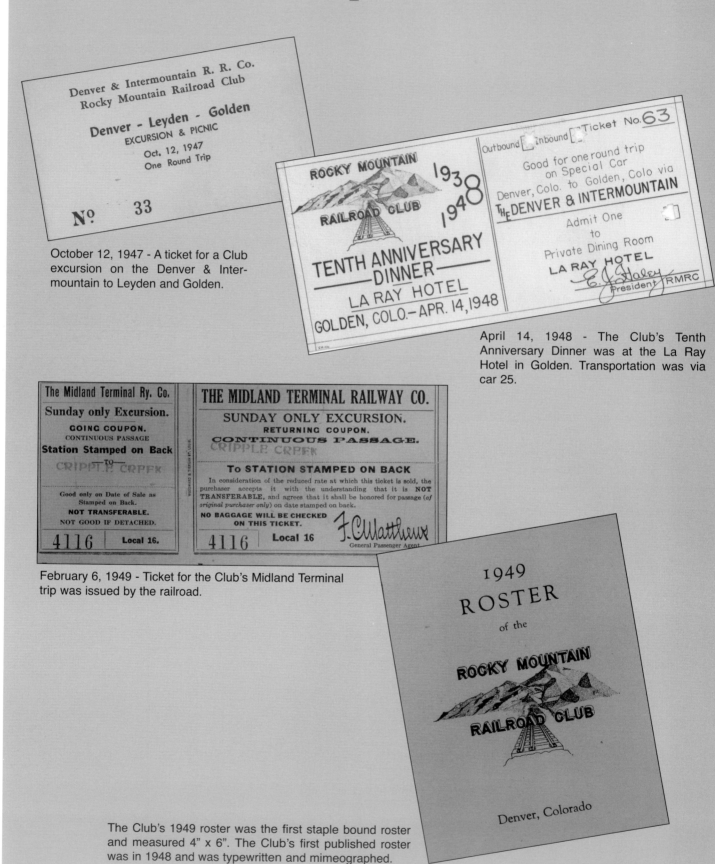

Denver & Intermountain R. R. Co.
Rocky Mountain Railroad Club

**Denver - Leyden - Golden**
EXCURSION & PICNIC

Oct. 12, 1947
One Round Trip

No. 33

October 12, 1947 - A ticket for a Club excursion on the Denver & Intermountain to Leyden and Golden.

ROCKY MOUNTAIN RAILROAD CLUB

1938
1948

TENTH ANNIVERSARY DINNER
LA RAY HOTEL
GOLDEN, COLO.- APR. 14, 1948

Outbound Inbound   Ticket No. 63
Good for one round trip on Special Car
Denver, Colo. to Golden, Colo via
THE DENVER & INTERMOUNTAIN
Admit One
to
Private Dining Room
LA RAY HOTEL
E. J. Haley
President RMRC

April 14, 1948 - The Club's Tenth Anniversary Dinner was at the La Ray Hotel in Golden. Transportation was via car 25.

The Midland Terminal Ry. Co.
**Sunday only Excursion.**
GOING COUPON.
CONTINUOUS PASSAGE
**Station Stamped on Back**
TO
CRIPPLE CREEK
Good only on Date of Sale as Stamped on Back.
**NOT TRANSFERABLE.**
NOT GOOD IF DETACHED.
4116 | Local 16.

THE MIDLAND TERMINAL RAILWAY CO.
**SUNDAY ONLY EXCURSION.**
RETURNING COUPON.
**CONTINUOUS PASSAGE.**
CRIPPLE CREEK
**To STATION STAMPED ON BACK**
In consideration of the reduced rate at which this ticket is sold, the purchaser accepts it with the understanding that it is **NOT TRANSFERABLE**, and agrees that it shall be honored for passage (of original purchaser only) on date stamped on back.
**NO BAGGAGE WILL BE CHECKED ON THIS TICKET.**
4116 | Local 16
F. C. Matthews
General Passenger Agent

February 6, 1949 - Ticket for the Club's Midland Terminal trip was issued by the railroad.

1949
ROSTER
of the

ROCKY MOUNTAIN
RAILROAD CLUB

Denver, Colorado

The Club's 1949 roster was the first staple bound roster and measured 4" x 6". The Club's first published roster was in 1948 and was typewritten and mimeographed.

# Photo Extra 1938 - 1949

1938-49

1950-59

1960-69

1970-79

1980-89

1990-99

2000-03

Color Extra

June 11, 1939 - Members drove to Brush to see a new centralized traffic control system operated by the Chicago, Burlington and Quincy. Left to right: unidentified. Jackson Thode, Everett Rohrer, Homer High, Forest Crossen, unidentified, William L. VanPatten. **R. H. KINDIG PHOTO**

August 27, 1939 - M&PP engine 3 waits at the top of Pikes Peak for the downhill departure of the Club's excursion. **R. H. KINDIG PHOTO**

May 5, 1946 - Big Boy 4012 is the backdrop for these members in Cheyenne. Left to right – John Maxwell, Betty Maxwell, Joe Schick, unidentified, Everett Rohrer, Otto Perry, Ed Haley, Dick Kindig, William VanPatten and Betty Logue.
**LES LOGUE PHOTO**

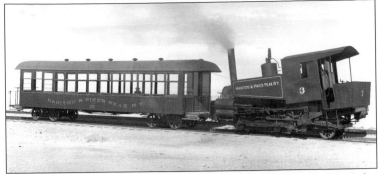

October 27, 1940 - Members tour the Denver & Salt Lake roundhouse and shops in Denver. **R. H. KINDIG PHOTO**

May 30, 1947 - In a classic and timeless pose, RGS engine 20 waits to depart Trout Lake with its four-car train.
**R. H. KINDIG PHOTO**

May 31, 1947 - D&RGW 319 was leased by the Rio Grande Southern to fill in for RGS engine 20 on the return trip from Dolores to Ridgway. Number 20 had developed steam leaks. This was the Club's only trip behind a C-18 class locomotive.
**R. H. KINDIG PHOTO**

September 7, 1947 – Members pose at Cimarron on the second day of an excursion over Marshall Pass and through the Black Canyon.
**E. J. HALEY PHOTO**

April 24, 1948 – A boulder at the entrance of a tunnel at Rock Creek Canyon slows, but does not halt the Club's trip on the Denver & Salt Lake. **C. S. RYLAND PHOTO**

April 25, 1948 – D&SL engine 119 awaits departure from the station in Craig. This was the Club's only trip with a Denver & Salt Lake locomotive. **RMRR CLUB ARCHIVES**

September 18, 1948 – D&RGW 494 slowly backs into the station at Crested Butte, the Club's only excursion to this station. **R. H. KINDIG PHOTO**

September 19, 1948 – Turning the Club's train at Cimarron. **M. C. POOR PHOTO**

September 19, 1948 – The "Silver Vista" was a favorite car that was used on many Club trips until it was destroyed by fire in 1953. **R. H. KINDIG PHOTO**

September 19, 1948 – D&RGW engine 361, a 2-8-0, eases the Club's special past the Cimarron Station. **RALPH HALLOCK PHOTO**

1938-49

1950-59

1960-69

1970-79

1980-89

1990-99

2000-03

Color Extra

February 6, 1949 – The Midland Terminal station still stands in Cripple Creek in 2003 as it did on this clear, cold February day. **R. W. ANDREWS PHOTO**

February 6, 1949 – Midland Terminal locomotive 59 thunders out of a tunnel on a day that delighted photographers with steam and smoke. **J. C. THODE PHOTO**

May 28, 1949 – Ingram Mountain forms a backdrop above RGS locomotive 74 and the Club's train at Pandora. Bridal Veil Falls are frozen in the distance. **JACK PFEIFER PHOTO**

May 29, 1949 – The Club's excursion train rescued disabled goose 4 at Matterhorn on the Rio Grande Southern. **J. C. THODE PHOTO**

May 29, 1949 – Creeping across this trestle above Ophir, RGS 74 is barely making five mph with the Club's train. R. H. KINDIG PHOTO

May 29, 1949 – RGS 74 pulls the five-car train across the spectacular trestle at Ophir. JACK PFEIFER PHOTO

May 29, 1949 – Ed Haley watches his wife carefully descend the steps of the "Edna" at Trout Lake. Can we tell from her dress the fashions of the day? JACK PFEIFER PHOTO

1938-49

1950-59

1960-69

1970-79

1980-89

1990-99

2000-03

Color Extra

May 30, 1949 – D&RGW engine 361 is shown with the nine-car train at Sapinero depot. **J. A. PFEIFER PHOTO**

August 28, 1949 – It's the end of the trip back in Denver after the Club's excursion behind D&IM motors 1107 and 1106. **GEORGE TROUT PHOTO**

September 25, 1949 – The Monarch Branch excursion climbs the 4.5% grade at the Maysville highway crossing. **JOSEPH SCHICK PHOTO.**

September 25, 1949 – Limestone destined for the Colorado Fuel and Iron mills in Pueblo is in gondolas adjacent to the Club's train at Monarch. **JACK PFEIFER PHOTO**

# Chapter 2: 1950 - 1959

**1950** **Meetings at the City and County of Denver Municipal Courtroom 101. Pres. Irv August; V-P. R. A. LeMassena; Secy. Herb O'Hanlon; Treas. R. H. Kindig. No monthly newsletter.**

During the 1950s and 1960s, while steam was still in operation, Otto Perry would usually buy a ticket for each trip, but instead of riding the train, he would follow it and photograph the trains at many locations. (Otto also took his cat "Mr. Nut" in his car on many of his photo trips.) This passion for photography resulted in a collection of over 20,000 negatives that later were acquired by the Denver Public Library, thanks to the efforts of the Club.

March – *Trains* magazine provided a very complimentary review of the Club's recent publication, *Denver South Park & Pacific*. In the reviewer's words, "Here is a book destined to become a collector's item within a year of publication."

April 1, 2 – The Club rode D&RGW trains 9 & 10 between Denver and Craig. Engine 801 (4-6-2) handled the train between Denver and Phippsburg on both days. Engine 1227 (formerly D&SL 407, 2-8-2) was used beyond Phippsburg each way. The train consisted of a baggage car, one coach and the open platform observation car "Spanish Fork Canyon," chartered by the Club. Thirty-five members and guests took the trip. A piece of tramp iron lodged in the firebox caused the grates to get cocked and the fire was lost at two locations. The train was delayed at Phippsburg changing locomotives because the stoker failed on engine 801. Overnight accommodations were at the Hotel Cosgriff in Craig. Heavy snow was encountered on the return at Winter Park. However, at East Portal the sky was clear and a group photo was taken.

April 12 – Annual dinner at the Holland House in Golden. Chartered D&IM Railroad car 25 again provided transportation.

April 16 – The world premier of the movie "A Ticket to Tomahawk" is shown in Durango featuring RGS locomotive 20.

*Trains* magazine carried an interesting article in the August 1950 issue about the D&RGW's sudden support of narrow gauge operations as a result of the film's popularity.

May 21 – D&RGW narrow gauge excursion from Salida to Monarch to Villa Grove and back to Salida using engine 489. Prior to the trip, the Salida shop painted the boiler jacket a dark green. This was probably the last D&RGW narrow gauge locomotive to have its jacket repainted. The train included baggage car 164, coaches 284, 320, 280 and 319 with the "Silver Vista" on the rear. Cost of the trip was $4.95 with an extra charge for the special bus, which provided transportation from Denver to Salida. The movements to manage this train reflect some of the complications on a trip on a branch line operation. Leaving Salida, the train consisted of the baggage car behind the locomotive, with the four

April 1, 1950 – D&RGW engine 801 (4-6-2) is shown handling the Craig train on the former D&SL near Volcano. **R. H. KINDIG PHOTO**

April 2, 1950 – Club members pose at the East Portal of the Moffat Tunnel on the return from an incident-packed D&RGW excursion between Denver and Craig. **J. C. THODE PHOTO**

1938-49
1950-59
1960-69
1970-79
1980-89
1990-99
2000-03
Color Extra

May 21, 1950 – D&RGW engine 489 at Villa Grove. **R. H. KINDIG PHOTO**

July 2, 1950 – D&IM narrow gauge excursion from Denver to Leyden to Golden and back to Denver. **N. R. MILLER PHOTO - KLINGER COLLECTION**

July 23, 1950 - D&RGW engine 3602 will assist the 16-car excursion from Minturn. Shortly after departure, a mechanical problem required that it be replaced by engine 3619. **R. W. ANDREWS PHOTO**

coaches and then the "Silver Vista." At Monarch, the engine and the baggage car were turned, now pulling the "Silver Vista" followed by the coaches. At Poncha Junction, the engine and baggage car were again turned. At Villa Grove, the wye was long enough for the entire train to be turned, arriving back in Salida in the same order as they departed.

June – The Club published *Steam Tramways of Denver*, by Morris Cafky. This pamphlet is listed as Volume III, continuing the newsletter numbering system established in 1949.

July 2 – D&IM narrow gauge excursion from Denver to Leyden to Golden and back to Denver. This was last run of narrow gauge electric interurbans. Fare was 50¢ for adults and 25¢ for children. A picnic lunch was held in Golden. Cars .02, .03 and 130 were used. The ticket for this trip read "This is the last D&IM Interurban trip and the last official street car movement in Denver."

July 23 – D&RGW standard gauge circle trip. The special train left Denver at 6:00 a.m. behind engine 1705 (4-8-4). A helper 3618 (2-8-8-2) was used to the East Portal of the Moffat Tunnel where it was cut off. Locomotive 1705 continued to Minturn where engines 3602 and 1803 (4-8-4) were put on the front replacing the 1705. Shortly after departure, 3602 suffered a mechanical problem and was replaced by engine 3619 that was dropped off at the summit of Tennessee Pass. The train continued to Pueblo behind the 1803 and back to Denver via the Royal Gorge route. The open platform observation car "Spanish Fork Canon" carried the Club's drumhead on the rear of the train. This was one of the largest trips ever run by the Club. The 16-car train carried over 555 passengers (although one source reported 595 passengers). The number of delays caused by engine problems, flooding near Florence and Pueblo and crew changes caused the special to return to Denver at about 1:00 a.m. Monday morning. Ed Haley recalled in 1988 that the return to Denver from Pueblo was made at high speed with the single Northern. He said that sparks flew out from under the wheels of all the cars on curves and that cars on the highway looked like they were going backwards. It was also on this trip that future Club Treasurer Ane Clint met her husband to be, David.

Fall – The *Denver South Park & Pacific* book sells out (1,000 copies).

October 7, 8 – The Club had planned to operate a narrow gauge excursion on October 7 from Alamosa over the narrow gauge San Luis Valley and Marshall Pass route to Gunnison. Flyers and tickets were printed for this excursion. However, ticket sales were slower than expected and the cautious and sound business mind of President August prompted the decision to cancel the trip. Had this trip operated, it would have been truly unique.

October 12 – The Club purchased Denver & Intermountain car 25 from the Denver Tramway Company for $150. It purchased the motors, separately, for $160.00. From this date until March 15, 1953, the car was stored in the D&IM car barn located at 2055 Myrtle Avenue (Myrtle Avenue and Zuni Street). After that, the car was stored in a lumber yard in Golden until it was moved to the Colorado Railroad Museum in 1958.

December 5 – The Club adopted its first formal set of bylaws. The bylaws would be revised in 1953, 1958, 1961, 1962, 1966, 1984, 2000 and 2003.

December 13 – Noted locomotive and railroad car designer Otto Kuhler presented the December program entitled "Trains That Were Never Built."

Although the exact date the Club started using PO Box 2391 is not certain, it was in use in 1950.

**1951**  **Meetings at the City and County of Denver Municipal Courtroom 101. Dues are $1.00 for Colorado residents and 50¢ for out-of-state members. Pres. R. A. LeMassena; V-P. George Trout; Secy. Herb O'Hanlon; Treas. R. H. Kindig. Listed for the first time in Club rosters is the position of "Secretary – Treasurer, Eastern Division," who was Michael Koch. Also, from 1951 through 1956, members who were also members of the Eastern Division were identified in the roster with the initials E.D. In 1951 Eastern Division (E.D.) members numbered 17; 1952 – 16; 1953-54 – 17; 1955 – 14; 1956 – 16. No monthly newsletter.**

February 25 – Farewell excursion of daylight service on the Colorado & Southern from Denver to Cheyenne and return. Travel was by trains 31 and 32 with a chartered D&RGW open platform observation car "Granite Canon" on rear. The roundtrip fare was $5.58.

Although this was the last Sunday run, the last day-time runs of these trains was on Wednesday, February 28. Tickets for the 240-mile trip were purchased at a station ticket window prior to the 8:45 a.m. departure. The route of the train was through Broomfield, Boulder, Longmont, Ft. Collins and Cheyenne. Passengers could mail postcards or letters to themselves by dropping them in the RPO in Cheyenne on the return of train 32. Locomotive 370 pulled the five-car train between Denver and Cheyenne.

March – Club members could purchase a 56-page booklet of locomotive photographs published by Club Member, Guy Dunscomb for $2.00 a copy.

May 6, 1951 - RMRRC and D&IM car 25 at Golden. **J. C. THODE PHOTO**

May 6 – Special "By Reservations Only" excursion on car 25 from Denver (14th and Valley Road) to Golden, the Remington Branch, the Morrison Branch and the Rubey Branch. A picnic lunch was held at a park in Golden and the fare was $1.00 for adults and 50¢ for children. Approximately 85 passengers rode this trip.

May 30 – Five-car excursion (two cabooses and three coaches) on the Colorado & Southern from Denver to Ft. Collins using engines 374 and 647. This was the first passenger train ever operated by the C&S over the Owl Canyon Branch, northwest of Ft. Collins. The trip went west through Owl Canyon to Rex with engine 647 on the head end and engine 374 on the rear with the train backing up. Upon reaching Rex, the end of the Ingleside Branch, the 674 was uncoupled and it returned backing down to Ft. Collins. Engine 374 pulled the train to Ft. Collins where the Club took a tour of the remaining operating lines of the Ft. Collins Municipal Railway on cars 25, 21 and 20. Leaving Ft. Collins the 374 ran to Windsor where the Great Western Railway provided engine 90 for a run to Johnstown and Longmont (via the Elm and Welty Branches). Combination car 100 was used on this portion. C&S engine 374 (which had run light between Windsor and

May 30, 1951 – RMRRC Excursion at Fort Collins before going on the C&S Owl Canyon Branch. D&RGW observation car is the "Granite Canon." **R. H. KINDIG PHOTO**

May 30, 1951 – Great Western car 01102 on rear of the train over the GW portion of the joint C&S/Great Western excursion. Rogers E. M. Whitaker ("E. M. Frimbo") stands on the rear platform. **R. H. KINDIG PHOTO**

May 30, 1951 – Ticket for the Club excursion over the Owl Canyon Branch of the Colorado & Southern. The ticket (not all pictured) was issued by the railroad for the trip.

Ft. Collins and then to Longmont over the C&S) returned the train to Denver from Longmont. Cost of the trip was $7.50 for adults and $3.75 for children. Passengers could also board the train at Ara (Boulder) or Longmont. The ticket for this excursion was 17 inches long and was provided by the C&S..

June 9 – The Eastern Division of the Rocky Mountain Railroad Club met at the home of Phil Ronfor near Boonton, NJ. The date the Eastern Division was first established is not known.

June 30 – Ft. Collins Municipal Railway car 22 made its last run. This trip was reportedly the last single-truck Birney to run in regular service in the USA as well as being the last streetcar to operate in Colorado. The Ft. Collins trolley systems ceased operations after this date.

June – Club published *The Colorado Eastern Railroad* by Charles Ryland. This pamphlet was listed as Volume IV (continuing the newsletter numbering system established in 1949).

July – Club membership numbered more than 350.

August 21 – Secretary Jackson Thode wrote a two page letter to Mr. T. A. Thompson containing a brief history of the Club and a summation of its activities. In it, Jack stated:

"The group's (Club's) purpose was, and remains, to promote interest in the railroads, past and present, of the Rocky Mountain Region, with particular emphasis on the railroads of Colorado. Interestingly enough, the members come from non-railroad walks of life – farmer, postal employee, lawyers, doctor, business-men, etc., with only one pensioned and one active railroad employee – bound together only by their intense fascination for trains. This preponder-ance of non-railroad peo-ple is still a major factor of the club's membership."

August – RGS locomotive 20 was used in the filming (near Hesperus) of the movie "Viva Zapata." Number 20 also had a leading role in "A Ticket to Tomahawk." as the "Emma Sweeney."

September 2, 1951 - The Club's train waits as two RGS geese pass at Placerville.
**W. W. KRATVILLE PHOTO**

September 1, 2 – The Club offered a two-day RGS nar-row gauge excursion from Ridgway to Telluride and Pandora Basin. Overnight accommodations (not part of the trip cost and at the member's own expense) were in Telluride. Engine 74 was used on this trip. This was the last steam passenger train operated by this road and included the business car "Edna," three gondolas and two cabooses.

September 1 - One hundred and thirty-seven riders paid $10.00 for this portion of the trip, from Ridgway to Telluride. Lillian Stewart, in 1987, recalled that since no hotel arrangements had been made, finding sleeping places was challenging. Since there was only one hotel in Telluride, some passengers slept on the "Edna" and others, who brought sleeping bags, slept on the ground in the park. Lillian and a dozen oth-ers slept in a former house of ill repute, which was opened for the travelers. Eight men slept in the maternity ward of the hospital while other passengers found space in the jail and the railroad station.

September 2 – The second day's trip was from Telluride over Lizard Head Pass and returned to Ridgway. Unlike the trip in 1949, no prob-lems with recalcitrant geese were encountered on this portion. This was the last steam passen-ger trip on the RGS.

October 13 – Twelve members of the Eastern Division of the Club met at the home of Morris Abbott in Milford, CT.

October 28 – Sixty-five Club members and guests rode car 25 on D&IM Route 84 from Denver to Golden. This was the second trip on what was now the Club's own

October 28, 1951 - D&IM car 25 near Golden.
**N. R. MILLER PHOTO - KLINGER COLLECTION**

interurban car. The tour included travel over the branch line to the Remington Arms Plant, now Denver Federal Center, the Morrison Branch and the Rubey Branch along Clear Creek.

November 26 – The Club purchased D&RGW narrow gauge caboose 0578 for $204 at Salida.

The November issue of *True* Magazine featured a paint-ing of Colorado & Southern engine 60 by member Phil Ronfor, on the cover. Ronfor was a well-known artist who did illustrations for *Railroad Magazine* and other publications, including advertisements for the Pennsylvania Railroad.

December 18 – An article in *The Denver Post* newspa-per describes the sincere but futile efforts by Club President to rally support to continue operations on the Rio Grande Southern. Debt on the line was accumulat-

1938-49
1950-59
1960-69
1970-79
1980-89
1990-99
2000-03
Color Extra

ing at the rate of $8,000 a month and repairs were needed all along the line. LeMassena attempted to get federal agencies and the affected counties to agree to hold off on tax claims. He proposed that minority bondholders operate the sixty-mile portion of the line between Dallas Divide and Lizard Head Pass. Unfortunately, Receiver J. Pierpont Fuller was forced to close down the line after sixty years of service in southwest Colorado.

**1952**　**Meetings at the City and County of Denver Room 186 (from December 1951 to May 1952) and then Municipal Courtroom 101 thereafter. Pres. Herb O'Hanlon; V-P. Charles Ryland; Secy. Morris Cafky; Treas. Arl Cuthbert. (No Eastern Division positions listed). No monthly newsletter.**

May 18 – Trip on the D&IM Railroad from Denver to Golden and return. Car 25 was used. Members took their own picnic lunches and the fare was $1.00 for adults and 50¢ for children.

May 30, 31 – The Club operated its first of many Memorial Day narrow gauge excursions on the D&RGW from Alamosa to Durango and return. Roundtrip fare was $12.00 for adults and $6.00 for children but did not include meals or accommodations. Tickets for the trip could either be purchased at the Rio Grande City Ticket Office at 1531 Stout St. in Denver, or by ordering through the Club. Passengers could either take a standard gauge train to Alamosa or go by car.

May 31, 1952 - A freight train derailment near Toltec, NM delayed the Club's excursion at Osier several hours while they waited for the track to be cleared. **R. H. KINDIG PHOTO**

January – Club created "General Instructions for Secretary and Treasurer." These procedures described the membership card numbering system as well as the method to continue or not continue member's numbers if they failed to renew their membership.

April 2 – Eighty members take a "Last Trip" to the Annual dinner at the Holland House, Golden with transportation via D&IM chartered car 25. The program consisted of three reels of movies on California logging, pictures of the RGS and an Otto Perry movie. This was the first "Last Trip" on car 25 (as reported by the *The Denver Post*). There were several "Last Trips" operated because the D&IM was in the process of abandoning their operations. The D&IM officially shut down effective March 16, 1953.

May 30 – The twelve-car train to Durango, pulled by engine 488, carried 366 riders. The train included cars in Pullman Green and cars that had been painted in the Rio Grande Gold scheme. Also included in the consist were business car B-7, the deluxe parlor car "Alamosa" and the glass-topped observation car "Silver Vista."

May 31 – The same twelve-car train returned to Alamosa using road engine 488 to Chama where engine 490 replaced 488. Engine 490 was used as the helper from Chama to the summit of Cumbres Pass. Engine 494 handled the train to Alamosa. A freight train derailment near Toltec, NM prompted the railroad to hold the train at Osier until the line was cleared.

The crew and passengers started a large bonfire using old ties. Everyone was able to keep warm and sang songs to stay in good spirits. After the train reached Antonito and proceeded towards Alamosa, Otto Perry and John Maxwell who were both following the train by car, swore that the train reached speeds of 60 mph as the crew tried to make up lost time.

June 23 – The Club purchased RGS engine 20 (formerly Florence & Cripple Creek) for $2,000 and business car 021 "Rico" for $400 in a Court administered sale. Pierpont Fuller, court appointed receiver of the RGS, had an appraisal that showed the value of engine 20 to be $1,300 and the business car to be $200. As the Club was bidding against Knott's Berry Farm and the City of Boulder, we were fortunate to pick up these pieces for the prices we did. Knott's Berry Farm purchased the business car "Edna" for $2,000 and Boulder bought engine 74 for $2,100.

June – Club published the pamphlet *Denver, Longmont and Northwestern* by B. L. "Billy" Boyles. This pamphlet is listed as Volume V (continuing the newsletter numbering system established in 1949).

July 20 – D&RGW standard gauge circle trip from Denver to Dotsero via the Moffat Tunnel and back to Denver via Tennessee Pass and the Royal Gorge and Pueblo. The train consisted of eight 900-series coaches, snack car 748, the open platform observation cars "Glenwood Canon" and "Ogden Canon," a diner-lounge, and the "Granite Canon." This was the first use of diesel power by the Club (locomotives 5554, 5553, 5552 and 5551) and the roundtrip fare was $12.00 for adults and $5.00 for children. In addition to the onboard handout, passengers received a set of two maps drawn by Ed Haley which were later reproduced for the *1956 Westerner's Brand Book*. The maps covered the west central portion of Colorado and a depiction of settlements of the Upper Arkansas River Valley.

September 10 – Members who purchased "salvage shares" of RGS engine 20, to enable the Club to buy this locomotive, were notified that "stock certificates" would be mailed as soon as ready. Shares sold for one dollar each (which was equivalent to $7.03 in 2003). That was a pretty hefty amount at that time. Those who purchased these shares, were entitled to receive a dollar back in five years for each share they bought. However, shareholders were not entitled to "cannibalize" engine 20.

October 19 – Club member David Clint was killed along with three crewmen when D&RGW locomotive 3703 is destroyed in a tragic explosion eleven miles south of Littleton. David, husband of Ane Clint (who would later become the first female officer of the Club) was traveling in the cab on the Pueblo bound freight. The accident was attributed to an inoperable water gauge, which registered full, although the water level in the boiler was below the crown sheet.

October 25 – D&RGW narrow gauge excursion from Alamosa to Chama, NM. Fare was $6.00 for adults and $3.00 for children. The nine-car train consisted of one baggage car, three old style coaches, four deluxe coaches and the parlor car "Alamosa." Passengers had to drive to Alamosa (or take the train on their own) to catch the narrow gauge train and had to provide their own meals, including lunch. This Fall Colors special operated behind engine 499 from Alamosa to Chama. Engine 488 was added as helper to Cumbres where it was dropped and 499 continued with the train to Alamosa.

October 28 – The Club operated a special run of car 25 from the D&IM shops at W. 14th Ave. and Valley Road along the Remington, Morrison and Rubey branches. Cost of the trip was $1.00 for adults and 50¢ for children. The trip was limited to 60 passengers and included a picnic lunch in Golden.

The Club was invited to become the Denver Chapter of the National Railway Historical Society but the Club's Board of Directors turn down the offer, preferring to remain independent.

December – Member Neal Miller gave those in attendance at the December meeting, an 8x10 black and white photo from his collection. This began a tradition that has continued regularly since that date continuing

October 25, 1952 - Mr. and Mrs. E. J. Haley stand on the platform of the parlor car "Alamosa" at Chama, NM. **R. H. KINDIG PHOTO**

1938-49

1950-59

1960-69

1970-79

1980-89

1990-99

2000-03

Color Extra

through December 2003. Neal has reproduced these photos at his own expense and has never asked for reimbursement. As he says, "I can't afford it, but I really get a kick out of it anyway. People like trains, so they get a train picture from me once a year." Neal recalls his first photo was Colorado & Southern engine 634 running with just a caboose in Longmont near 3rd Avenue.

December – Former RGS business car 021 "Rico" was moved to Golden and its temporary home on the campus of the Colorado School of Mines.

Throughout most of these years, Club meetings featured 16mm films taken by Otto Perry or movies and slides taken by Club members of trips and events of interest to all. This format made many meeting nights similar to the "potpourri" nights the Club holds today.

**1953** **Meetings at the City and County of Denver Municipal Courtroom 101. Pres. E. L. Rohrer; V-P. Charles Ryland; Secy. John Maxwell; Treas. John Ryland; Secy-Treas. – Eastern Division – Michael Koch; Other Eastern Division Directors included Morris Abbott and Philip Ronfor. No monthly newsletter.**

February 3 – The *Empire* magazine of the *The Denver Post* contained a lengthy article by Bernard Kelly about the Club including the Club's formation, early trips and the qualifications to become a member, "The important thing is, do you love railroads enough to be a little crazy about them?"

February 20 – An article appeared in the *Hustler* a neighborhood newspaper in the Denver area. Members Otto Perry, Francis Rizzari, Everett Rohrer, Josie Crum, Ed Haley are profiled and several other prominent members mentioned. As the article states, "If heraldry were in use today, the members of the Rocky Mountain Railroad Club, 350 strong would have emblazoned on their shields a steam locomotive rampant, a great plume of smoke trailing behind it. For, as former secretary Morris Cafky once said, they are absolutely devoted to steam, steel and the flanged wheel."

March 8 – Last revenue run of car 25 on a D&IM standard gauge excursion from Denver to Golden and over the Morrison Branch and back. Two runs were made, one at 9:00 a.m. and one at 2:00 p.m. Rental of car 25 for this trip was $40. It is odd that rental was paid as the Club had purchased the car in October 1950. Perhaps the $40 paid was to operate on the D&IM. The ticket read "Last run on the D&IM."

March 11 – Fifteenth Anniversary Banquet was held at the Holland House in Golden, with travel via car 25. The roundtrip and dinner was $3.50. The trip was covered by the *The Denver Post* with an often-reproduced

photo of past President Herb O'Hanlon in front of car 25 with Route 84 numberboards. Sixty-five members and guests rode the car. On board was D&IM Trainmaster C. L. Matthews, who retired five days later after thirty-four years of service. Members unanimously voted him a life member in the Club at the Wednesday evening dinner. It is interesting to note that the Club Archives has a ticket for the Fifteenth Anniversary Dinner that is actually dated April 13, 1954 to be held at the Chamber of Commerce Building at 13th and Welton in Denver. The actual date of the Fifteenth Anniversary Dinner was March 11, as noted here. These "erroneous" tickets are somewhat mysterious and were clearly a typographic error.

March 15 – The *Otto Perry Catalogue* listing for the Denver & Intermountain Railroad Co. indicated a Club special was operated on this day using car 25. This was the last run of car 25. The D&IM officially closed down their operations effective March 16, 1953.

April – Club moves locomotive 20 to the Alamosa narrow gauge yards.

April – The Club purchased Ft. Collins Municipal Railway car 22 from the Southern California Division of the Electric Railroaders Association. The SCERA purchased four of the five remaining Birneys from the Ft. Collins Municipal Railway after the Birneys were taken out of service. None were relocated until each was sold. All were eventually sold to various buyers and societies and all have been preserved. The Club paid $115 for our car 22, which was paid in installments. This car last operated June 30, 1951.

May 17 – The Club's first Union Pacific excursion, this one from Denver to Laramie and return. Challenger engine 3967 (4-6-6-4) was used. The train consisted of eleven cars (a baggage-buffet car, a baggage car, three coaches, a snack car, three more coaches, a baggage car and Agricultural Improvement car 200 – with the Club's drumhead on the rear). Routing was Denver to LaSalle to Buford (where a two-hour stop was made to observe mainline traffic) and then over Sherman Hill. Tours of the roundhouse and shops at Laramie were provided. Cost was $10.00 roundtrip for adults and $5.00 for children. The train connected with the eastbound "National Parks Special" at LaSalle and continued back to Denver on the Dent Branch. Jim Ehernberger and four other passengers boarded at Borie for the trip, which cost them $2.20 plus 33¢ federal tax. The menu in the snack car included: sandwiches at 33¢ to 35¢, and ice cream bars, coffee or large donuts for a dime). The Club paid the Union Pacific Railroad $1,591.37 for this trip.

June 13 – Engine 20 (formerly Rio Grande Southern) was relocated to the Mt. Blanca and Western Railroad at the Narrow Gauge Museum in Alamosa.

November 1, 1953 - Club members make up the Mt. Blanca and Western engine-house forces in repainting former RGS engine 20 at the Narrow Gauge Museum in Alamosa. The tender was lettered "Florence and Cripple Creek" and the cab had the name "Portland." Engine 20 had been acquired by the Club the previous June. **J. C. THODE PHOTO**

August 14 – Members hiked the Colorado Midland right-of-way to Hagerman and Busk-Ivanhoe tunnels.

August 23 – Excursion on the M&PP to the summit of Pikes Peak. Two trips were made using engine 5. Snow was encountered at the top.

August 29 – "Mac" Poor led a number of members on a hike to the Alpine Tunnel.

September 26, 27 – D&RGW narrow gauge excursion from Alamosa to Durango and return. The fare was $13.00 ($6.50 for children) The sold out train had 14 cars, including business car B-7, "Silver Vista" and parlor car "Alamosa" and over 400 riders. Refreshments were available at Chama. Many people were turned away. Members drove to Alamosa and had to provide their own overnight accommodations in Alamosa and Durango. Tickets could be purchased through the Club or at the Rio Grande Ticket Office at 1531 Stout Street, in Denver. A passenger, 15 year-old Dorothy Mann, died on Monday the 28th following her arrival in Durango on the excursion train. An autopsy was performed but no cause of death was determined.

> September 26 – Engine 488 powered the fourteen-car train from Alamosa to Durango. Business car B-7 and the "Silver Vista" were on this trip. This would be the last trip for the glass-topped observation car which was destroyed by fire on September 30.

> September 27 – The return train used engine 488 as the road engine to Chama. There, the 486 was added as helper to the summit of Cumbres Pass. Engine 488 completed the remainder of the trip to Alamosa.

November 1 – Over a dozen Club members worked on

repainting Club engine 20 in Alamosa.

November and December – Club members were able to receive a discount by showing their membership cards to the cashier at the Vogue Art Cinema, 1465 South Pearl, to see the new movie, "The Titfield Thunderbolt."

December 8 – The Club renewed its insurance policy covering D&IM car 25 ($500) located at the Duvall Davison lumber yard in Golden; RGS business car 021 "Rico" ($1,000) and D&RGW caboose 0578 ($300), both located next to the experimental mill at the Colorado School of Mines in Golden. A separate policy issued on December 10, provided $500 all-risk coverage on the Club's Bell & Howell movie projector.

December 31 – The Club's bank balance at the end of the year was $802.68.

**1954    Meetings at the City and County of Denver Municipal Courtroom 101. Dues are $2.00 for Colorado residents and $1.00 for out-of-state members. Pres. E. L. Rohrer; V-P. Francis Rizzari; Secy. John Maxwell; Treas. G. S. Barnes. Secy. -Treas. – Eastern Division – Michael Koch; Other Eastern Division Directors included Morris Abbott and Philip Ronfor. No monthly newsletter.**

As early as 1954, application for membership in the Club was limited to persons eighteen years of age or older. Individual membership applications were approved by action of the Board of Directors.

January 24 – Club members took the *Ski Train* along with Colorado Mountain Club to Winter Park (fare was $2.60). The D&RGW locomotives used on this trip were 5534 (EMD F3 built in November 1946), 5573 and 5574 (EMD F7s built in February 1949).

February 20 – Philip Ronfor was hosted at a buffet dinner at the M. C. Poor home where Mr. Ronfor received the "Medal of Honor" for his support of Club activities. Superintendent of Dining Service and Maitre de Hotel, Cleta Poor, arranged for a memorable dinner. While wives of notable members did the culinary arts, their husbands dispensed firewater, restoratives, wine and potable waters. C. Ryland offered "Retrospective Remarks" and Maestro D. Peterson at the console directed group singing. Later in the evening, E. Haley presented a movie starring Clara Kimball Young in "Dark Silence."

April 17 – Robert W. Richardson reported in the March 1954 issue of the *Narrow Gauge News* that the Club would hold its Annual dinner in Boulder. Transportation was via a special Colorado & Southern steam powered train (locomotive number unknown) and cost

May 29, 1954 - The Club's Alamosa - Silverton excursion train waits at Chama, NM during the servicing and lunch stop. The railroad provided spare cabooses on many trips during these years to increase the seating capacity. **R. H. KINDIG PHOTO**

was $3.00. This seems to conflict with the information contained below.

April 26 – The Annual Dinner was held in Denver, at the Chamber of Commerce Building on April 26, not on April 13, as indicated by a preprinted ticket in the Club archives. The postcard announcement for the dinner indicates the cost was $6.00 per person. UP steam movies were shown at the dinner.

May 29, 30, 31 – Annual D&RGW narrow gauge Memorial Day excursion from Alamosa to Durango to Silverton and return. The fare for this trip was $18.00 and members had to drive to Alamosa and provide their own overnight hotel accommodations. Smoking Stack Press in Golden printed the handout for this trip. Member Charles Ryland was proprietor and printer "devils" were Dick Kindig, Ed Haley and Richard Ronzio. More than 300 passengers took the trip.

> May 29 – This day's fourteen-car train consisted of one reefer, eleven passenger coaches and two cabooses on the rear end. Locomotive 487 pulled the train from Alamosa to Durango.

> May 30 – This day's train added one more caboose for the run to Silverton and back. Engine 476 (painted as the 7 for a movie) was assisted by U.S. Army diesel 4700N. Diesel 4700N served as helper on portions of the trip but was uncoupled and run out of sight for photo run-bys of the steam locomotive.

> May 31– Fourteen cars again made up this train powered by road engine 487 with the 492 serving as helper from Chama to Cumbres.

August – The Club decided not to pursue publishing Mrs. Josie Crum's book *The Rio Grande Southern Story*. It was later published by Dr. A. G. Chione in Illinois

> In January 1955, President Irv August in a letter to all members, discussed this issue in some detail. He said:

> "… Directors were unable to reach an agreement with the author concerning the extent of editing required. The author insisted on retention of proven erroneous information and possibly libelous material and it was decided that the book would not meet the high standards required for publication under the Club's imprint."

October 31 – UP excursion using two chartered cars on the Cheyenne local train 57 from Denver to Cheyenne. Engines 2888 and the 812 were on the northbound leg. The Club returned to Denver on train 52 behind engine 2888. While in Cheyenne, members were allowed in the roundhouse and shop areas without escorts.

December – The Eastern Division of the Club was temporarily "abandoned" due to difficulty in coordinating meetings and locations.

> Club members who were well-known authors or historians but who did not live in Colorado and were unable to attend regular Club meetings formed this Division in the 1950s. These members attempted to maintain contact with each other by holding periodic meetings at their homes, but because they were widely separated across the eastern and midwestern states, it proved too difficult.

**1955** **Meetings at the City and County of Denver Municipal Courtroom 101. Dues are $2.00 ($1.00 out-of-state) – Pres. Irv August; V-P. E. J. Haley; Secy. M. C. Poor; Treas. R. H. Kindig. Secy.-Treas. – Eastern Division – Michael Koch; No monthly newsletter.**

In a January letter Club President August solicits suggestions from Club members for ideas for trips and activities. He also reports that a Book Committee, headed by Ed Haley, was established and will publish Morris Cafky's book *Rails Around Gold Hill*.

February 12 – The Eastern Division of the Club is reactivated, with plans to meet at least twice a year.

> At some later point in the Club's history, the Eastern Division will disappear, although no specific record notes the fact. In 2001, the Board revised the Bylaws to take away the concept of out of state divisions.

March 2 – Annual Banquet was held at the American Legion Club in Lakewood. Cost of the dinner was $2.50. Ms. Helen Tatum provided movies on the Colorado & Southern South Park Division.

April 13 – Seventeen year old Jim Ehernberger commuted to Club meetings from his home in Cheyenne. He worked for the UP and normally would take train 52 leaving Cheyenne at 2:45 p.m. arriving in Denver at 5:20 p.m. Motive power at this time was one of the last Pacific class locomotives (4-6-2). He would then hike up 17th Street to the meeting at the City and County Building, crossing Larimer Street (which was not the nicest neighborhood in those days) and getting a snack along the way. After the meeting Jim would either catch a Greyhound bus (that left at 10:00) or take a Trailways bus at 11:59 p.m. or stay overnight with friends and take train 57 at 8:10 a.m. Jim reported to work on Tuesday at 11:59 p.m., and was scheduled to work sixteen hours until 3:59 p.m. on Wednesday afternoon. As Club meetings were on Wednesday, Jim had to get someone to cover the last of his shift to catch the train to Denver. If he took the bus back to Cheyenne after the meeting, he didn't get home until after 2:45 a.m. on Thursday, to get ready for another shift that would begin at 3:59 p.m. Talk about dedication!

May 28, 29, 30 – D&RGW narrow gauge Memorial Day excursion from Alamosa to Durango, to Silverton, back to Durango and return to Alamosa. Both nights were in Durango and the cost was $18.00. Passengers had to make their own overnight arrangements in Durango as well as provide their transportation to Alamosa. The train was sold out. Each passenger received a commemorative envelope and piece of stationary for this trip.

May 28 – Engine 499 powered this fifteen-car train, consisting of ten coaches, three cabooses, business car B-7 and a reefer for baggage from Alamosa to Durango.

May 29 – Road engine 476 was assisted by 478 to Silverton. Business car B-7 was on the rear end.

May 30 – Engine 499 pulled the train to Chama, where the 486 was added as helper to Cumbres Pass. The 499 continued alone to Alamosa with all fifteen cars.

July 13 – At this month's meeting, there was a "grab bag" auction of thirty-four copies of *Poors* and *Moodys* railroad manuals. Chances were $1.00 each.

July 16 – D&RGW standard gauge circle trip excursion from Denver through the Moffat Tunnel to Dotsero and back to Denver via Tennessee Pass, Salida, the Royal Gorge and Pueblo. Diesel locomotive 5571 led the power on this 508-mile trip.

August 6 – Club members, led by M. C. "Mac" Poor, explored an uncompleted portion of the South Park line near Baldwin, recently re-discovered by Robert W. Richardson. The section included nearly 300 feet of rockwork similar to that found at the "Palisades" portion of the line west of the Alpine Tunnel.

September 23, 24, 25 – D&RGW standard gauge and narrow gauge "Fall Foliage" excursion from Denver to Chama, NM via a special train from Pueblo, Walsenburg and LaVeta Pass to Alamosa.

September 24, 1955 - Dick Kindig, Club Treasurer, standing in parlor car "Alamosa" on the Chama "Fall Foliage" excursion. **J. L. EHERNBERGER PHOTO**

September 23 – Diesel power (F-7s), coach and sleeping car accommodations were on the standard gauge portion of this special train to Alamosa. Jack Morison recalls that the excursion left Denver (with Pullmans) Friday evening about 8:00 p.m. with the "Granite Canon," open platform observation car, as the last car, arriving in Pueblo around 10:30 p.m. There the D&RGW took the special train to Walsenburg and on to Alamosa arriving by 3:00 a.m. Participants could sleep on the standard gauge coaches or Pullman cars overnight in Alamosa. The fares varied between $18.00 and $36.00 depending on sleeping arrangement each night. The choice of coach or Pullman dictated the difference in fares.

September 24 – The eleven-car train was pulled by engine 490 from Alamosa to Chama and back late in the afternoon. The train consisted of baggage car 126, coaches 306, 320, 284, 319, 312, 327, 323 and the parlor car "Alamosa" (in that order). One hundred ninety-eight riders rode the narrow gauge portion, of which 150 had come by standard gauge to Alamosa. A number of the riders were from the Illini Railroad Club.

September 25 – The D&RGW special then departed early Sunday morning for Pueblo via LaVeta Pass. The passage over LaVeta Pass was completely obscured by low clouds and fog eliminating any opportunities for photo run-bys. In Pueblo, an hour and a half layover allowed members to take photographs. Jack Morison recalled the roundhouse was filled with steam locomotives. The special then left about 3:30 p.m. to return to Denver.

December – The Club published Morris Cafky's book, *Rails Around Gold Hill*. Pre-publication price was $8.50 with a normal price of $10.00. A set of three color prints could be purchased separately for $1.25. World Press was again selected to do the printing and included three full color paintings by Richard Ward. The cover jacket painting featured Florence & Cripple Creek locomotive 20. Ed Haley did the maps for the book. The cost of printing approximately 2,750 copies was $18,850 not including advertising brochures, boxes and postage for mailing. By December 7, 1,935 copies had been sold.

In 1956 and the year or two preceding it, M. "Como" Poor and E. "Jefferson" Haley hosted periodic get togethers for individuals who were recognized by the Club for support of Club activities. These meetings took place at "Delaney's Saloon" of which E. J. Haley was Proprietor. The Loyal Sons and Daughters of the Rusty Spike to the Poor House, who attended these activities, were attended to by Barkeep, C. S. Ryland, entertained by Organist, D. K. Peterson, and kept in line by R. H. Kindig, the Gentle Bouncer.

**1956** **Meetings at the City and County of Denver Municipal Courtroom 101. Pres. R. A. LeMassena; V-P. W. J. Gordon; Secy. R. A. Ronzio; Treas. J. O. Riley. Secy.-Treas. – Eastern Division – Michael Koch; Other Eastern Division Directors included Morris Abbott and Philip Ronfor. No monthly newsletter.**

President LeMassena reported in his January "newsletter" that the Club received a gift of an auditorium size Kodak projector from World Press. He also noted that the Colorado & Southern was using 2-8-0's on their Sheridan Blvd. and Buchtel Blvd. branches and that the CB&Q closed its Denver steam shops.

March 11 – UP standard gauge excursion from Denver to Cheyenne via the Dent Branch and LaSalle and return using engine 9000 (4-12-2) which was enroute to Pomona, CA for permanent display. Wind chill was in the minus numbers for several runbys of this nine-car train. 215 members and guests took this trip, despite the snow. Cost was $6.00 for adults and $3.00 for children. At the last minute, the Union Pacific notified the Club that it was taking engine 9000 off the train and substituting a 4000-class Big Boy instead. President LeMassena contacted the UP immediately and convinced them that since a large number of out-of-state visitors were already enroute to ride behind this specific locomotive, it was necessary to leave engine 9000 on the train. The UP agreed. Members also had a chance to visit the roundhouse and shop area while in Cheyenne. Locomotive 9000 ran light from Cheyenne to Denver and then returned the day following the trip at the head of a manifest freight.

March – The Club's book, *Rails Around Gold Hill*, was sold out.

April 11 – Annual Dinner was at the American Legion Club in Lakewood (1655 Simms). Cost was $2.50. The program consisted of movies and slides of D&RGW narrow gauge.

May – The Club authorized the publication of the *Pictorial Supplement to Denver South Park & Pacific* a supplement to the *Denver South Park & Pacific* history.

May – President LeMassena wrote a one-page glossy format "newsletter" with local information as well as describing future Club activities for the remainder for the year. Unfortunately, a number of the proposed activities, such as an excursion behind a D&RGW 3600-class locomotive did not materialize.

March 11, 1956 - Club drumhead is mounted on the front of Union Pacific 9000 in Cheyenne. Moisture collected on the drumhead causing the canvas to wrinkle, a condition that was never corrected. **MIKE TRENT PHOTO**

March 11, 1956 - Union Pacific engine 9000 on a run-by at Dent during this below zero degree day. **MIKE TRENT PHOTO**

June 2, 3 – Annual D&RGW narrow gauge excursion from Alamosa to Durango and return. The cost was $15.00 and 182 passengers rode the 11-car train. A commemorative envelope was prepared as a cachet for this trip (postage was 3¢). Passengers drove to Alamosa and had to provide their own hotel arrangements.

June 2 – Engine 490 pulled the eleven-car train from Alamosa to Durango. The train consisted of one combination car, one baggage car, seven coaches, the parlor car "Alamosa" and a red freight gondola on the rear end.

June 3 – The same train returned to Alamosa behind the 490, with engine 488 as helper

added at Chama for the portion to the summit of Cumbres Pass.

June 16 – A Memorial Dinner was held celebrating the publication of *Rails Around Gold Hill*. Special attendees included author, Morris Cafky, Editors Ed Haley and Dick Kindig, Artist Richard Ward and the printer (World Press), the engraver (Capitol Engraving) and the binder (Dieter Bookbinding).

August 4 – UP standard gauge excursion from Laramie, WY to Northgate, CO over the Coalmont Branch (former Laramie, North Park & Western) using engine 535 (2-8-0). The cost was $6.00. Six cars made up the train, all Harriman style coaches with one baggage car. The handout for this trip was printed on glossy paper and included photos, a map, roster information and text provided by Dick Kindig and Jim Ehernberger. The trip notice recommended several ways to get to Laramie, including driving or taking the train. Schedules for UP trains 9 and 10 and 17 and 18 were included. Pullman cars were also available to passengers for $26 to $29 depending upon accommodations.

September – The meeting notice for this meeting indicated the Club has available for 25¢ a four page history of the Laramie, North Park and Western Railroad, as well as Bulletins No. 3 and 4 *Steam Tramways of Denver* and *The Colorado Eastern Railroad* for fifty cents each.

November – The Club publishes *The Case of Train Number 3* about the flood in Pueblo in 1921. The cost was $2.00.

November 14 – Members who attended the regular meeting could purchase a copy of *The Case of Train Number 3*. Hard cover copies could be obtained by paying $3.00.

December 8 – The Club renewed its insurance policy on car 25 (stored in the yard of the Duvall Davison lumber company, 1313 Ford St., Golden), business car 021 "Rico" and caboose 0578 (both stored adjacent to the experimental mill at the Colorado School of Mines) and the Birney (stored at the Golden Waterworks), west of the city limits of Golden. Total cost of the policy was $1,876.

Charter member Everett Rohrer left the Club to focus upon the new Rocky Mountain Steam Traction Society based in Denver.

1938-49

1950-59

1960-69

1970-79

1980-89

1990-99

2000-03

Color Extra

**1957** **Pres. W. J. Gordon; V-P. John Maxwell; Secy. Charles Max; Treas. George Trout. No further listing of Eastern Division Directors or Officers. No monthly newsletter.**

March 1 – Program Chairman, Ross Grenard, sent a letter out to Club members describing the new policy on programs for monthly meetings during the coming months and years. He explained that members will make slide presentations or guest speakers will present topics of interest. He also solicited suggestions for future programs, much the way the current program activities are arranged.

March – To support the publication of the *Pictorial Supplement to Denver South Park & Pacific*, Book Committee Chairman, Dick Kindig appealed to members to submit relevant material to M. C. Poor.

April 10 – Annual Dinner at the Republican Club (1544 Lincoln St.) in Denver. Cost was $3.50 and the program "A History of the Development of Union Pacific Motive Power" by a representative of the railroad.

May 31, June 1, 2 – D&RGW narrow gauge Memorial Day excursion, Alamosa to Silverton. Cost was $20.00 for adults and $10.00 for children, which did not include overnight accommodations. There were 347 riders on the trip.

> May 31 – The eleven-car train, with a red freight gondola on the rear end, was pulled by engine 489 from Alamosa to Durango.

> June 1 – Engine 478 served as road engine for the train. The 476 was the helper to Silverton and it returned light to Durango.

> June 2 – The eleven-car train left Durango at 7:00 a.m., behind road engine 476. At Chama, engine 486 was added as helper to Cumbres with the train returning to Alamosa at 4:40 p.m. Passengers had to drive back to Denver as regular standard gauge service had been suspended in 1953 and no special was provided this year as was done in 1955.

June 30 – Colorado & Southern standard gauge excursion from Denver to Fort Collins and Greeley. Engine 909 (USRA 2-10-2) was used on the five-car train (consisting of one heavyweight green baggage car and four coaches in the CB&Q silver color) between Denver and Ft. Collins. Engine 648 (2-8-0) was used from Ft. Collins to Greeley and return. Engine 909 pulled the

June 30, 1957 - Colorado & Southern engine 909 arrives in Denver in the early evening. This was the Club's only trip behind a USRA 2-10-2-type locomotive. **R. H. KINDIG PHOTO**

train back to Denver. Roundtrip fare was $5.00 and the train departed Denver at 8:00 a.m. and was scheduled to return by 5:00 p.m.

August – The first of a two-part article on the Colorado Midland Railroad by Morris Cafky appeared in *Trains* magazine. The second part was in the next month's issue.

September 15 – UP standard gauge excursion. Laramie, WY to Northgate, CO over the Coalmont Branch. Engine 535 was used. The six-car train included five streamlined coaches (of which one was an observation car) and an open gondola. Fare for the trip was $6 for adults and $3 for children. Dick Kindig and Jim Ehernberger prepared oversized glossy handout for this trip. It included a number of photos, as well as a map, text and roster of Laramie, North Park & Western Railroad.

December – The Club's year-end bank balance was $1,919.71.

**1958** **Meetings at the Denver Public Library, 14th and Broadway. Dues were $2.00 for in-state members $1.00 for out-of-state members. Pres. W. J. Gordon; V-P. John Maxwell; Secy. Ross Grenard; Treas. Morris Cafky. No monthly newsletter.**

**and**

February 8 – The Board sent out a letter to all members describing the Club's upcoming activities for 1958. This letter was in the format that would be adopted the next year when monthly newsletters began to be published. The letter also contained a plea for more members to support the trips being planned.

April 9 – The 20th Anniversary Banquet was held at the Holland House in Golden. Transportation was via a Colorado & Southern standard gauge chartered train

May 31, 1958 - D&RGW excursion near Bondad on the Club's only trip over the Farmington Branch. **R. H. KINDIG PHOTO**

1938-49

1950-59

1960-69

1970-79

1980-89

1990-99

2000-03

Color Extra

same trip on April 8, 1959 using Colorado & Southern locomotive 809. Engine 646 was later transferred to Cheyenne where it operated in switching service for another year.

May 30, 31, June 1 – Three-day D&RGW narrow gauge Memorial Day excursion scheduled from Alamosa to Durango to Silverton. However, due to flood damage on the Silverton Branch, the special was diverted to Farmington, NM instead. This was the Club's only trip over the Farmington Branch. Cost of this trip was $20.00. Two nights were spent in Durango at members' own expense and transportation to Alamosa was also the members' own responsibility.

May 30 - Engine 476 was used on the eleven-car train from Alamosa to Durango and return (which included a red freight gondola on the rear end to Durango).

May 31 – Engine 493 pulled the train to Farmington. Only the engine was turned and the train was pulled backward to Durango, with the gondola behind the locomotive.

June 1 – Engine 476 pulled the train to Chama where the 499 was added as helper to the summit of Cumbres Pass. Engine 499 was cut off there and the 476 continued to Alamosa.

Note: North Jersey Recording Associates recorded a 12" 33-1/3 rpm high fidelity record on this trip which was sold for $4.95, postage paid.

May – The Club established the Equipment Restoration Fund.

July 27 – Combined Colorado & Southern and Great Western Railway excursion from Denver to Longmont on the C&S and then to Eaton and to Loveland on the GW. From Loveland the C&S took the train back to Denver. C&S engine 900 and GW engine 90 were used on each road's segment. Equipment for the trip included a D&RGW heavyweight coach, three CB&Q green heavyweight coaches with one baggage car. On the GW, that road added a caboose behind the locomotive. Club member Ernie Peyton set up a lunch counter at Eaton where passengers were allowed 50 minutes for the meal. A tour of the shops in Loveland permitted members the opportunity to photograph locomotives and equipment. Cost was $6.00 for adults and $3.00 for children, (lunch not included).

using engine 646. Cost was $4.00 and was limited to 200 (although 208 actually rode). The four-car train departed Denver Union Station at 6:00 p.m. and returned just after midnight. As there was no wye in Golden, the train backed all the way back to Denver. The cold weather had caused a switch to freeze, delaying the return to Denver. Shrimp cocktail, filet mignon, vegetables, and fancy ice cream were included in the dinner. An editorial article in the *The Denver Post* on April 11 covered the trip, as reporter William Barker had been a passenger. He noted that "Mac" Poor was huddled in a vestibule with his microphone as he was tape recording the sounds of the train and its whistle. Ed Haley said that the trip had been sold out for weeks and included one passenger who drove in a snowstorm from Wichita to make the trip. Barker reported that another passenger, "A pretty girl, her dark hair stirred by the vestibule breeze stared out at Golden as we moved away, clickety-clack, clickety-clack. 'Coors brewery looks like some grim castle through the black mist,' she said. 'And the eerie town lights… We could be moving through some place in Middle Europe. This is the Orient Express and we're all sinister characters in a Hitchcock movie.'" This was reported as the last passenger train between Denver and Golden in an article in the *The Denver Post* on April 10. However, the Club made the

August 24, 1958 - The Club's first Chicago, Burlington & Quincy excursion using Colorado & Southern engine 646 is shown in Longmont.
**N. R. MILLER PHOTO - KLINGER COLLECTION**

August 24 – The Club's first Chicago, Burlington & Quincy excursion operated from Denver to Lyons via Lafayette, Erie and Longmont and return using Colorado & Southern engine 646. The five-car train included two streamline coaches and three heavyweight cars. The cost of this trip over the freight-only Lyons branch was $5.00. Guests brought picnic lunches. Due to the hot weather and quality of fuel, the 646 (an oil-burning locomotive) caused a number of fires along the trip. While stopped at Church's Lake (near the present day Highway 36 overpass) the fireman was sprayed with oil that ignited. He jumped into the lake and extinguished the fire with no injuries. The train was also stopped in Broomfield by Fire Department authorities who were upset by the fires. The Lyons Fire Department provided water for the tender during the two and one half-hour layover for lunch.

Late August – Club completed moving caboose 0578 and business car 021 "Rico" from the experimental mill at the Colorado School of Mines to the Colorado Railroad Museum. By the end of the month, all Club equipment was located at the Colorado Railroad Museum. The two narrow gauge cars as well as car 25 had all been vandalized. However, insurance covered the replacement of broken windows and other damage. In a letter to all members dated November 20, the Club summarizes the negotiations with the Iron Horse Development Corporation (Museum) that has allowed locating the Club equipment in Golden. The same letter encourages members that there is much to be done to preserve these pieces and seeks volunteers and funding to help restore the equipment.

"Mac" Poor ended the letter with the simple statement, "Mark your check, 'Equipment Restoration Fund!" This is still true today!

September 7 - Slides in the Ed Haley collection at the

Colorado Railroad Museum indicate that Club took a trip on the M&PP this day. This was the last run of steam locomotive 4, which handled only one coach. Numerous runbys were provided. No other details have been located.

Late fall – The Club took advance orders for the *Pictorial Supplement to Denver South Park & Pacific* priced at $12.50 if ordered by December 31, 1958.

November 2 – President Bill Gordon and Museum President Robert Richardson turned the first shovel-full of dirt for the new Colorado Railroad Museum building, using a shovel used 76 years earlier on the never-finished Ohio Pass extension of the Denver, South Park & Pacific.

December – For any person who has served as an unpaid volunteer for any organization, including the Club, there are times when the level of frustration overcomes one's patience. Treasurer Morris Cafky included the following statement in the Club's ledger for the end of 1958:

> "At this point, I give up as I am completely confused and baffled. The bank statement shows $3,589.20 on deposit on November 28, 1958 whereas my figures are nearly $1,000 below that. And my monthly balance sheets don't seem to agree with the bank statements either, though closer to them than the check stub balances. I freely admit that I am a complete idiot when it comes to keeping books."

There is no written record of what the Board of Directors did to placate Morris, but in 1959, Ane Clint began serving as Treasurer, a position she held for ten years. No doubt Ms. Clint had her share of frustrations as well, as have many Treasurers subsequent to Morris and Ane.

**1959** **Meetings at the Farmer's Union Auditorium at 16th and Sherman St. Dues are still $2.00 for in-state members and $1.00 for out-of-state members. Pres. M. C. Poor; V-P. D. K. Peterson; Secy. Mike Blecha; Treas. Ane Clint. Dave Gross is elected Board member and at age 18 was the youngest to ever serve in that position up to that date. Beginning in July, a periodic informational letter (normally a one sheet, two-sided document) was prepared and distributed by the President. Newsletter numbering began with issue 4 in October.**

This year Ane Clint became Treasurer. She was the first woman to become a Club officer. Ane served in this role through 1969. She also helped type and proof read the Club newsletter from 1960 until 1975. She arranged for the printing of the newsletter through her company at no cost to the Club. She also volunteered for many other tasks. Ane continued her membership until her death in 1983. Ane and her husband David joined the Club in 1951. David was killed October 19, 1952 when the boiler of D&RGW engine 3703 exploded south of Littleton.

February 1 – The Board of Directors published a letter to all 660 members describing upcoming trips and Club activities. Vice President Daniel Peterson stated:

> Plans are being made for several steam trips this year over both standard and narrow gauge lines, assuming that steam will be available. The way the "infernal" combustion engines are invading our very back yard, all of us had better make this year a "Ride It Now" year, before we have any regrets.

> President Poor notes that 2,060 copies of the *Pictorial Supplement to Denver South Park & Pacific* had been ordered as of that date.

April 8 – Annual Dinner in Golden. A steam powered Colorado & Southern four-car train pulled by engine 809 was used to transport guests to the Holland House and the total cost of transportation and dinner was $5.00. The trip was limited to 200 guests. Dick Kindig presented the program, which included Georgetown Loop comparison slides taken in 1939. The train returned to Denver about 12:35 a.m.

April – The Club mailed a letter to all members on upcoming excursions and included a reminder that dues are due!

May 29, 30, 31 – Annual D&RGW narrow gauge Memorial Day excursion from Alamosa to Durango to Silverton and back. The trip was sold out. Playing card-sized souvenir timetables were given each ticket holder. The timetable featured a glossy, black and white photo of engine 477 with four cars of the "San Juan," which was train number 116, near Cresco, NM. Roundtrip fare was $20 for adults and $10 for children. Passengers had to make their own travel arrangements from Denver to Alamosa, where the train left for Durango at 8:00 a.m. on Friday. The next morning, departure for Silverton was at 8:00 a.m. On Sunday, the train to Alamosa left Durango at 7:00 a.m. The Club's profit for this trip was $1,727.

> May 29 – Engine 476 pulled the twelve-car train from Alamosa to Durango. A caboose was behind the locomotive and an open red freight gondola was the rear car.

> May 30 – Engine 473 handled the train of eleven cars to Silverton, assisted by 476 which returned light to Durango.

> May 31 – Engine 476 pulled the thirteen-car train, which included the private car "Nomad." At Chama, engine 498 was added as helper to Cumbres.

**The following trips are often identified as Club sponsored excursions, but they were actually operated by the CB&Q as part of their public relations program.**

> June 9 – Colorado & Southern standard gauge excursion from Denver to Colorado Springs and return. One streamline vista dome car was in the consist. The price of the ticket ($3.00) included a chuck wagon dinner in Colorado Springs. Engine was CB&Q 5626 (4-8-4) which showed Club members speed with steam. In Colorado Springs members could continue on a second leg of the trip via D&RGW standard gauge to Alamosa. The train returned to Denver about 11:00 p.m.

> June 10 – Colorado & Southern standard gauge excursion from Denver to Ft. Collins using CB&Q engine 5626. The price of this trip was $3.00 and tickets were purchased at the C&S city ticket office. The train left at 5:00 p.m. returning at 11:00 p.m. taking the place of the regular Club meeting which would have been held that night.

June 9 – The Club executed a License Agreement with the Iron Horse Development Corporation (later to be known as the Colorado Railroad Museum) permitting the Club to store and keep on its premises, Club equipment, engine 20, the "Rico," car 25, Birney 22 and caboose 0578. The Club agreed to pay $1.00 annually, each January, for the privilege of using the museum's site. In fact, it was the support of members Ed Haley, Dick Kindig, Bill Gordon and "Mac" Poor working with Robert Richardson and Cornelius Hauck that resulted in the purchase of the farm at 17155 W. 44th Ave, that became the Colorado Railroad Museum. This agreement and fee are still in effect. This demonstrates the long-standing and mutually beneficial relationship between the Club and the Museum, which is nearly fifty years old.

June – The Club acquired a standard gauge boxcar body from the Colorado & Southern for use as a tool and equipment storage car at the Colorado Railroad Museum. The car was repainted and stenciled with the old C&S emblem.

July 19 – Colorado & Southern standard gauge excursion from Denver to Ft. Collins to Rex to Cheyenne and back to Denver. C&S engine 647 was used northbound and engine 900 operated southbound. The train consisted of one baggage car and four heavyweight coaches. The cost of the trip was $7.50 for adults and $4.00 for children. The Club paid the railroad $1,478 but the income was $1,610 for a profit of $132.

August – The Club distributed the D&RGW souvenir edition of the *Green Light* with the August newsletter, thanks to Jack Thode.

October 25 – CB&Q standard gauge excursion from Denver to Burns Junction to Longmont and then to Lyons and return using Colorado & Southern engine 647. The train consisted of a baggage car, two Burlington and two D&RGW heavyweight coaches. One hundred seventy-four passengers rode the train and the temperature was 80 degrees. The Lyons Fire Department provided water while passengers picnicked in Meadow Park during the two and a half-hour layover. Cost was $5.00 for adults and $2.50 for

children. The Club lost $237.55 on this trip.

November 22 – Workday at the Colorado Railroad Museum to work on the Birney car 22.

December 9 – Clarence S. Jackson, son of William H. Jackson, presented the Club a large framed photograph of the elder Jackson. This photo is on display at the Colorado Railroad Museum.

The Club published the *Pictorial Supplement to Denver South Park & Pacific*. All costs of publishing (done by World Press) were paid by September 1960. The price was $15.00 and included a painting by Phil Ronfor on the jacket cover, as well as six other full color paintings by Ronfor and Richard Ward. Ed Haley prepared maps that were provided in a special map pocket in the back of the book.

# S c r a p b o o k

Commemorative envelope given riders of the May 28-30, 1955 Memorial Day trip.

Embossed membership card.

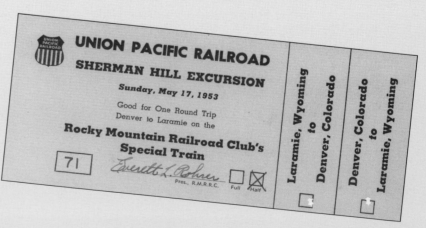

May 21, 1950 – Passengers inside the "Silver Vista" enjoyed a nearly unobstructed view of the scenery on this rare trip to Villa Grove. **E. J. HALEY PHOTO**

July 2, 1950 – End of the line at Leyden. Three rail operation is clearly seen in this view looking east. **GEORGE TROUT PHOTO**

July 2, 1950 – Car .02 of the Club's three-car excursion to Leyden prepares to leave the Central Loop Station in downtown Denver. PHOTOGRAPHER UNKNOWN. **ANE CLINT ALBUM - DARRELL ARNDT COLLECTION**

July 2, 1950 – Members await reboarding cars .02, .03 and 130 at Arvada. **N. R. MILLER PHOTO - KLINGER COLLECTION**

THE ROCKY MOUNTAIN RAILROAD CLUB INVITES YOU TO A

## Rail Excursion

### THRU THE ROCKIES

**Sunday, July 23, 1950**

Over 300 members of the Rocky Mountain Railroad Club, the most active rail fan group in the nation, will take a one-day excursion over Rio Grande's scenic mainline, July 23, 1950. They invite you to enjoy these spectacular features of Rocky Mountain rail travel:

**MOFFAT TUNNEL ROUTE** Leave Denver Sunday morning, traversing Rio Grande's Scenic Shortcut through South Boulder Canyon and the 6.2 mile long Moffat Tunnel to Dotsero.

**ROYAL GORGE ROUTE** Return via the Royal Gorge Route over 10,241 foot Tennessee Pass, past Mt. Elbert and Mt. Massive, America's second and third highest peaks, and through America's best-loved travel wonder, the Royal Gorge of the Arkansas River to arrive at Denver Sunday evening.

**GIANT STEAM LOCOMOTIVES** Giant Rio Grande mountain-type steam locomotives, the famous 3600's, in action over the highest standard-gauge mainline in the country.

**PHOTO STOPS** Photo stops at points en route— including the Royal Gorge, Moffat Tunnel, and Tennessee Pass—will be made for convenience of passenger photographers.

**LUNCH CAR** Air-conditioned equipment and a sip-and-snack car serving lunches, coffee, soft drinks, and sandwiches.

*One-Day Trip Over the Scenic Line of the World...Only $10.00, with meals extra.*

**MAIN LINE Rio Grande THRU THE ROCKIES**

**DENVER AND RIO GRANDE WESTERN RAILROAD**
THE DIRECT CENTRAL TRANSCONTINENTAL ROUTE

H. F. ENO, Passenger Traffic Manager
Denver & Rio Grande Western Railroad
Rio Grande Bldg. - 1531 Stout Street
Denver, Colorado

**RESERVATION STUB**

I. E. August, President
Rocky Mountain Railroad Club
2645 Steele St., Denver 5, Colo.

Please reserve..............tickets for the Circle Trip from Denver excursion Sunday, July 23, 1950.

Amount Enclosed
$............

Signed.................
Address.................

*Make your reservation now by returning attached coupon*

July 23, 1950 – The "Circle Trip" waits at East Portal with the Club's drumhead clearly visible on the last car. Dress for this outing was not just casual. **R. W. ANDREWS PHOTO**

July 23, 1950 – Announcement in *Trains* magazine describes what some consider the Club's most unusual standard gauge steam trip.

July 23, 1950 – D&RGW locomotives 3618 and 1705 wait for clearance to enter the Moffat Tunnel westbound at East Portal. The former Denver and Salt Lake grade over Rollins Pass is visible above the last car of the train. **RMRR CLUB ARCHIVES**

July 23, 1950 – D&RGW locomotive 3618 waits for the go ahead at East Portal. PHOTOGRAPHER UNKNOWN. **ANE CLINT ALBUM - DARRELL ARNDT COLLECTION**

September 1950 – Open platform wooden car 306 shows off new Rio Grande Gold colors at Durango. These cars were constructed in the 1880s and some are still operating on the Durango & Silverton Narrow Gauge Railroad. **R. C. GRAY PHOTO**

May 30, 1951 – C&S engine 374, a 4-6-2, waits in Denver Union Station for departure of the Club's excursion on the Owl Canyon Branch. **R. H. KINDIG PHOTO**

```
ROCKY MOUNTAIN RAILROAD CLUB
Farewell excursion Colorado & Southern Ry.
daylight service between Denver & Cheyenne
Sunday February 25, 1951 Lv. Denver 8:45 A.M.
Arr. Cheyenne 12:10 P.M. Lv. Cheyenne 12:20 P.M.
Arr. Denver 3:35 P.M.
     Special car for club members will be carr-
ied on trains 31 & 32. Round trip fare $5.58
tax included. Please bring your own lunch as
train schedule does not allow for same enroute.
     Enjoy a 240 mile trip with the Snowy Range
Mountains in view all the way.
     Notify Herb O'Hanlon 2695 Bellaire Street
Denver, Dexter 3256, if you plan to make the
trip. Tickets should be purchased at station
ticket window before boarding train.
                    Bob LeMassena, President
```

February 25, 1951 – Club members received penny postcards notifying them of Club meetings and trips. **RMRR CLUB ARCHIVES**

May 30, 1951 – Members stand on the platform of the Great Western combination car at Elm. The drumhead reads "Dead Beet Express."
**GEORGE TROUT PHOTO**

September 2, 1951 – RGS locomotive 74 slowly crosses one of the trestles at Ophir on the Club's last steam passenger trip on the RGS. **R. H. KINDIG PHOTO**

April 2, 1952 – Left to right, Ed Gerlits, behind the door, Neal Miller, Loren Weed and Conductor Matthews ride car 25 to Golden for the Annual Banquet. **GEORGE TROUT PHOTO**

May 30-31, 1952 – The Club's first of many successful and memorable Memorial Day weekend excursions is shown in the Otto Perry view (above) as it crests the summit of Cumbres Pass. On the following day, Dick Kindig recorded the train at the Durango depot.

1938-49

1950-59

1960-69

1970-79

1980-89

1990-99

2000-03

Color Extra

October 25, 1952 – D&RGW engines 488 and 499 double-head the excursion train near Windy Point. **R. H. KINDIG PHOTO**

1953 – The Club roster shows eighteen members of the "Eastern Division." This photo taken in Irv August's home in Longmeadow, MA shows, left to right, Phil Ronfor, Stanley Bradley, Michael Koch, Thomas Gilbert, Irv August, John Krause and Morris Abbott enjoying a meal with "imported" beer. **ANDREW WITTENBORN PHOTO**

May 17, 1953 – Challenger locomotive 3967 simmers at La Salle enroute to Laramie, WY on the Club's first Union Pacific mainline excursion. **R. H. KINDIG PHOTO**

May 17, 1953 – Five passengers (including the infant in the man's arms) got on and off the special train at Borie Tower, WY instead of going all the way to Denver. The tower was taken down a few weeks later. **J. L. EHERNBERGER PHOTO**

May 30, 1954 – U. S. Army diesel 4700N double-heads with D&RGW engine 7 at Silverton. Number 7 was in reality engine 476 and had been painted for a movie. **R. H. KINDIG PHOTO**

October 31, 1954 – UP engine 2888 double-heads with Northern 812 on train 57, shown here at Greeley, with extra cars for the Club's excursion to Cheyenne. **R. H. KINDIG PHOTO**

WORLD PRESS, INC. *Printers Publishers*

1340 SPEER BOULEVARD · DENVER 4 COLORADO

LOUIS J. DOUGHTY, Pre

PHONE MAIN 4

February 3, 1955

AGREEMENT

The World Press, Inc. agrees to manufacture for the Rocky Mountain Railroad Club a book entitled "Rails Around Gold Hill" which will incorporate the following specifications:

```
Page size.....................8½x11
Number of pages..............400
Type size....................12 on 14 - 30 ems
Paper stock..................70# No. 1 enamel
End pages....................front and back
Jacket (two color)...........70# enamel
Tip-ins (four color).........3 on 70# enamel
Halftones....................62 full page,
        6½x9; 39 half page, 4¼x6½; 43 1/3
        page, 2½x6½; 4 end page, 8x10
        3 four-color process, 9x12 (approx)
Binding......................Buckrum - gold
                             stamped
```

The World Press, Inc. will be responsible for the cost of all corrections. Alterations will be chargeable to the Rocky Mountain Railroad Club.

Terms of payment are understood to be as follows: One-third on or before February 15, 1955. One-third after all corrections have been made and page proofs approved. Final one-third upon completion of the book.

The prices listed below include all the specifications listed above and the World Press, Inc. guarantees first-class workmanship. Deviations from above specifications will be chargeable or deductible as the case may be.

1,000 copies....$8260.00    1,500.....$10,085.00

2,000.......$11,750.00

The World Press agrees to complete publication within 60 days after final page proofs are submitted by the Rocky Mountain Railroad Club.

Final determination of the number of copies to be made at the time the book goes to press.

*M. Baar, Sec.*

*Irving E. August, Pres.*

*E. J. Haley, V. Pres.*

*Louis J. Doughty, Pres. World Press, Inc.*

*R. H. Kindig, Treasure*

February 3, 1955 – Contract for the publication of *Rails Around Gold Hill* contains the signature of all the Club officers.

May 28, 1955 – The annual Memorial Day excursion leaves Alamosa, passing the Narrow Gauge Motel and Museum with 15 cars and going about 25 mph. **R. H. KINDIG PHOTO**

1938-49
1950-59
1960-69
1970-79
1980-89
1990-99
2000-03
Color Extra

May 29, 1955 - The Club's Memorial Day weekend special is seen at Rockwood behind D&RGW engines 478 and 476. **R. H. KINDIG PHOTO**

May 28, 1955 – A day earlier than the photo above, members enjoy a leisurely ride on the rear platform of D&RGW business car B-7 along the three-rail mainline headed toward Durango from Alamosa. **JOHN KRAUSE PHOTO**

May 29, 1955 – D&RGW engine 476 leads the train on the high line above Rockwood. **R. H. KINDIG PHOTO**

May 30, 1955 – D&RGW engine 499 is serviced at Chama, NM. **N. R. MILLER PHOTO - KLINGER COLLECTION**

March 11, 1956 – The Union Pacific had 88 three-cylinder locomotives with the 4-12-2 wheel arrangement, the longest rigid wheel base of any steam locomotive built. The 9000, built in 1926, was the last survivor when it operated on the Club's excursion. This view (upper right) shows the freshly painted locomotive enroute to Denver on March 9. **MIKE TRENT PHOTO**; Two days later the temperatures dropped to near zero, but that didn't stop 215 hearty passengers from taking the only excursion with a locomotive of this type. The train is shown (above left) unloading passengers near La Salle for a photo run-by. These locomotives had an unusual off-beat exhaust sound because of the three-cylinders. **R. H. KINDIG PHOTO**

March 11, 1956 – The Union Pacific generously provided a special drumhead for the Club's excursion. That was why the Club's drumhead was mounted on the front of locomotive 9000.
**GEORGE TROUT PHOTO**

September 15, 1957 – Union Pacific engine 535 takes water at Spring Creek, WY, prior to going to Northgate via the Coalmont Branch. **MIKE TRENT PHOTO**

1938-49
1950-59
1960-69
1970-79
1980-89
1990-99
2000-03
Color Extra

June 1, 1957 – D&RGW engine 476 takes water at Needleton Tank; then the second engine, the 478, will fill its tender before the train resumes its journey to Silverton.  R. H. KINDIG PHOTO

June 30, 1957 – With bell ringing and the engineer and fireman watching the photographer, C&S locomotive 909, a 2-10-2, slowly begins its departure from Ft. Collins, bound for Denver.
MIKE TRENT PHOTO

March, 1958 – Ed Haley sent Jack Thode this photo post card with the following note: "Dear Jack, I sincerely feel that I must comment upon the poor beds and service encountered on these narrow-gauge Pullmans of the D&RGW."  E. J. HALEY PHOTO

September 15, 1957 - On the departure from Laramie, the Union Pacific added six cars of cattle to the Club's excursion. They were set out sixteen miles west and the train continued to Northgate. The Club lost money on this trip. When a well-intentioned Club officer suggested to the railroad that they help cover the loss, executives in Omaha quickly turned down the request.  J. L. EHERNBERGER PHOTO

May 31, 1958 – D&RGW engine 493 leads the Club's only excursion over the Farmington Branch. Seen here near Inca, NM, flood damage forced the railroad to cancel the trip on the Silverton Branch. **R. H. KINDIG PHOTO**

July 27, 1958 – C&S locomotive 900, a 2-10-2, is seen leaving Boulder with five cars for the joint C&S/GW trip. **R. H. KINDIG PHOTO**

July 27, 1958 – Great Western 90 was used on a number of Club excursions, including the combined C&S/GW trip on this date. This photo, taken in December, 1958, clearly shows the lines of the only Decapod to operate in Colorado. **R. H. KINDIG PHOTO**

March 9, 1959 – Irv August sent this three cent postcard to all members of behalf of the Equipment Committee, notifying members that all the Club's equipment was now at the Colorado Railroad Museum. Thus began decades and many thousands of hours of volunteer labor to preserve and maintain the equipment.

# ROCKY MOUNTAIN RAILROAD CLUB

Now that all of the Club's Equipment has been brought to the site of the Colorado Railroad Museum, at 17555 West 44th Avenue, the Equipment Committee is looking for volunteers to help restore our rolling stock. If you are interested in helping, please check the item that you are willing to help out on.

Or you are welcome to come out any time that you have a few hours to spare. Mr. Bob Richardson has been appointed Foreman at the Museum and will be happy to see anyone come out. He will be able to give information as to what needs to be done.

There is a big job ahead of us and we are going to need all the help we can get to put the equipment back into the condition it was in when in service.

I. E. AUGUST
Chairman, Equipment Committee.

1938-49
1950-59
1960-69
1970-79
1980-89
1990-99
2000-03
Color Extra

June 10, 1959 – CB&Q Northern 5626 shows its powerful lines leaving Boulder, northbound. The trip from Denver to Ft. Collins and back replaced the Club's regular evening meeting. **R. H. KINDIG PHOTO**

May 31, 1959 – D&RGW engines 498 and 476 climb Cumbres Pass above Labato, NM with 12 cars on this Memorial Day special. **R. H. KINDIG PHOTO**

June 10, 1959 – Ghostly images seem to be looking over CB&Q locomotive 5626 as it sits in Ft. Collins prior to its departure to Denver. **OTTO PERRY PHOTO**

July 19, 1959 – C&S locomotive 647 is headed northbound on the Owl Canyon Branch and then went to Cheyenne with four silver coaches and a traditional green baggage car. Engine 900 took the train back to Denver from Cheyenne. **R. H. KINDIG PHOTO**

# Chapter 3: 1960 - 1969

**1960** Meetings at the Farmer's Union Auditorium, 16th & Sherman. Due to an increase in postage and payments of rent, dues are raised to $3.00 for in-state members and $2.00 to out of state members. Pres. R. H. Kindig; V-P. W. J. Gordon; Secy. Mike Blecha; Treas. Ane Clint. An informal informational letter was prepared by the President and distributed every month except April.

February – Over 3000 copies of the *Pictorial Supplement to Denver South Park & Pacific* were sold.

April 13 – Annual Dinner at the Harvest House in Boulder. The trip was made behind Colorado & Southern engine 638, pulling one baggage car and five coaches. This train was the last passenger train ever to run in to the old Boulder Station. Cost was $6.00 for filet mignon and train trip. Jim Ehernberger presented the program titled "Trains Made Smoke." The Club lost $1,177 on this trip, of which $600 was for repairs to the locomotive.

May 28, 29, 30 – The Club's D&RGW narrow gauge Memorial Day excursion from Alamosa to Durango to Silverton and back. Two nights were spent in Durango and cost of the ticket did not include overnight accommodations. The trip handout was reproduced from *Over the Range to the Golden Gate* which was a 1903 tourist's guide. 375 passengers from 27 states and England rode this trip. Fares were $21 for adults and $11 for children.

> May 28 – The twelve-car train, pulled by engine 483, included caboose 0574 on the head end and freight gondola 9605 was the rear car between Alamosa and Silverton.
>
> May 29 – The Durango to Silverton leg was powered by engine 473 in road service with the 478 as helper.
>
> May 30 – The return to Alamosa was behind engine 491 with the 476 added as helper at Chama to the summit of Cumbres Pass.

July – The Colorado Railroad Museum established an entrance fee of 25¢. However, Club members were admitted free if they showed a current membership card.

July – The Boy Scout Jamboree, held near the Air Force Academy in Colorado Springs required 64 special trains with over 900 passenger cars to handle all the scouts participating.

October 2 – Joint Colorado & Southern and Great Western Railway excursion from Denver to Longmont on the C&S where the train was turned over to the GW. The excursion continued to Eaton with a number of photo stops before returning to Loveland where the C&S took the train back to Denver. C&S engines 638 and GW engine 90 were used on each road's segment of this six-car train, two of which were heavyweight Pullmans. Passengers were able to tour the GW's shops in Loveland. Cost was $6.00 for adults and $3.00 for children.

October 2, 1960 - The Club's C&S and Great Western excursion ticket.

October 23 – Work day at the Colorado Railroad Museum.

November 20 – First Rocky Mountain Railroad Club excursion on the Union Pacific using engine 844. The 560-mile trip ran from Denver to Rawlins, WY and return. Engine 844 operated between Cheyenne and Rawlins. Diesels pulled the train from Denver to Cheyenne and back. The $20.00 fare ($12.50 for children) included all meals served in the style made popular on the streamliner "City of Las Vegas." In other words, meals were available in a lunch-counter car on trays that could be carried to one's seat. The Union Pacific Railroad donated the original front number plate from engine 843 for the Club to raffle to paid passengers of this excursion. Member Bob Riley won the number plate for his $1.00 chance.

December – Year-end membership was 837 and the bank balance stood at $8,723.58. Income this year included $32 from "Train Chasers," persons who did not ride the excursions but purchased tickets nonetheless and followed the train taking pictures.

September 10, 1961 - C&S engine 638 on the Arkins Branch west of Loveland.
**N. R. MILLER PHOTO - KLINGER COLLECTION**

**1961** **Meetings at the Farmer's Union Auditorium, 16th & Sherman. Dues $3.00. Pres. J. O. Riley; V-P. Charles Max; Secy. Ed Lewandowski; Treas. Ane Clint. A periodic informational letter (normally a one sheet, two-sided document) was prepared and distributed by the president.**

April 12 – Annual Dinner was at the Harvest House in Boulder. Colorado & Southern engine 638 was used for the five-car roundtrip train. All equipment was D&RGW, including one vista dome coach. One surprise photo stop was provided for evening photography. Engineer Mickey Hansen was the Road Foreman of Engines for the C&S, a man known for his musical skill with a whistle and smooth handling techniques. The program was a slide and tape recording program presented by "Mac" Poor, Dan Peterson and Dave Gross, titled "Mountain Railroading in Sight and Sound." More than 240 attendees paid $6.00 for dinner (deluxe broiled filet mignon with side dishes).

May 27, 28, 29 – Annual D&RGW narrow gauge Memorial Day excursion from Alamosa to Durango the first day, from Durango to Silverton and return the second day and then Durango to Alamosa the third day. Three hundred and eighty-eight passengers paid $21.00 ($11.00 for 23 half-fare children) for this trip. Twenty-two states and Canada were represented, with 45 passengers from California alone. Hotel accommodations and meals were left to each passenger. Information provided in the handout was taken from the 1903 tourist's guide *Over the Range to the Golden Gate*.

May 27 – The thirteen-car train, including two cabooses and a freight gondola were pulled by engine 488 from Alamosa to Durango.

May 28 – Engine 478 was the road engine to Silverton, assisted by the 473.

May 29 – The same thirteen-car train returned to Alamosa behind engine 488. At Chama, engine 499 was added as helper to the summit of Cumbres Pass.

July – Because of recent examples of persons being apprehended for removing lights from locomotives in the Colorado & Southern yards in Denver, the Club restated its policy:

"Any member of the Club who becomes involved is such a misdeed, or who becomes involved in a similar misdeed, will automatically be asked to resign from the Club. If such an individual refuses to resign from the Club, proceedings will be initiated to remove him involuntarily."

September 10 – Joint Colorado & Southern and Great Western Railway excursion from Denver to Loveland behind C&S engine 638, where the train was turned over to the Great Western. GW engines 51 and 75 double-headed on that road's segment to Eaton and returned to Longmont. The 638 then brought the train back to Denver. 296 passengers (of which 125 were children) paid $7.00 ($4.00 for children) to ride. The train consisted of six cars, a baggage car and a mixed compliment of heavyweight and smooth-side cars. Each passenger received a copy of the booklet *Where Steam Still Serves* produced by the Great Western Railway.

September – *Trains* magazine article by Dick Kindig "Mudhens and Sport Models" described in outstanding detail the 2-8-2 narrow gauge locomotives used by the D&RGW's Durango line and featured many Club trips.

September 10, 1961 - Great Western engines 51 and 75 double-head the Club's excursion south of Johnstown. Photographer R. H. Kindig noted "Six cars, 20 mph."

October 22 – Workday at the Colorado Railroad Museum.

December 12 – The Club received one of the 1961 Awards of Merit of the American Association for State and Local History for its publication of the *Pictorial Supplement to Denver South Park & Pacific*. The presentation of the award was at the December meeting of the State Historical Society of Colorado.

**1962** **Meetings at the Farmer's Union Auditorium, 16th & Sherman. Dues $3.00. Pres. J. C. Thode; V-P. Jack Morison; Secy. Ed Lewandowski; Treas. Ane Clint. A monthly newsletter was prepared by the Secretary and it was distributed every month beginning an unbroken practice continued to the present. Ed Lewandowski was the first newsletter Editor of this series.**

March – Membership exceeded 800 with members in 42 states, Canada, Venezuela, France, England, New Zealand and Australia.

April 11 – Annual Dinner was held in Boulder. The roundtrip was on a Colorado & Southern special train using engine 638 (with engineer Mickey Hansen). Almost 300 attended. The cost of dinner (filet mignon) was $5.00 and the train added another dollar for a total of $6.00. The program that evening was a showing of the movie "Roaring Rails." The Club paid the C&S $652 for use of the train on this trip.

May 27, 28, 29 – D&RGW narrow gauge Memorial Day excursion from Alamosa to Durango. Numerous photo stops were arranged, including "meets" with freight trains. About 300 fans rode and paid $21 for adults and $11 for children. Hotel accommodations and meals were left to each passenger. Information provided in the glossy, 28-page handout was taken from the 1903 tourist's guide *Over the Range to the Golden Gate*. It also included a number of photos and drawings of locomotives and equipment.

May 27 – The first day, engine 487 took the eleven-car train from Alamosa to Durango.

May 28 – Locomotive 473 took the train (with ten cars) to Silverton and back, without a helper.

May 29 – Engine 487 returned the excursion train to Alamosa, with engine 491 helping from Chama to

Rocky Mountain Railroad Club
"THE COLORADO ROAD"
The Colorado & Southern Ry. Co.
STEAM EXCURSION
LAST RUN OF C.& S. 638
DENVER to TRINIDAD, COLORADO
LEAVING DENVER AT 7:30 A.M., DEC. 16, 1962
(STEAM ENGINE ON SOUTHBOUND TRAIN ONLY)
Nº 475
Half Fare If Punched
President R. M. R. R. C.

TRINIDAD to DENVER
ON SPECIAL TRAIN
Half

PUEBLO to TRINIDAD
ON SPECIAL TRAIN
Half

COLORADO SPRINGS to PUEBLO
ON SPECIAL TRAIN
Half

DENVER to COLORADO SPRINGS
ON SPECIAL TRAIN
Half

Cumbres. Newly painted observation car 9605 was now in Grande Gold. It had previously been red. It was the last car on this eleven-car consist.

July – The Club acquired the J. Foster Adams glass plate and photo collection through the efforts of Dick Kindig. Adams was a long-time resident of Portland Oregon who photographed trains using glass plates. The Club's portion of the collection numbered more than 400 photos. The balance of the Adams collection was given to the State Historical Society of Wisconsin (now on loan to the Mid-continent Chapter of the NRHS).

July 22 – CB&Q six-car excursion from Denver to Lyons via Lafayette, Erie and Longmont and return using Colorado & Southern engine 638. Again, Mickey Hansen was at the throttle of this train with all heavy-weight cars. Mickey, a Club member, was also Road Foreman of Engines for the C&S in Denver. About 250 railfans enjoyed this Sunday trip and picnic in Lyons. Cost was $4.00 for adults and $2.00 for children. The 8:30 a.m. departure was arranged to allow out-of-town travelers arriving in

September 9, 1962 - Last combined C&S/GW steam excursion operated by the Club. Mickey Hansen was engineer on C&S engine 638. **R. H. KINDIG PHOTO**

1938-49

1950-59

1960-69

1970-79

1980-89

1990-99

2000-03

Color Extra

Denver that morning to connect with the special train. A tragic footnote accompanies this trip. Locomotive sparks started a number of fires along the route, including one next to the Boulder Turnpike overpass. Heavy smoke obscured a portion of the turnpike and as a car slowed to pass through the smoke, a chain reaction occurred involving six cars. One person was killed and fourteen injured in the accident. Smoke and excessive speed (approximately 70 miles per hour) contributed to the situation according to the Colorado State Patrol. Due to the fire conditions, only two photo run-bys were made.

July – An audit of the Club's finances reported total assets of slightly over $20,000 with no liabilities. Of this amount $9,639.23 was listed as investments in Club equipment.

August 17 – The Board decided to refrain from running a Union Pacific steam excursion to Rawlins this year, due to the railroad's requirements for fares and guarantees.

September 9, 1962 - The Club's last steam excursion on the Great Western Railway was behind engine 90, a 2-10-0, the only Decapod locomotive in Colorado, seen here near Mead. **R. H. KINDIG PHOTO**

September 9 – Joint Colorado & Southern and Great Western Railway excursion from Denver to Longmont behind the C&S engine 638 where the six-car train (one baggage and five coaches) was turned over to the Great Western. GW engine 90 continued on that road's segment to Eaton and to Loveland where the 638 brought the train back to Denver. Fare was $7.00 for adults and $4.00 for children. The train departed Denver at 8:00 a.m. and returned at 7:00 p.m. The Club reimbursed the Great Western Railway $670 for their portion of the trip.

October 10 – Author Richard Overton spoke on "Some Untold Chapters of the Burlington" at the

Club's regular meeting.

October 21 – Five past officers and Club members traveled to the Westall Monument in the Platte Canyon to do minor repairs and to mount a bronze plaque commemorating the death of Engineer Westall who died one day after a wreck at this location on August 28, 1898 on the Denver Leadville & Gunnison Railway.

October – Club member Edward T. Bollinger and his associate Frederick Bauer, were recognized by the American Association for State and Local History. They received the Award of Merit for the book titled *The Moffat Road*.

October – All copies of *Pictorial Supplement to Denver South Park & Pacific* were sold out by the end of this month.

November 14 – Colorado & Southern excursion to Golden to tour the Coors Brewery. Engine 638 was used on this late afternoon/night run. This was the last Denver area run of this locomotive. Members "in good standing" were limited to one guest and overall the trip was limited to 200. Members of the NRHS and National Model Railroad Association were also invited to attend. The special departed Denver at 6:00 p.m. arriving in Golden at 7:15. The evening's events included tours of the brewery, a movie titled "Colorado – The Favored Land," refreshments, dancing and a short business meeting. The train returned to Denver about midnight. Roundtrip fare was $3.50.

December 16 – Colorado & Southern excursion from Denver to Trinidad. This was the last run of engine 638, because the locomotive was going to be donated to Trinidad. Engine 638 already had its rods removed and the cab boarded before the decision was made to run this trip. Ed Haley was responsible for the arrangement of this final C&S steam excursion. The six-car train (one baggage and five coaches) was limited to what 638 was capable of handling over Palmer Lake summit. An auxiliary water tender provided additional capacity. Coal was added to the tender at Pueblo with a crane. Approximately 356 passengers rode on various segments of the trip. One coach was reserved for passengers boarding at either Colorado Springs or Pueblo. Roundtrip adult (children fares were one-half) fare from Denver, was $12.00; from Colorado Springs $10.00; or from Pueblo, $8.00. After a special ceremony in Trinidad where they formally accepted engine 638, the train returned to Denver behind C&S SD9 diesels at maximum track speed. An 8x9-inch souvenir drawing on C&S letterhead was given to passengers who rode the train. Each letterhead was numbered and required an on-board date stamp to be authentic.

**1963**  **Meetings at Western Federal Savings and Loan Association at 17th and California St. Dues $3.00 and membership more than 900. Pres. J. C. Thode; V-P. Richard Ronzio; Secy. and Ed. E. R. Lewandowski; Treas. Ane Clint.**

The January meeting had 175 attendees at the new Western Federal location.

April – Club membership numbered nearly 900.

May 3 – In a letter responding to an inquiry made by Ed Haley concerning the availability of a steam locomotive for a future trip, The Great Western Railway Company wrote:

"We are endeavoring to dispose of some of our steam equipment and have asked for bids to see if anyone desires to buy the equipment prior to disposing of it as scrap. Under the circumstances, we do not desire to run any excursions other than one which was committed some time last year. Storing and maintaining this outdated equipment is extremely costly to us and any benefits that we derive from an excursion or two are so minimal that we are planning to discontinue them completely." The trip on September 9, 1962 was the last steam powered trip operated by the Great Western for the Club.

May 11 – For the 25th Anniversary Banquet, the Club arranged a Colorado & Southern special train Denver to Colorado Springs using CB&Q engine 4960 (2-8-2). The Club issued a souvenir timetable for this trip with historical information on previous excursions. This Silver Anniversary Dinner was at the Antlers Hotel. The trip and movie were all for $6.00! More than 450 people attended. A memorable point, of sorts, for many members

May 11, 1963 - 25th Anniversary Dinner and excursion ticket was printed on silver paper.

was when the train ran out of water at the Air Force Academy on the way to Colorado Springs. The train stopped at the wastewater treatment facility where the locomotive engineer called the Academy for assistance. Thanks to the Fire Department of the Academy, the tender was replenished from a pumper truck and auxiliary tanker (8,000 gallons of water) and the trip continued. The CB&Q charged the Club $1,736.35 for the use of the train. The net loss to the Club for this event was $1,207. The Intermountain Chapter had already reserved the locomotive for a trip on this date for their organization, but discussions between NRHS Chapter President William Jones and Club President Thode negotiated the change.

May 13 – As part of a "Salute to Steam Railroading Month" the Burlington provided a number of excursion trips to Denver area school children. The railroad ran three trains on Monday, May 13 from Denver to Tampa curve, near Keenseburg, and back. Tickets were $1.50 (strictly for children and teachers) and were purchased directly from the Burlington's travel office.

May 30, 31, June 1 – D&RGW narrow gauge Memorial Day excursion from Alamosa to Durango the first day, from Durango to Silverton and return the second day and then from Durango to Alamosa the third day. The three-day trip covered more than 490 miles. This was the first revenue service of two new all-steel narrow gauge coaches built by the railroad. Nearly 500 railfans were on the sold-out twelve-car trip. Fare was $21.00 for adults and $11.00 for children. Overnight accommodations (not included in the fare) were available in Durango. The on-board souvenir flyer *Journey to Yesteryear* included a reprint of *Denver & Rio Grande Railway Timetable No. 19* dated July 23, 1882. Also in this same flyer was a poem written by W. P. Johnston, Sr., "Railfan's Refrain." Gene Johnston sent the poem to the Club shortly after his father's death. The poem describes the Durango to Silverton line and in the closing sentence, reflects a sentiment shared by most Club members, "...And I hope this famous railroad in the Rockies never dies." The train cost the Club $6,721 and the Club realized a profit of $1,895 on this trip.

May 30 – Twelve-car train, including two cabooses and a freight gondola, was pulled by engine 488. At Dulce, NM there was an Indian encampment.

May 31 – Engine 478 handled the twelve-car train without assistance to from Durango to Silverton and back.

June 1 – Engine 488 handled the same consist as was used on May 30 from Durango to Alamosa. Engine 498 was added as helper at Chama to Cumbres.

1938-49
1950-59
1960-69
1970-79
1980-89
1990-99
2000-03
Color Extra

May 30, 1963 - Club excursion stopped in Dulce, NM where Indians performed ceremonial dances for the passengers.
R. H. KINDIG PHOTO

This trip was the first revenue run for two new all-steel coaches, 330 and 331, as well as reconditioned coach 350, formerly the parlor car "Alamosa," rebuilt baggage car 126 and recently restored business car B-7.

May – The monthly newsletter contained the most recent issue of the D&RGW employee's newsletter *Green Light*. This issue commented on trips sponsored by the Club and also included photos of the new, all-steel narrow gauge coaches being built at the Burnham Shops in Denver.

May was designated "Salute to Steam Railroading Month" by Governor John Love as a result of initiatives by the Club and specifically, Director Ted McKee.

May – Club published a reprint of the *Denver & Rio Grande Railway Timetable No. 19,* July 23, 1882, in commemoration of "Salute to Steam Railroading Month." All passengers who rode the Memorial Day trip received copies. On every excursion passengers were provided attractive printed hand-outs.

May – All members received a copy of the special timetable used for the 25th Anniversary Banquet and steam trip with their newsletter mailing.

June – The Club published the 1963 roster. Printed by Hotchkiss Inc. at a cost of $232.33, the roster continued a tradition of printed rosters, which began in 1948. In that year only, the roster was a three page mimeo-graphed handout listing members names and home-towns. Beginning in 1949, the roster was generally printed annually or combined to cover two years until 1989-90. The roster was not printed again until 1998 in commemoration of the Club's 60th Anniversary. The cost of the 1998 roster was in excess of $1,800, most of which was covered by advertising revenue. That was the first time paid advertising was solicited for the roster, which included many photographs and display ads.

September – Club members began construction of 600-foot section of trolley track line at Colorado Railroad Museum. Cost was approximately $2,400. The intent was to operate the Club's Birney car 22. Supplies for the work were purchased from the D&RGW and CB&Q railroads. Laborers hired from the D&RGW provided a portion of the construction.

September – October - The Club announced a contest jointly sponsored by *Trains* magazine and the Club soliciting photographs for the upcoming special article in *Trains* magazine commemorating the Club's 25th Anniversary. Twenty-one winners were to be selected with prizes ranging from $25 to honorable mention. Each photographer whose photo was selected would receive a copy of the Club's new Hotchkiss map. Deadline for submittals was November 20.

October 12 – The Club's members completed construction of 600 feet of standard gauge track at the Colorado Railroad Museum. Poles and wire remained to be erected.

October – The Club, in conjunction with Hotchkiss, Inc., published a "Hotchkiss 'Historical Map of Colorado Railroads, 1913." Ed Haley traced active and abandoned rail routes on a map originally published in 1913 by Clason Map Company of Denver. The reprint included enlarged sections (on the reverse of the map) depicting selected sections of the state with concentrations of railroads. The map sold for $4.74 (flat) and $5.00 folded. Copies were numbered.

November – The Club acquired 55 year-old nine-inch gauge 4-4-0 steam locomotive 999 from Mrs. George Lindsay. Mr. Lindsay built this locomotive in 1907 where it originally operated at Denver's Manhattan Beach until 1910. This locomotive is on display at the Edgewater Museum near Sloans Lake.

December 8 – President Thode and his wife Joyce hosted officers and members of the Board at the Mt. Vernon County Club as a way of saying thanks for their support during this year. The cost of the Sunday brunch was $2.50 per person.

**1964**  **Meetings at Western Federal Savings. Dues still $3.00 for in-state and $2.00 for out-of-state members. Pres. Ted McKee; V-P. Herb O'Hanlon; Secy. R. A. LeMassena (who resigned in March and was replaced by Fay McKee); Treas. Ane Clint; Ed. J. C. Thode.**

January 8 – Charles Ryland presented a program "Adventure in West Virginia" that was "depicted with coloured lantern slides and expounded in all its boring detail!". He printed a special card given to members at that evening's program that illustrated both his sense of humor and skill as a printer.

March 11 – *Trains* magazine Editor (and Club member) David P. Morgan honored the Club by awarding special prizes to members whose photos were selected for the magazine's September issue recognizing the Club's 25th Anniversary.

April 13 – As part of the pre-publication coordination needed for the upcoming Colorado Midland book, Messers. Cafky, Haley and Kindig sent a telegram to artist Phil Ronfor, as follows:

PAINTING FOR BROCHURE COVER URGENTLY NEEDED. PAGE PROOFS COMPLETED. BROCHURE WRITTEN, QUANTITY OF BOOKS SET BY BOARD OF DIRECTORS. CLUB IS IN FINANCIAL PINCH. DUE TO OUR INABILITY TO ANNOUNCE PREPUBLICATION BOOK SALE. WIRE COLLECT EARLIEST POSSIBLE DATE OF COMPLETION, AS DECI-

September 13, 1964 - Souvenir Union Pacific ticket featured advice for riders like original Overland tickets.

SION IS PENDING RE USE OF PHOTOGRAPHS OR OTHER PAINTING ON BOOK ANNOUNCEMENT.

April 13 – Phil Ronfor responded by telegram:

UNWORTHY PERSON HERE IN QUANDARY. STOP. CAN FINISH TEN DAYS. STOP. NO SOONER. STOP. SELLING HOUSE MOVING WORKING LIKE HECK. STOP. FULL OF SHAME. STOP. YOU DO WHAT'S BEST. STOP. REGRET TROUBLE CAUSED. PHIL

Needless to say, Mr. Ronfor's painting was completed and made part of the brochure and adorned the cover of the book. Although owned by the Club, Morris Cafky was loaned the painting to display in his home. Upon his death in 2002, the Club retrieved the painting and it is now on display at the Colorado Railroad Museum.

May 29, 30, 31 – D&RGW narrow gauge Memorial Day excursion from Alamosa over Cumbres Pass to Durango the first day, from Durango to Silverton and return the second day and back to Alamosa from Durango the third day. Two nights were spent in Durango (not included in the ticket price). More than 300 railfans paid $21.00 for the trip. Club member Tom Cox presented three sound-color movies for guests on Saturday evening, the 30th of May in the Diamond Circle Theater. Each passenger received an 8 1/2 by 11 handout, which included photos, maps, an excursion timetable and a copy of the reprinted *Denver & Rio Grande Timetable No. 19*, July 23, 1882.

1938-49
1950-59
1960-69
1970-79
1980-89
1990-99
2000-03
Color Extra

May 29 – Engine 488 pulled the eleven-car train from Alamosa to Durango.

May 30 – Engine 476 pulled the train to Silverton and return unassisted.

May 31 – Engine 487 served as road engine from Durango to Alamosa and the 480 was the helper from Chama to Cumbres.

September – *Trains* magazine featured a special section devoted to the Club's 25th Anniversary, which included photos selected as part of the Club's contest.

September 13 – Union Pacific excursion from Denver to Cheyenne (behind diesels) and from Cheyenne to Rawlins and return behind engine 8444. Number 8444 was previously the 844 but an extra numeral four was added since a GP30 held the new number 844. The nine-car train carried 237 passengers. Returning from Rawlins, many miles were clocked at 42 seconds or 85.7 mph. The roundtrip fare was $12.00 for adults and $12.50 for children. Over 300 of the 560 miles were behind steam. All meals were included buffet-style. The foot-long souvenir ticket included advice to riders similar to that provided on original Overland train tickets, such as "Shooting buffalo from train window strictly prohibited."

December 31 – Year-end financial statement showed cash assets of $7,430.31 and capital assets of $12,817.93.

**1965**  **Meetings at Western Federal Savings Building. The Club lists 949 members in roster. Pres. Ted McKee; V-P. Herb O'Hanlon; Secy. R. H. Kindig; Treas. Ane Clint.; Ed. J. C. Thode.**

January 31 – Bert Fullman died. Bert served as a director, served on newsletter mailing committee and was a former Denver & Salt Lake Railway engineer.

February – First appearance of the now familiar Club logo appeared on the first page of the newsletter.

March – The Club published roughly 6,100 copies of Morris Cafky's book *Colorado Midland*. Pre-publication price was $12.00 and the regular price was $14.00. Total cost of the publication, including original oil paintings prepared by Howard Fogg and Philip Ronfor was in excess of $60,000. However, more than $33,000 worth of books was pre-sold. This included a set of four-color prints that sold separately for $2.00. All in all, the Club netted nearly $30,000 from the sale of this book.

Ed Haley, Dick Kindig and Bill Gordon spent five evenings the last week of March packing books (three nights), stuffing newsletters and

preparing the Memorial Day Trip Announcements for mailing (Thursday) and then on Friday, attended a Board of Directors meeting that lasted until 12:30 a.m.

Breakeven point for the book was somewhere between 4,700 and 4,800. This includes discounts, review copies, returned copies (damaged by the Post Office) or defective copies.

April 11 – In a lengthy reply to a letter from Mr. Alexander Crosby, Newsletter Editor Jackson Thode stated:

The reproduction work (of the newsletter) is entirely the result of the skills of our invaluable Treasurer – Mrs. Ane Clint – a tremendously capable person who manages to handle all the Club's financial affairs, maintains the bookkeeping records in form and accuracy which pass an annual CPA audit, handle excursion ticket orders in complete detail, supervises the typing, multilithing and folding of the newsletter, in addition to other Club work of a similar nature. And since the loss, which is felt so keenly, of our esteemed old-timer, Bert Fullman, Ane and I have been stuffing, sorting and mailing our 950 newsletters each month. I might add that Mrs. Clint also works at a full time job to earn her living!

April 17 – The Club received a 9-inch gauge 4-4-0 live steam locomotive from Mrs. Joan Humphrey. This locomotive was lettered for the Denver, Northwestern & Pacific and numbered 210. It operated at Elitch Gardens from 1893 to approximately 1935. This locomotive is displayed at the Colorado Railroad Museum. It should be noted that that the 4-4-0 locomotives of the Denver, Northwestern and Pacific were actually numbered 390 and 391. The number 210 would have been, in real life, a 2-6-6-0 mallet.

April 30 – As of this date, the Club's finances showed a total bank balance of $3,913.80. Receipts for the month were $4,158.10 (including two trips) and expenditures were $2,058.77. The Club kept routine expenses separate from the equipment restoration fund (a balance of $515.65) and the book fund (a deficit of $223.35 that month).

May 2 – Special excursion on the D&RGW from Denver to East Portal and return behind ex-Great Western steam engine 51 (owned by member John Birmingham). The three-car special (limited to this number due to the low tractive effort of the 51) actually lost money (approximately $1,041) with empty seats leaving Denver. Only 131 passengers took this trip. The rental for this locomotive and train was

$2,900 for 240 guaranteed reserved seats. A second section was powered by diesel 5311, which carried a tender, a water car, a baggage car and a caboose to handle any fires. Twenty small fires were extinguished during the trip. When water was needed by the 51, the second section would pull adjacent to the tender at a siding to make a transfer from the water car. For this trip, engine 51 still carried lettering for the Colorado & Southern as make-up for its part in the movie "Cat Ballou" recently filmed near Canon City.

May 16 – The Sunday edition of *The Denver Post* contained an article in the *Empire* magazine about Ane Clint.

May 2, 1965 - D&RGW three-car special behind former GW steam engine 51 operated from Denver to the East Portal of the Moffat Tunnel. Engine 51 still carried the Colorado & Southern lettering from its recent filming in "Cat Ballou." **R. H. KINDIG PHOTO**

May 29, 30, 31 – D&RGW narrow gauge Memorial Day excursion from Alamosa over Cumbres Pass to Durango to Silverton. 389 railfans were on the thirteen-car train. Fares were $21.00 for adults and $11.00 for children. Club member Don Smith presented a program entitled "History and Activities of the Ghost town of St. Elmo" on Saturday evening, May 30th. After all expenses were paid, the Club made a profit of $1,310 on this trip. Jack Morison recalls a story about Mac Poor on this trip that is humorous as well as insightful about Mac. Jack was awed, as were many members, by the importance and stature that Mac Poor held in the Club. While riding on the trip, Jack decided to say hello to Mac, but was uncertain how to approach him. So, while Jack and Mac were riding in the same vestibule, Jack says to Mac, "Looks like good fishing in that river, doesn't it?" Mac looked at Jack, and with a frown said, "Goddamit, I could care less if there's a fish in that river. I'm a railroad fan and I could care less about fishing." He then turned and walked back into the car. As Jack noted in 1987, it was a bit intimidating in the late 1950's to be a new member in the midst of well-known authors, photographers and famous persons who were Club members.

May 29 – Engine 483 pulled the thirteen-car train that included two covered gondolas (open-side, roofed observation cars 450 and 451) from Alamosa to Durango.

May 30 – Engine 476 was the lone locomotive on this eleven-car train to Silverton and back (one covered gondola). A coach and observation car were left in Durango since

the 470-series locomotives were limited to eleven cars on this branch.

May 31 – Engine 483 again served as road engine on the return to Alamosa with 498 in helper service from Chama to Cumbres Pass.

June 16 – Heavy rains of more than 12 inches in six hours caused Plum Creek to rise rapidly eventually reaching the Platte River in Denver. The flooding covered most of the yards in the central Platte Valley. Nine days after the flood, a single-track line was opened between Denver and Pueblo. All Colorado & Southern, Santa Fe and Rio Grande traffic was routed via the Moffat Tunnel, to Dotsero, Minturn Salida and the Royal Gorge. All along the Platte River north and east of Denver, traffic was affected on the Union Pacific on the old Kansas Pacific line and on the Rock Island as well as the CB&Q. For several days trains were routed through Cheyenne including a 37-car consolidated *Denver Zephyr* and *California Zephyr*. The August newsletter contained as an insert, the D&RGW house organ, *Green Light,* which covered the flood's devastation in detail.

June 26 – Annual Banquet was held at the Hochlandhof in Winter Park. A special seven-car diesel-powered train carried 267 members and guests to West Portal over the D&RGW. Included in the consist were two domes and five modern lightweight stainless steel coaches. The locomotives used were an Alco PA in service with a new GP35. Also, a former tender from one of the 3700-class Baldwin 4-6-6-4s was used as a steam generator car. Transportation and dinner were $7.00. The program was by Dow Helmers who presented information on the historic Alpine Tunnel. The

1938-49
1950-59
1960-69
1970-79
1980-89
1990-99
2000-03
Color Extra

# Rocky Mountain Rail Report

**The Rocky Mountain Railroad Club**

P.O. Box 2391    Denver, Colorado 80201

MAY 1966                No. 81.

CURRENT NEWS AND HISTORICAL NOTES OF
ROCKY MOUNTAIN RAILROADING PUBLISHED
MONTHLY FOR ITS MEMBERS BY THE ROCKY
MOUNTAIN RAILROAD CLUB

MEETING NOTICE: DATE....WEDNESDAY, MAY 11, 1966
TIME....8:00 P.M.
PLACE...WESTERN FEDERAL SAVINGS
BUILDING (BASEMENT
MEETING ROOM),
717-17TH ST., DENVER

EDITOR --- TED MCKEE

January, 1966 – The words "Rocky Mountain Rail Report" first appear as the masthead of the Club's newsletter.

D&RGW charged the Club $1,050 for a guaranteed minimum of 300 seats. Meals were $3.50 each for prime rib dinners. The total loss to the Club was $266.

June – Club made available "Scotchlite " reflective stickers with the Club's logo, in either front adhesive or back adhesive styles.

July – The Club started mailing the newsletters first class rather than third class, as done previously.

August 27 – *The Denver Post* incorrectly reported that the Club operated a special, private excursion behind engine 51 from Denver to Golden and return. The locomotive had been recently cleaned and worked on to clean out silt and June flood damage, which occurred where it was stored at the Colorado & Southern Rice yard along the Platte River. Club President McKee states: "The Club never has operated, and never will operate, an excursion that is not open to the entire membership and their guests."

August 29 – Excursion from Denver to Longmont and return ran behind ex-Great Western engine 51 (owned by Singing Rails). Over 250 fans rode the five-car train consisting of four D&RGW heavyweight coaches and one combination coach car and paid $6.00 ($3.00 for children). Mickey Hansen was the engineer and the town of Longmont rolled out the red carpet and a Pierce-Arrow automobile to greet the train. Fire engines, square dancers, singing and horse drawn coaches were all part of the one and a half-hour layover for a picnic lunch. Numbers were drawn from ticket holders for chances to ride in the cab of the 51 at different times. In the flyer announcing the trip, it was stated "This is the Club's 'Do

or Die' attempt at this type of trip. If a sufficient number of passengers turn out to enable us to come close to breaking even, trips of this type will continue to be run. However, if your support is not forthcoming, the Club's officers and directors will probably not attempt to run further excursions with this locomotive. It is your decision to make." The thirty tons of coal required for the trip was donated by the Pittsburgh-Midway Coal Company.

August – The newsletter reported that the synthetic reproduction of engine 20, used in some scenes of the movie, "A Ticket to Tomahawk" is currently being used for still shots in the TV program "Petticoat Junction." This replica "Hooterville Cannonball" cost nearly $80,000 to build in 1951.

October 17– Eight-car excursion on the Union Pacific from Denver (behind diesels) to Cheyenne and then to Rawlins and return behind engine 8444. The cost was $21.00 for adults and $11.00 for children. Nearly 200 passengers (including Club Member David P. Morgan editor of *Trains* magazine and his wife) took this trip which included meals in the style of the famed "Las Vegas Diner." At times, speeds of 80 miles per hour were reached. Passengers who wanted to ride the steam only portion of the trip from Cheyenne to Rawlins paid $20 for adults and $10 for children. The Club paid the Union Pacific $4,838 for the train and meals and lost about $574 on this trip after all revenue and expenses were balanced.

November 7 – Charter member Les Logue died. Les served as Treasurer and was very active in early trips. He was one of the adventurous members to explore the Alpine Tunnel with Irv August and Ed Haley in 1948.

November 13 – Workday at the Colorado Railroad Museum.

December – Club membership reached 1001, in 43 states and 17 foreign countries. The Club established the Bert Fullman Memorial Fund to accumulate funds with which to purchase rail and history volumes to give to the Denver Public Library's Western Collection. Commemorative bookplates were created to be placed into any donated publication. The bookplate depicted D&SL locomotive 203 exiting the Moffat Tunnel. This same logo appeared on the masthead of the *Rocky Mountain Rail Report* beginning July 1969.

**1966**    **Meetings are held at the Western Federal Savings Building. Pres. (and newsletter editor) Ted McKee; V-P. Ed Schneider; Secy. R. H. Kindig; Treas. Ane Clint.**

January – The words "Rocky Mountain Rail Report" first appeared as the masthead of the Club's newsletter. Also, the Club initiated a "Swap N Shop" section in the newsletter where members can advertise at no cost for items they have for sale or want to buy.

February 4 – Member Lucius Beebe died. Well known railroad author (over 30 books), iconoclast, bon vivant and historian, Beebe co-authored many books with Charles Clegg. In a letter written earlier this year, he commented, "Denver is declining, like everything else, into a dreariness of sub-mediocrity. Too much of everything, mostly people."

March – The CB&Q announced the retirement of its last two steam locomotives, numbered 4960 and 5632.

April 17 – Special steam-powered excursion on the D&RGW Railroad behind ex-Great Western sixty-year old locomotive 51 (owned by John Birmingham and Dr. James Arneill). The trip was delayed more than thirty minutes as the crew had to clean the engine's grates after a yard crew used a clamshell to fill the tender with coal from a pile on the ground which included several inches of dirt. The first planned photo stop at Clay was cancelled due to fog and snow. The second stop at Plainview allowed photographers little more in their viewfinders than a disembodied headlight. Roundtrip tickets to the Moffat Tunnel were $10.00 for adults and $6.00 for children (no meals included). More than 250 passengers rode this four-car train with heavyweight coaches. Again, Mickey Hansen was the engineer on this special. Because of the low speeds (6-8 mph) due to stiff grades, the accompanying diesel (GP9 5943) with water car and caboose was used as a helper upgrade

May 28, 1966 - The last Club excursion on the D&RGW from Alamosa to Durango. Engine 483 approaches Cumbres Pass.
**J. L. EHERNBERGER PHOTO**

May 28, 1966 - D&RGW engine 483 and 344 railfans visit Florida, east of Durango. Two days later the train went east for the last time for the Club.
**J. L. EHERNBERGER PHOTO**

after Plainview. For photo run-bys the diesel was cut off and on the return the diesel followed the special. The photo runby above Tolland was shrouded in fog and snow was falling intermittently at East Portal. On the return, the train executed a running meet with a westbound freight. The excursion arrived in Denver only 20 minutes behind schedule, despite all the challenges. The May issue of the D&RGW's internal organ *Green Light* featured an article on the trip.

May – The Club's newsletter now carried a drawing of locomotive 20, on the Florence & Cripple Creek, which was created by member Tom Gray. 8x10 and postcard prints of the drawing were made available to members for $1.00 and 10¢, respectively.

May 28, 29, 30 – D&RGW narrow gauge Memorial Day excursion from Alamosa over Cumbres Pass to Durango and to Silverton. Three hundred and forty-four railfans from twenty-four different states rode on this trip. Fares were still $21.00 for adults and $11.00 for children. This was the last Club sponsored trip on the D&RGW

1938-49

1950-59

1960-69

1970-79

1980-89

1990-99

2000-03

Color Extra

July 17, 1966 - Ex-Great Western engine 51 pulled the Club's special on the CB&Q's Lyons Branch, seen here near Longmont. **R. H. KINDIG PHOTO**

Ticket for the July 17 steam special, Denver to Lyons.

over Cumbres Pass. (In the future, the Cumbres & Toltec Scenic Railroad would again operate over Cumbres Pass). Club member Ron Ruhoff presented a program entitled "Ten Ways to the Rockies" Saturday evening, May 29th. The Club paid the railroad $5,644 for the train on this trip. In conjunction with this 15th annual Memorial Day narrow gauge trip, the Club offered a commemorative souvenir envelope. Mailed from Silverton, the cachets numbered in the thousands and collectors bought many for their collections.

> May 28 – The eleven-car train was pulled by engine 483 from Alamosa to Durango. Two covered gondolas were in the consist.

> May 29 – Engine 476 provided the sole motive power to Silverton and back.

> May 30 – Engine 483 was the road engine from Durango to Alamosa with the 487 as a helper from Chama to Cumbres.

June 11 – Workday at the Colorado Railroad Museum.

July 17 – Steam-powered excursion behind ex-Great Western engine 51 (still owned by two Club members –

John Birmingham and James Arneill). Following the Colorado & Southern line from Denver to Burns Junction, the five-car train used CB&Q trackage to Lafayette, Longmont, and Hygiene to Lyons. The roundtrip was $7.00 for adults and $3.50 for children. Over 225 riders enjoyed this trip covered by local news celebrity Starr Yelland, who rode with a cameraman and sound engineer. The use of the locomotive was $850 (including insurance). As a guarantee of 250 tickets was made with the CB&Q, the 84 unfilled seats resulted in a deficit of $875.

September 24, 25 – Two days of excursions over the Colorado and Southern and Union Pacific Railroads.

September 24 – Colorado & Southern trip from Denver through Broomfield and Longmont to Boulder. Numerous photo-stops were made culminating with the Annual Banquet held at the Boulder Harvest House. Motive power for the four-car special was locomotive 51. Cost for the train trip and dinner was $10.00. Bill Gordon presented movie footage of D&RGW and Union Pacific steam in action for the night's program. The cost of renting the locomotive on this trip was $420 plus an additional $350 for insurance. More than 360 passengers took this trip. The cost for three 41-passenger buses to shuttle guests from the station to the Harvest House was $94. Guests returned to Denver in the same train, however it was diesel powered. Engine 51 could not be turned in Boulder and it operated backwards all the way to Denver.

September 25 – Excursion on the Union Pacific using engine 8444. The trip from Denver to Cheyenne was via the Dent Branch. A trip over Sherman Hill was included returning to Cheyenne where diesel power was substituted for the 8444. Roundtrip fare, which included meals all day in the cafeteria style diner, was priced at $17.00 for adults and $8.50 for children. A standing room only crowd filled the sold out thirteen-car train. The cost for the train and meals was $5,534. The consist for this train was (in order) baggage car 5716, coaches 5452, 5555, 5520, diner 4806, lunch counter diner 4000, coaches 5405, 5494, 5492, 5502, 5432 and lounge car 6203 – all Union Pacific cars. This trip made money for the Club.

If passengers purchased tickets for both the September 24 and 25 trips, a package price of $24.00 for adults and $16.00 for children was offered.

On August 13, 1967, an article appeared in the

*New York Times* written by Jack Goodman, a reporter, who rode the UP portion of the trip. Written in a light vein, he commented that "I am still bewildered by the whole thing....Let it be said that the word 'odd' must be used advisedly when referring to the ladies and gentlemen from 30 states, Canada and even Australia who turned up for the trip."

October – The Club's "General Store" offered twenty-three different items to members. These included books, 33 1/3 rpm, 12 inch hi fi recordings, postcards, decals, engineer hats, and other merchandise.

November 17 – The Club purchased from Howard Fogg an original oil painting of two Moffat Road engines working upgrade on the Rollins Pass line for $150 for the Fullman Memorial at the Denver Public Library. Howard was willing to donate the painting, but Dick Kindig felt it was only fair to pay some amount for the artwork.

**1967**  **Meetings at Western Federal Building. Dues remain $3.00. Pres. E. E. Schneider; V-P. Tom Gray; Secy. R. A. Cordill; Treas. Ane Clint. Ed. (January through March) Ted McKee. Temporary Editor from April to December E. E. Schneider.**

Irv August recalled that at a meeting held at the Western Federal Savings Building (year unknown) Otto Perry was scheduled to show movies at a Club meeting. Yet, Otto was not present. Irv went upstairs and found Otto who had just arrived on his bicycle with the movies. Otto was concerned what to do with his bike, so Irv took the bicycle downstairs to the meeting room where Otto then showed the movies. Irv also recalled Otto's comments during his programs were always interesting and filled with humor.

February – The D&RGW stunned the Club and rail community by discontinuing all narrow gauge excursions on the Alamosa to Durango line.

April – The Club turned down an offer from the owners of ex-Great Western locomotive 90 to purchase it for $20,000. It was sold to the Strasburg Railroad in Pennsylvania.

June 3, 4 – Excursion on the Union Pacific behind engine 8444 from Denver to Rawlins, WY. Routing was from Denver to Speer via the Dent Branch then west to Rawlins. Return the next day was from Rawlins to Speer to Dent and back to Denver. Cost was $25.00 roundtrip for adults and $17.00 for children and included all meals for both, but not overnight accommodations in Rawlins. Two hundred and forty-three passengers took this trip. The Club lost $575 on this trip.

Cost for the locomotive and train was $6,792.

June – Club donated a watercolor original "Mallet at Yankee Doodle Lake" to the Denver Public Library Western History Department. The Howard Fogg painting was given in appreciation of the research assistance provided by library staff.

August – Workday at the Colorado Railroad Museum.

September – The D&RGW Railroad notified the Club that the "The Rio Grande no longer will run special or excursion passenger trains on its standard gauge lines, and will not consider any proposals for the operation of such trains."

October 12 – Club donated $500 towards a $3,500 feasibility study of rail transportation in the South Platte River Valley.

November – Club announced intent to establish a library of 8mm and 16m movies to preserve important railroading films. Members were encouraged to contact the Club about the no cost copy service that the Club would provide to obtain movies.

June 3-4, 1967 - Brochure advertising the Club's excursion behind Union Pacific Railroad engine 8444.

1938-49

1950-59

1960-69

1970-79

1980-89

1990-99

2000-03

Color Extra

December 9 – Annual Banquet at the Hyatt House (1790 Grant St.) in Denver. Cost was $5.00 per person. Bill Gordon showed historic movies of the Colorado & Southern under steam. Each of the 90 ticket holders was entitled one chance to win a copy of Morris Cafky's *Rails Around Gold Hill*. This dinner resulted in a slight loss to the Club of $25 after all expenses were deducted from revenues.

July 12, 1968 - Cripple Creek & Victor engines 1 and 3 with two cars at Cripple Creek.
R. H. KINDIG PHOTO

**1968** **Meetings at the Western Federal Building. The dues remain $3.00 for Colorado members and $2.00 for out-of-state members. Pres. E. E. Schneider; V-P. Tom Gray; Secy. R. A. Cordill; Treas. Ane Clint. Although he was titled "Temporary Editor," E. E. Schneider served in this role from April 1967 until May 1970.**

January 20, 21 – Club chartered three cars that were added to the *Yampa Valley* (trains 9 and 10) to Craig (overnight). The F unit led (A-B-B configuration) train included one baggage car and the "Silver Sky" vista dome observation car for the regular train, with three additional stainless steel cars for the Club. Roundtrip fares were $16.00 for adults and $8.00 for children. The 173 passengers carried their own lunches or could order lunches from the conductor to be placed on the train at Orestod.  Passengers had to make their own hotel reservations. On April 8 of this year, the D&RGW discontinued passenger train service to Craig.

May 11, 12 – Union Pacific steam excursion behind engine 8444 from Denver to Rawlins via the Dent Branch and return. Members and guests paid $26.00 for the train only (accommodations in Rawlins were extra) – children were $17.00. All meals were included in the price of the ticket and the buffet style placed no limit on the number of "seconds" a person could take. The twelve-car train carried just over 400 passengers. The cost of the train to the Club was $10,269.29. This was the Club's 85th train or trolley trip.

July 12, 13 – Dinner, melodrama and steam railroading at Cripple Creek. For $11.00 the 52 members had a buffet-style dinner, hotel accommodations and rides on the two-foot gauge Cripple Creek & Victor Railroad all day on the 13th.  Club member John Birmingham operated both his 2-foot gauge steam locomotives, saddle tank engine 3 and Mallet engine 1.

July – The Cafky book *Colorado Midland* sold out.

November 2 – Annual Banquet was held at the Quality Courts Motel at I-70 and Chambers Road.  Only 39 members and guests participated this year. The cost of the sirloin steak dinner was $4.75.

November – Club members received copies of a booklet titled "New Ways to Run Railroads" published by Alco Products, Schenectady, NY, thanks to Irv August.

December – The Club, in cooperation with the Denver Posse of the Westerners, reprinted Lester L. Williams' book *Disaster at Fountain* with complimentary copies given to members whose dues were paid by March. The original edition was printed in 1965.

**1969** **Meetings at Western Federal Building. Pres. Jim Ehernberger; V-P. Carl Carlson; Secy. R. A. Cordill; Treas. Ane Clint; Asst. Treas. W. L. Van Patten; Temporary Editor E. E. Schneider. Dues were $3.00 for in-state members and $2.00 for out-of-state members.**

January – Members whose dues were paid could receive a copy of the Union Pacific Railroad's Centennial Calendar. The cost was 50¢ for mailing and was limited to the first 400 requests. Club member Howard Fogg did the paintings for this calendar.

April – The Club donated $250 to Colorado Railroad Museum.

May – The Club endorsed state efforts to save the narrow gauge lines west of Antonito. This is the first political effort ever made by the Club and letters were sent to state legislators in support.

May 30 – Excursion on the Union Pacific behind engine 8444 from Denver to Laramie and return via the Dent

Branch. Fare was $20.00 ($14.00 for children) on this sold–out trip for which people were turned away. Three meals were provided as part of the ticket price. Approximately 450 passengers were on the train, which included one baggage car, nine coaches, a buffet diner and a lounge car.

June 12 – The Club purchased former Los Angeles Municipal Railway PCC car 3101 for $200 from the First National Bank of Cripple Creek. This 3-1/2 foot gauge car was built in 1943 and moved to Cripple Creek for use at the Gold Camp Railroad and Museum.

June 15 – Rocky Mountain Railroad Club Day was held at the Colorado Railroad Museum. A steam-up of the museum's engine 346 was included.

July – The *Rocky Mountain Rail Report* masthead changed from engine 20 to a drawing of Denver & Salt Lake engine 203 emerging from the Moffat Tunnel. This drawing was the same as the bookplates developed for books obtained and donated to the Denver Public Library as part of the Bert Fullman Memorial Fund.

July – Club acquired a five-inch gauge 2-6-0 live model narrow gauge Colorado & Southern steam locomotive 4 from the widow of Bill Soper. The model featured a "beartrap" cinder catcher. The model is on display at the Colorado Railroad Museum.

July 19, 20 – Excursion to Cripple Creek for dinner, melodrama and unlimited rides on the Cripple Creek & Victor Narrow Gauge Railroad between Cripple Creek and Anaconda. The route followed the abandoned Midland Terminal Railway. Prices were $15.00 for all events which included train riding all day, both days as well as brunch on Sunday. More than 40 members participated. The low turn out initially discouraged the Board from making plans to do this again, yet the following year the trip operated with success.

September 13 – Annual Banquet was held at the Ramada Inn in Evans, CO. A special steam-powered train was operated over the Union Pacific from

# Rocky Mountain Rail Report

### The Rocky Mountain Railroad Club
P.O. Box 2391    Denver, Colorado 80201
JULY 1969                              No. 119

CURRENT NEWS AND HISTORICAL NOTES OF ROCKY MOUNTAIN RAILROADING PUBLISHED MONTHLY FOR ITS MEMBERS BY THE ROCKY MOUNTAIN RAILROAD CLUB

EDITOR - - - ED SCHNEIDER

MEETING NOTICE:  DATE . . . . . . WEDNESDAY, JULY 9, 1969
                 TIME . . . . . . 8:00 P.M.
                 PLACE . . . . . WESTERN FEDERAL SAVINGS BLDG., (LOWER LEVEL MEETING ROOM), 17TH & CALIFORNIA STS., DENVER

PROGRAM NOTES:   CLUB MEMBER JOHN M. BIRMINGHAM, OPERATOR OF THE CRIPPLE CREEK AND VICTOR NARROW GAUGE RAILROAD, WILL PRESENT A TALK WITH SLIDES ON HIS ROAD. JOHN WILL ANSWER QUESTIONS ABOUT THIS RAILROAD SO YOU'LL BE READY FOR THE CLUB'S "WEEKEND OF STEAM", SATURDAY AND SUNDAY, JULY 19 AND 20.

* * * * *

ON THE LEFT (BELOW) IS A VIEW OF THE CLUB'S THREE LIVE-STEAM MODEL ENGINES, 999, 210, AND C.& S.4, AT THE COLORADO RAILROAD MUSEUM. A CLOSER VIEW OF OUR LATEST ACQUISITION, COLORADO AND SOUTHERN 4, IS SHOWN AT THE RIGHT.

CLUB ACQUIRES BEAUTIFUL MODEL NARROW GAUGE C. & S. OPERATING STEAM LOCOMOTIVE. MRS. WILLIAM H. SOPER, WIDOW OF THE LATE BILL SOPER, A MEMBER OF THE ROCKY MOUNTAIN RAILROAD CLUB UNTIL HIS DEATH FOUR YEARS AGO, HAS PRESENTED THE CLUB WITH AN EXTREMELY WELL DETAILED 5-INCH GAUGE LIVE STEAM ENGINE ALONG WITH SEVERAL SECTIONS OF TRACK. THE LOCOMOTIVE WAS MODELED AFTER COLORADO & SOUTHERN NARROW GAUGE ENGINE NO. 4, WHICH WAS BILL'S FAVORITE WHEN HE WORKED AS CRANE AND WRECKER OPERATOR ON THE SOUTH PARK LINE AS A YOUNG MAN. HE LEFT THE RAILROAD IN 1924. BILL LOVED STEAM AND HIS LAST JOB BEFORE RETIREMENT WAS AS A STATIONARY ENGINEER AT THE DENVER FEDERAL CENTER. ALL PARTS OF THIS LOCOMOTIVE WERE CAREFULLY TURNED OUT BY BILL IN HIS HOME MACHINE SHOP. THE PROJECT WAS COMMENCED IN 1960 AND COMPLETED 3 YEARS LATER. BILL OPERATED HIS ENGINE ON A CIRCLE OF TRACK IN HIS BACK YARD. IT IS PLANNED TO HOLD A FORMAL PRESENTATION OF THIS LOCOMOTIVE TO THE ROCKY MOUNTAIN RAILROAD CLUB AT THE COLORADO RAILROAD MUSEUM, WITH MRS. SOPER AND OTHER RELATIVES PRESENT AT THE CEREMONY AS SOON AS SPACE AND A SUITABLE GLASS CASE CAN BE PROVIDED.

* * * * *

July, 1969 - *The Rocky Mountain Rail Report* masthead changed to a drawing of Denver & Salt Lake engine 203 prepared by Club member Tom Gray. The front page reports the Club's acquisition of a live steam scale model of C&S engine 4.

Denver to Evans via the Dent Branch behind engine 8444. The return was over the mainline through Brighton. Cost of the trip and meal together was $7.50. Over 310 passengers took this trip. Ron Parkhurst gave an historical presentation on the Gilpin Country Tramway. Unfortunately, the meal was a disappointment, due to small portions. As one observer noted, the walk from the train, to the Ramada Inn, four blocks away, "...looked like Moses leading the children of Israel to the Promised Land." The corporate offices of the Ramada Inn later apologized for the meal and refunded the Club a portion of the cost. A special item of note was that the event was one hundred years to the day after the first rail of the Denver Pacific Railway was placed near Cheyenne on what became the first railroad to construct into Denver.

1938-49
1950-59
1960-69
1970-79
1980-89
1990-99
2000-03
Color Extra

October 19 – This was Rocky Mountain Railroad Club Day on the Colorado Central Narrow Gauge Railroad in Central City. The cost for unlimited rides was $2.00 for adults with children free.

October – The Club relocated PCC car 3101 from Cripple Creek to the Colorado Railroad Museum. The move was performed by Duffy Moving and Storage for $1,032.75.

October 19, 1969 - Colorado Central Narrow Gauge locomotive 44 makes a dramatic run-by on Club Day at Central City. A clear day following an early snow storm provided great steam and smoke effects. **J. L. EHERNBERGER PHOTO**

# Scrapbook

Rocky Mountain Railroad Club № 449

UNION PACIFIC STEAM EXCURSION
DENVER, COLORADO
TO
RAWLINS, WYOMING
AND RETURN

Leaving Denver at 8:20 A.M., M.D.T., June 3, 1967
Leaving Rawlins at 8:00 A.M., M.D.T., June 4, 1967
Meals Included in Cost of Ticket

Half Fare
If Punched
President R. M. R. R. C.

LARAMIE, WYOMING TO DENVER, COLORADO
RAWLINS, WYOMING TO LARAMIE, WYOMING
LARAMIE, WYOMING TO RAWLINS, WYOMING
DENVER, COLORADO TO LARAMIE, WYOMING

UNION PACIFIC NO. 8444, NEAR EDSON, WYO.
OCTOBER 1965

Through the years, the Club issued black & white glossy pocket calendars depicting various railroad locomotives and trains.

CRIPPLE CREEK & VICTOR
NARROW GAUGE RAILROAD
ROUND TRIP
CRIPPLE CREEK STATION TO
POVERTY GULCH · PISGAH JUNCTION · YELLOW BIRD MINE · POINTER MINE · ANACONDA · MARY McKINLEY MINE · ELKTON · VICTOR JUNCTION · VICTOR, COLORADO
AND RETURN
№ 10515

Rocky Mountain Railroad Club № 392

SPECIAL TRIP
DENVER TO CRAIG, COLO.

JANUARY 20-21, 1968

USING D.&R.G.W. "YAMPA VALLEY"

Half Fare
If Punched
President R.M.R.R.C.

CRAIG TO DENVER, COLO. ON D.&R.G.W. NO. 10 LV. 9:50 A.M., JAN. 21, 1968
DENVER TO CRAIG, COLO. ON D.&R.G.W. No. 9 LV. 9:05 A.M., JAN. 20, 1968
Half     Half

1938-49

1950-59

1960-69

1970-79

1980-89

1990-99

2000-03

Color Extra

May 28, 1960 – D&RGW engine 483 exits Toltec Tunnel with 12 cars on the Club's annual Memorial Day excursion. **R. H. KINDIG PHOTO**

May 29, 1960 – Locomotives 478 and 473 double-head the Club's train at Hermosa, enroute to Silverton. **R. H. KINDIG PHOTO**

October 2, 1960 – C&S engine 638 steps briskly southbound, near Berthoud. The seven-car train was returning from Loveland after the Great Western portion of the trip had been completed. **J. L. EHERNBERGER PHOTO**

October 2, 1960 – Engine 90 is seen east of Loveland with the seven-car train on the Great Western portion of the joint C&S/GW trip this clear day. **R. H. KINDIG PHOTO**

November 20, 1960 – Union Pacific 844 is spotless in this classic photo taken in Cheyenne. The first Club trip behind this locomotive would lead to more than four decades of steam excursions sponsored by the Club and other organizations. **LOU SCHMITZ PHOTO**

November 20, 1960 – Union Pacific engine 844 basks in the light of the Cheyenne roundhouse after its return from the Club's first excursion behind this four-eight-four Northern. **JACK JORDAN PHOTO**

September 10, 1961 – C&S engine 638 crosses the Big Thompson River near Wilds on the Arkins Branch with the Club's six-car train. **R. H. KINDIG PHOTO**

July 22, 1962 - The Club's final excursion using C&S engine 638 on the CB&Q Lyons Branch set several grass fires along the way because of dry weather conditions. **R. H. KINDIG PHOTO**

September 9, 1962 – C&S 638 (upper right) and Great Western 90 (above) head up the Club's last joint trip on these two railroads. Number 638 would continue in service until December of this year. Number 90 did not operate another Club trip. **R. H. KINDIG PHOTOS**

May 11, 1963 – Chicago, Burlington & Quincy locomotive 4960 powered the Club's 25th Anniversary Dinner train. In this photo, taken in Centralia, IL in November, 1954, the Mikado's 2-8-2 wheel arrangement is clearly seen. **J. L. EHERNBERGER COLLECTION**

October 1963 – Ed Haley was a cartographer for the U. S. Bureau of Reclamation. His detailed maps were used in many trip publications and Club books. He was largely responsible for the reprinting of the *Hotchkiss Historical Map of Colorado – 1913*.

1938-49

1950-59

1960-69

1970-79

1980-89

1990-99

2000-03

Color Extra

**ADVENTURE IN WEST VIRGINIA** DESCRIBING *PERILOUS PEREGRINATIONS* THROUGH **FOREST AND GLEN** DEPICTED WITH *COLOURED LANTERN SLIDES* AND EXPOUNDED IN ALL ITS **BORING DETAIL ! !** BY C. S. RYLAND JANUARY 8, 1964 FOR THE ROCKY MOUNTAIN RAILROAD CLUB

Elk River No. 3 at Swandale, W. Va. May 3, 1957

January 8, 1964 – Charlie Ryland's program flyer for the Club's January meeting conveys the creativity of his work as a graphic artist and printer.

May 31, 1964 – During the decade of the 1960s, the Club's reputation was solidified by both its mainline trips and Memorial Day narrow gauge excursions on the D&RGW. Locomotives 480 and 487 are seen near Windy Point as they lift their train over Cumbres Pass. **F. H. BAHM PHOTO**

September 13, 1964 - Oily smoke flows over the Club's nine-car train at a photo run-by near Rock River, WY. **R. H. KINDIG PHOTO**

September 13, 1964 – Union Pacific 8444 stands in between the *City of Los Angeles* and Big Boy 4023 (left) as passengers take a brief stop in Cheyenne. The locomotive carries an extra "4" to differentiate it from UP GP30 diesel 844, whose class carried this series of numbers. **R. H. KINDIG PHOTO**

May 31, 1965 – The Club's Memorial Day excursion powered by D&RGW 483 passes the water tank at Navajo, NM. **R. H. KINDIG PHOTO**

July 17, 1966 – The tender is lettered "Colorado & Southern" but the locomotive carries number 51. The former GW 51, owned by two Club members, pulls the five-car special on a trip that operated to Lyons and back.
**R. H. KINDIG PHOTO**

September 24, 1966 – The last Club trip behind former Great Western 51 was for the Annual Dinner to Boulder's Harvest House. This locomotive (photographed at Loveland on October 6, 1957) was still owned (in 2003) by former Club member John Birmingham and is stored at Mead.
**R. H. KINDIG PHOTO**

1938-49
1950-59
1960-69
1970-79
1980-89
1990-99
2000-03
Color Extra

June 3, 1967 – This year the Club ran a two-day trip from Denver to Rawlins, WY and return behind locomotive 8444. Photographer Jim Ehernberger captures the big Northern crossing the wooden trestle over the South Platte River on the Dent Branch.

May 11, 1968 – In a repeat of the previous year's trip, 8444 is moving at 20 mph crossing the South Platte River at Welby. The train will continue to Rawlins, WY for an overnight stay and return the next day to Denver. **R. H. KINDIG PHOTO**

September 13, 1969 – Members were treated to a rare trip behind engine 8444 as more than 310 passengers rode to Evans for the Annual Dinner. Although the meal did not meet quality expectations, no one was disappointed by the trip. The route to Evans was via the Dent Branch where this photo was taken at Eastlake. The return to Denver was via Brighton. **R. H. KINDIG PHOTO**

# Chapter 4: 1970 - 1979

**1970** **Meetings at Western Federal Building with dues still at $3.00. Pres. Jim Ehernberger; V-P. Stuart Anderson; Secy. W. J. Gordon (a position he would hold until his death in 1997); Treas. Ted McKee; Assist. Treas. W. L. Van Patten; Ed. E. E. Schneider (January through April); then Bruce Black became the newsletter Editor. Junior memberships were established for person 14-18. Their dues rate were set at $2.00 per year.**

February 15 – Dedication at Colorado Railroad Museum of live steam locomotive 4 received as a gift from the widow of Bill Soper.

March – Trip Chairman Ed Haley conducted a survey of members concerning their thoughts on trips (results in May newsletter).

May 30 – Memorial Day excursion (12 cars) on the Union Pacific behind engine 8444 from Denver to Laramie and return via the Dent Branch and LaSalle. All meals were provided (breakfast, lunch and dinner). Fare was $27.00 for adults and $18.00 for children. Trip was sold out with some passengers standing the whole way. The Club reimbursed the Union Pacific Railroad $9,744.98 for the cost of the train. The consist for this train, in order, was baggage 5716, coaches 5407, 5424, 5437, 5505, lunch counter diner 4003, lounge 6201, coaches 5510, 5497, 5479, 5494 and 5414 – all Union Pacific cars.

August 12 – The Club moved meetings back to City and County of Denver Courtroom (100-E) at 1460 Cherokee St. The Western Federal location (for more than 10 years) was unable to host the Club due to changes in the bank's policies.

August 16 – This was Rocky Mountain Railroad Club Day at the Colorado Railroad Museum. Engine 346 is steamed up. The Club paid $54.06 for the coal used for this steam up.

August 22 – Cripple Creek & Victor Rocky Mountain Railroad Club Day. Unlimited rides were $5.00 with a current membership card.

September 6 – The Club was to operate an excursion on the Durango to Silverton line and was to be the second section of the day's normal trips. Fare was $7.50 for adults and $5.00 for children. However, heavy rains and flooding on September 5 caused a number of washouts. This was the only excursion where passengers had traveled to the originating point and the trip had to be cancelled the scheduled day of operation. This was a first in over 33 years of operating these trips.

May 30, 1970 - Union Pacific engine 8444 pulls a 12-car special that was standing room only in this scene near Perkins, WY. **J. L. EHERNBERGER PHOTO**

September – The Club received a 16mm movie on the Bonhomie and Hattiesburg Southern Railroad from Club member Joe Thompson for the Club's archives.

September 18 to October 5 – Although not an officially "sponsored" trip, many Club members rode 28 different steam and electric railroads, cog roads, aerial trams and a number of steamboats in Switzerland.

October 11 – Club Day on the Colorado Central Narrow Gauge Railroad in Central City. Cost for unlimited rides was $2.00 for adults with children free.

December – Club members received a complimentary copy of the D&RGW internal organ the *Green Light* marking the line's 100th anniversary. A D&RGW narrow gauge equipment roster was also included.

December 23 – Famous photographer and charter member Otto Perry died. Otto's photographs and movies made him famous. They have made it possible for the Club to offer unique historical videos of his work.

During 1970, the Club decided to publish Mallory Hope Ferrell's book on the Rio Grande Southern.

**1971** Meetings at the City and County Bldg. and dues were $3.00 for all members, in-state or out-of-state and "Junior Memberships" were $2.00. The usual $1.00 enrollment fee for new members remained in effect. Pres. L. Wilson Ruid; V-P. Charles Max; Secy. & Equip. Chair W. J. Gordon; Treas. Arl Cuthbert; Asst. Treas. W. L. Van Patten; Ed. Bruce Black.

January – The Club solicited photos for the new book on the Rio Grande Southern.

March 28 – Excursion on the Union Pacific behind engine 8444 from Denver to Laramie and return. Tickets were $33.00 for adults and $20.00 for children. Buffet style meals were included in the ticket price. Routing was via Dent Branch to LaSalle and to Laramie via Sherman Hill for the twelve-car train. The Club paid $12,917 for this trip but made a slight profit of $156.

June 18 – Workday at the Colorado Railroad Museum.

June – Long time Club member and author of the book *The Giant's Ladder*, Harold Boner died.

July 17, 18 – Field trip to the West Portal of the Alpine Tunnel.

July – The Club decided against publishing the new book by Mallory Hope Ferrell, the *Silver San Juan* due to the long time expected to recover its investment.

August 11 – The Club moved to new meeting location at Christ Episcopal Church on University Boulevard.

August 14, 15 – Cripple Creek & Victor sponsored Rocky Mountain Railroad Club Day. Rides were free with a current membership card.

August – The Club purchased the Otto Perry collection of 16mm films from his estate for $3,000.

September 4, 5 – This two-day trip on the Cumbres & Toltec Scenic Railway and the D&RGW were available as separate trips or as a package of $23 for both trips. Riders provided their own transportation and accommodations.

September 4-5, 1971 - Advertising brochure for the "Journey to Yesteryear on its Narrow Gauge Holiday."

September 4 – Trip on the Cumbres & Toltec Scenic Railway from Chama, NM over Cumbres Pass to Big Horn and return. A number of runbys were made of the train powered by engine 483. Fare was $15.00.

September 5 – Roundtrip excursion on the second section of the D&RGW's Durango and Silverton line using engine 478. Following the regular train, the Club's special made a number of photo stops. Fare was $10.00.

September – The Club decided to erect trolley poles and wiring on their trackage at the Colorado Railroad Museum. "Olie" Larsen, legendary highline boss for Public Service Company, oversees construction.

September 4, 1971 - Cumbres & Toltec Scenic Railway at Sublette, NM.
**J. L. EHERNBERGER PHOTO**

September 5, 1971 - D&RGW 478 crosses the relocated line and bridge south of Elk Park.
**J. L. EHERNBERGER PHOTO**

September 4, 1971 - Cumbres & Toltec Scenic Railway engine 483 crossing the Cascade Creek iron bridge. **J. L. EHERNBERGER PHOTO**

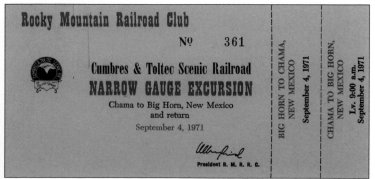

Rocky Mountain Railroad Club

Nº 361

**Cumbres & Toltec Scenic Railroad**
**NARROW GAUGE EXCURSION**
Chama to Big Horn, New Mexico
and return
September 4, 1971

President R. M. R. R. C.

BIG HORN TO CHAMA, NEW MEXICO
September 4, 1971

CHAMA TO BIG HORN, NEW MEXICO
Lv. 9:00 a.m.
September 4, 1971

Ticket for the "Journey to Yesteryear on its Narrow Gauge Holiday."

December 31 – The Club had $24,094 in its bank account at year's end.

**1972**  **Meetings at Christ Episcopal Church. Dues remain the same. Pres. Carl Carlson; V-P. Charles Max; Secy. W. J. Gordon; Treas. Arl Cuthbert; Assist. Treas. W. L. Van Patten; Ed. Bruce Black.**

May 28 – Excursion on the Union Pacific behind engine 8444 from Denver (via the Dent Branch) to Cheyenne and over Sherman Hill to Laramie and return. With the train sold out, more than 150 others had to be turned away. Fares were $20.00. Passengers could order box lunches for the trip. Engine 8444 was used on Amtrak trains 6 and 5 on May 26 and May 29 to shuttle the locomotive from Cheyenne to Denver and back as positioning for the Club's trip. The Club paid the railroad $7,625 for the use of the train.

June 24 – Special excursion (Club's first) on the Black Hills Central Railroad, which operated on the Burlington Northern's Deadwood Branch from Hill City to Deadwood, SD using tank engine 104 (2-6-2T) and five cars. 176 members rode this train. Cost was $15.00 per person and the Club paid the railroad $2,400 for use

1938-49

1950-59

1960-69

1970-79

1980-89

1990-99

2000-03

Color Extra

May 28, 1972 - The Club's Union Pacific trip behind engine 8444 was sold out. Many of those turned away and others who wanted to watch the great locomotive in action followed the trip in their own vehicles. An accompanying parade of vehicles is common on Club-operated excursions. **DARRELL ARNDT PHOTO**

June 24, 1972 - Engine 104 and five cars carried 176 members on a special excursion on the Black Hills Central Railroad from Hill City to Deadwood, SD. **R. H. KINDIG PHOTO**

of the train. The trip had originally been planned to use the Keystone Branch of the Burlington Northern, but flooding caused the change.

July 16 – Rocky Mountain Railroad Club Day at the Colorado Railroad Museum. Engine 346 was steamed up and the Club's business car "Rico" and a caboose were used to haul passengers.

July 26 – Workday at the Colorado Railroad Museum.

August 6 – Club sponsored a "get-together" at the West Portal of the Alpine Tunnel.

September 1, 2 – The Club again operated the two-day trips on the Cumbres and Toltec and D&RGW. These back to back excursions cost $24 for a two-trip package

or were priced separately. Passengers had to provide their own transportation and hotel accommodations.

September 1 – The Club ran a 16-car doubled-headed train from Chama to Cumbres Pass and return. A total of 115 passengers were on this train. Fare for this trip was $16.

September 2 – On this trip 158 passengers rode the Durango to Silverton special, which followed the regular morning train. The cost was $10 for the Durango-Silverton portion, if purchased separately from the previous day.

October 2 – Trip Chairman Ed Haley reported in a letter to Club members, "The 1972 excursions have been a financial disaster for the Club, accruing a deficit of $1,558." The Silverton trip lost $2,362 and the Black Hills trip was $256 in the red. $1,060 was realized as profit from the UP trip, however. Blaming himself for this situation, Ed resigned the position he held since 1947.

(Author's Note: Ed was unfair to blame himself as the cost of trip operations increased greatly with insurance and liability concerns. The loss of regular mainline steam operations and the establishment of tourist railroads had decreased the uniqueness of some of the trips the Club had operated in the past. No one can fault his 25 years of planning and organizing excursions for which the Club became famous).

Members whose dues were paid as of October 1, received a complimentary copy of Jackson Thode's *A Century of Passenger Trains*. With special permission of Denver Westerners, this portion of the larger book was reprinted especially for Club members. The cost to the Club for 1,124 copies was $834.30. Extra copies were available for $2.50.

**1973** **Meetings at Christ Episcopal Church. Dues remain $3.00 for regular members and $4.00 for new members. Pres. Charles Max; V-P. E. J. Haley; Secy. & Equip. Chair W. J. Gordon; Treas. W. L. Van Patten. Ed. Bruce Black (from January to March). Darrell Arndt became editor in April.**

April 17 – M. C. Poor, long-time member and author the *Denver South Park & Pacific* book died. "Mac's" knowledge of railroading history was remarkable and he held many leadership positions in the Club.

May 12 – Club celebrated its 35th Anniversary with a Banquet at Stouffers Denver Inn. Price was $6.50.

September – Guiseppe's Old Depot Restaurant opened in Colorado Springs in the former D&RGW station.

October – The last copies of the *A Century of Passenger Trains* were sold.

**1974    Meetings at Christ Episcopal Church.  Dues are the same.  Pres. Charles Max; V-P. E. J. Haley; Secy. W. J. Gordon; Treas. Carl Carlson; Assist. Treas. W. L. Van Patten; Ed. Darrell Arndt.**

January 20 – Excursion on the Union Pacific behind engine 8444 from Denver, over Sherman Hill to Laramie via Dent Branch to LaSalle and Speer.  Half a dozen run-bys gave photographers the opportunity to take remarkable steam and smoke filled photographs. This trip cost $25.00.  Bernard Kelly of the *The Denver Post* wrote an article on the trip in the March 17, 1974 edition of *Empire* magazine.  The train's consist included all Union Pacific cars in the following order baggage 5716, coaches 5483, 5480, 5484, 5475, 5482, dome-lounge 9004, coaches 5468, 5472, 5473, 5486 and 5474.

More than 250 members and guests watched a slide presentation by Dick Kindig and Ed Haley.  Door prizes included copies of *Rails Around Gold Hill, Colorado & Southern* by Hol Wagner, *Pictorial Supplement to Denver South Park & Pacific* and slices of DSP&P rail from 1883.

May 19 – The Club purchased a Sears brand manual typewriter for $161.70 to be used by Club Secretary Bill Gordon.   The typewriter was replaced in June 1987 with a Macintosh computer.

May 27 – Excursion on the Union Pacific behind engine 8444 from Denver to Laramie via the Dent Branch and return.  Roundtrip was $25.00 for adults and $20.00 for children.  More than 440 passengers rode the train.  The train's consist, in order using all Union Pacific cars was one 5700-series baggage car, coaches 5486, 5473, 5474, 5483, 5480, dome-lounge 9004, coaches 5475, 5484, 5472, 5468 and 5482.

May – Heavy rains and melting snows again brought flooding along the Platte River Valley in Denver.  Waters covered the floors of the Colorado & Southern roundhouse and adjacent facilities, and nearly reached the Big Boy on display at the Forney Museum.  The events were reminiscent of the floods of 1965.  Also in May, lightning struck the smokestack of the Tramway Cable building at 18th and Lawrence (now the Old Spaghetti Factory).  $3,500 was spent to repair the stack.  Another stack, this one at the Burlington shops beneath the 20th Street viaduct was toppled.  The 220-foot high structure had become unsafe. As the railroad no longer needed the power plant, it was demolished.

September 1 – Club's second trip on the Black Hills Central in South Dakota on the Deadwood Branch of the Burlington Northern. The cost was $15.00 and included sightseeing in Lead and Deadwood.

September – Denver voters approved the construction of a $1.56 billion light rail system.

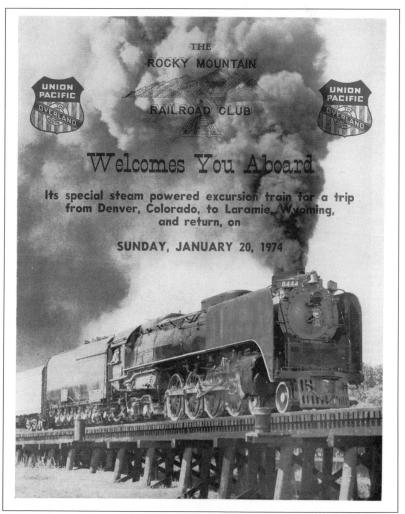

THE
ROCKY MOUNTAIN
RAILROAD CLUB

UNION PACIFIC THE OVERLAND ROUTE     UNION PACIFIC THE OVERLAND ROUTE

Welcomes You Aboard

Its special steam powered excursion train for a trip from Denver, Colorado, to Laramie, Wyoming, and return, on

SUNDAY, JANUARY 20, 1974

January 20, 1974 - A four-page glossy "Welcomes You Aboard" flyer (above) was used on a number of the Club's mainline excursions that used engine 8444.

1938-49

1950-59

1960-69

1970-79

1980-89

1990-99

2000-03

Color Extra

April – Charles Ryland, Dick Kindig and Ed Haley originally produced membership cards. Member's names were individually lettered by hand using a Leroy lettering set. This month, Jim Trowbridge, using special equipment at his Trowbridge Press, began printing membership cards.

April – The newsletter reported why some railroads don't like railfans on their property. Union Pacific special agents recently caught a rail enthusiast lying down between the rails at North Platte waiting for engine 8444 to pass over him so he could photograph it.

May – The Board decided to reprint the Club's *Denver South Park & Pacific* book by Mac Poor as a "Memorial Edition."

June 28 – More than 200 members and guests rode the Black Hills Central special between Hill City and Deadwood, SD. Locomotive 104 (2-6-2T) was used and a picnic lunch was held in Rochford. Tickets were priced at $15 for adults and $10 for children. Passengers had to make their own arrangements for transportation to the Black Hills, for meals and overnight accommodations.

July – Club meeting changed to the second Tuesday of each month, instead of the second Wednesday, due to a conflict with the church's needs.

July 21 – Rocky Mountain Railroad Club Day at the Colorado Railroad Museum. Activities included a steam up of engine 346. However, the Museum was issued a cease-and-desist order by the Jefferson County Health Department as a local resident had complained about the smoke drifting across the boundaries of the museum property.

August – The Club's car "Rico" was used along with other museum cars in the filming of a Johnny Cash TV show "The Great American Train Story or Riding the Rails" at the Colorado Railroad Museum (televised on November 22).

October 6 – Special diesel-powered trip on the Manitou & Pikes Peak cog railway. More than 60 members and guests participated. Cost was $8.00 for adults and $4.00 for children.

October 12 – Annual Banquet was held at the Stouffers Denver Inn. Ed Gerlits and Jim Ehernberger gave a movie and slide presentation on South American railroads. The roast baron of beef dinner was $8.00 per person.

October – The Union Pacific announced that Big Boy engine 4023 would be placed on display in Omaha and Challenger engine 3985 placed on display in Cheyenne. Engine 3985 would later be restored to service and used by the Club on many future excursions.

December – The Club provided an 18-foot Christmas tree at Union Station. This was part of larger project involving cash donations, food and decorations provided also by Intermountain Chapter NRHS, Amtrak staff, Brotherhood of Railway and Airline Clerks and the station gift shop.

**1975**    **Meetings at Christ Episcopal Church. Dues $3.00, $4.00 for new members. Pres. Eldin C. "Olie" Larsen; V-P. Jim Trowbridge; Secy. W. J. Gordon; Treas. Carl Carlson; Ed. Darrell Arndt. The position of Assist. Treas., held by W. L. Van Patten was changed to "Headstuffer" as Bill had been responsible for stuffing and mailing newsletters.**

March – This newsletter was the last one typed and proofread by Ane Clint. Ane had performed this task for 15 consecutive years.

April 13 – The Club hosted an open house for the *Nebraska Zephyr* train set at Union Station. More than 140 guests participated.

April – The Club had received pre-publication orders for 1,508 copies of the *Memorial Edition Denver South Park & Pacific* book.

May 20 – Denver voters defeated a proposal to purchase Union Station for use as a transportation center. (It was passed in 2001).

June 15 – Club members attended a public open house hosted by Ralph McAllister in Boulder who operated his 1/2 mile, 3-inch scale, 14 1/8" gauge railroad. Over a thousand visitors stopped by to see Mac's amazing railroad and collection of locomotives. Perhaps his most impressive locomotive was his 2-8-8-2 mallet which Ralph built from scratch. With a tractive effort of over 2,000 pounds, it operated with 200 psi boiler pressure, was 32 feet long (engine and tender) and weighed over ten tons fully loaded.

June 28 – Excursion over the Burlington Northern's Deadwood Branch from Hill City to Deadwood and return on a special Black Hills Central train using engine 104 (2-6-2T). Cost was $20.00 for adults and $15.00 for children. Excursion passengers were also able to ride free their regular train between Hill City and Custer on Friday, June 27th by just showing their Club excursion ticket. Passengers also had to provide their own transportation to Hill City, meals and overnight accommodations. Two hundred and seventy-three passengers rode behind the steam engine. Unfortunately a Club member from Albuquerque (Armand Forbes) was murdered east of Rapid City in a fight with a drunk. The assailant was apprehended, later convicted and sentenced to 32 years for first degree manslaughter. On October 5th, Bernard Kelly of

June 28, 1975 - The Club's train had a long delay at Mystic, SD when a portable pump refused to pick up water from a nearby stream. The trip was on the Burlington Northern's Deadwood Branch using Black Hills Central equipment. **J. L. EHERNBERGER PHOTO**

portion of the historic, 93-year-old D&RGW narrow gauge station in Silverton.

September 12, 13, 14 – First "Utah Fall Spectacular" excursion on Amtrak to Ogden, UT. Visits to the Salt Lake, Garfield and Western Railroad and the Wasatch Mountain Railway were arranged, with return to Denver on the *Rio Grande Zephyr*. Cost was $119.00 per person, double occupancy. Hotels in Provo and Salt Lake City were included. 70 members participated. Tours in the Ogden area were provided to a number of rail related sites.

October 4 – Diesel-powered excursion on the Manitou & Pikes Peak cog railway in three chartered cars. The outing included dinner at Giuseppe's Depot Restaurant and the opportunity to view the American Freedom Train behind engine 4449. Cost for the train was $8.50 and included a tour of the M&PP shops.

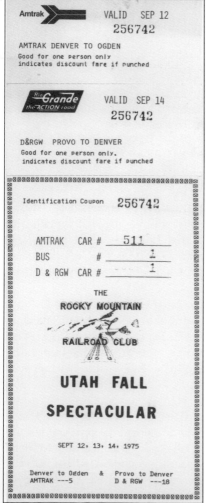

September 12-14, 1975 - Ticket for the first "Utah Fall Spectacular" excursion on Amtrak to Ogden, UT.

*The Denver Post* covered this trip with an article in the *Empire* magazine.

June – The DSP&P depot in Bailey was razed.

July 13 – Rocky Mountain Railroad Club Day at the Colorado Railroad Museum. Free admission with membership card.

July – Hatch's Book Store in Cinderella City offered Club members a 10% discount on railroad books through the end of December by showing a current membership card.

August 17 – A fire believed to have started by an arsonist heavily damaged portions of the historic ex-Santa Fe depot in Colorado Springs.

September 12 – A bomb explosion destroyed a

October – The Club received a donation of the color movie "Rivers of Silver, Ribbons of Steel" from William Loeffler.

October 11 – Annual Banquet was held at Henrici's Hilton Inn. Price was $6.75 and the program was by Mel Patrick on "Chicago Union Station" and "Zephyr West."

November – As the result of the donation of two copies of two books, *Denver South Park & Pacific*, and Jose Crum's *Rio Grande Southern Story*, the Club established a raffle wherein members could buy chances at $2.00 each for these books as part of their dues renewal process. Thomas Streeter donated the books in memory of his uncle Charles Cheney. Over the next several years the Club raffled copies of various Club publications to raise funds. Tickets ranged from $1.00 to $2.00 and were available only to Club members during dues renewal. This began a tradition that continues to today, although videos have been added to the items in the annual drawing.

**1976** **Meetings at Christ Episcopal Church – dues raised to $4.00. Pres. Eldin C. "Olie" Larsen; V-P. Jim Trowbridge; Secy. W. J. Gordon; Treas. Carl Carlson; Ed. Darrell Arndt.**

January 16 – Charter member Dick Kindig retired from Western Electric after 39 years of service.

January – The Colorado Railroad Historical Foundation purchased all the assets of the Colorado Railroad Museum to ensure the perpetuity of its operations.

1938-49
1950-59
1960-69
1970-79
1980-89
1990-99
2000-03
Color Extra

Robert Richardson and Cornelius Hauck (both Club members) formed the foundation in 1965 with the intent of purchasing the museum.

April 13 – The first annual book drawing took place, and Robert Wengler of Golden won the *Denver South Park & Pacific* book. Phillip Marceau of Port Orchard, WA won the *Rio Grande Southern Story*.

April 17 – Members were invited to tour the Uhrich Locomotive Company in Strasburg. Inclement weather discouraged some, but the opportunity to see a 15-inch gauge, coal-fired scale model of D&RGW K-27 (2-8-2) was well worth the effort for those who attended.

May 30 – Excursion on Union Pacific from Denver over Sherman Hill to Laramie via the Dent Branch behind steam locomotive 8444. The cost was $30 roundtrip for adults and $25 for children and the trip was sold out. Passengers arranged for their own lunches. Photo stops were made at many locations. The Club made a profit of $2,315 on this trip.

June 12, 13 – Two-day steam-up on the Cripple Creek & Victor Railroad. For $5.00 Club members could have unlimited rides on both days. Four steam locomotives were operating.

July 18 – Rocky Mountain Railroad Club Day at the Colorado Railroad Museum. "Cinderburgers" were available for a nominal price for members and their guests (prepared by Erwin and Bobbie Chaim and assisted by Bob Luttrell).

July 22 – Long-time member and railroad historian Dow Helmers died in Colorado Springs.

August 7, 8 – Club member Stuart Anderson hosted an open house in Boulder for Club members who wanted to view his Avery steam tractor. There was no charge for this outing.

August 14 – Field trip along the abandoned route of the Colorado Midland Railroad to the Carlton Tunnel and to the Hagerman Tunnel. More than 75 members participated.

August 28 – The Georgetown, Breckenridge & Leadville Railway (Georgetown Loop) hosted Rocky Mountain Railroad Club Day at Silver Plume. A $5.00 pass allowed unlimited rides behind engine 44 operating on the road. It would not be until 1984 that the High Bridge would be completed, allowing a trip on the Georgetown Loop in its entirety.

September 19 – Member Ralph McAllister hosted a public open house at his live steam operating railroad in Boulder. Approximately 200 attended, many of whom were Club members.

August 14, 1976 - More than 75 members participated in a hike along the abandoned route of the Colorado Midland Railroad near Hagerman Tunnel. **DARRELL ARNDT PHOTO**

September 20 – Reverend Gerrit Barnes died. It was his avid enthusiasm for railroading that brought the Club meetings to Christ Episcopal Church in 1971. Rev. Barnes served as founding pastor until 1974. Barnes Hall where the Club holds its monthly meetings was named for him.

September 25 – Diesel powered excursion in the new articulated two-car train set on the Manitou & Pikes Peak cog railway. Cost was $8.50 for adults and $4.25 for children. The trip included a visit to the shops, as well.

October 2 – Annual Banquet held at Henrici's Hilton Inn, Denver. Cost was $7.50 and the program was by Neal Miller "Last Passenger Train on the Midland Terminal" and the Buster Keaton movie "The General."

December – The Club published the *Memorial Edition Denver South Park & Pacific*. Pre-publication price was $19.00 and regular price was $24.50. Six thousand copies were printed. A small number of defective copies were sold to members for $17.00.

**Meetings at Christ Episcopal Church. Dues remain $4.00 per year for past members. Pres. Jim Trowbridge; V-P. Ed Gerlits; Secy. W. J. Gordon; Treas. Carl Carlson; Ed. Darrell Arndt.**

May 14 – Excursion on the Manitou & Pikes Peak cog railway. Fares remained $8.50 for adults and $4.25 for children (the same as last year's trip). Members were invited to stop by Guiseppe's Old Depot Restaurant in Colorado Springs following the trip.

July 16 – The High Country Railroad at Heritage Square hosted an open house for Club members. Cost for unlimited rides was $5.00.

July 19 to 24 – Club members served as volunteers for the National Model Railroad Association's "Rocky Rails '77" at Denver's Currigan Hall.

August 5 – Otto Kuhler distinguished artist and designer died.

August 6 – Club members walked the abandoned Denver, South Park & Pacific (C&S) roadbed in the Platte Canyon starting at Waterton. Trip was arranged by Denver Water Board employee and Club Treasurer Carl Carlson who secured special permission to enter the canyon. Cost was $4.00 for members riding the bus but no charge if you provided your own transportation.

August – The Western History Department of the Denver Public Library made available a catalog of photographs taken by Otto Perry. Three Club members (Dick Kindig, Jack Thode and Ed Haley) spent many hours indexing the collection.

September 2 to 5 – A number of Club members attended the Midwest Old Settlers Threshers Association reunion at Mt. Pleasant, Iowa. Travel was by Amtrak. The price was $125 not including Amtrak sleeping accommodations.

October 15 – Annual Banquet was held at Henrici's Hilton Inn in Denver. Cost was $9.50 and Ed Gerlits hosted the movie "The Titfield Thunderbolt."

November 26 – Steam-powered excursion behind engine 8444 from Denver, over Sherman Hill to

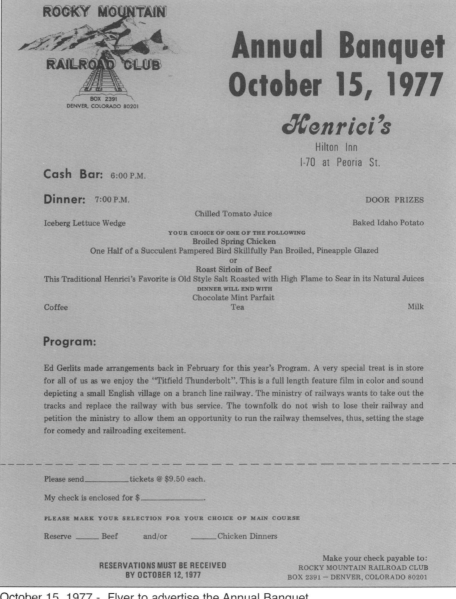

ROCKY MOUNTAIN RAILROAD CLUB

BOX 2391
DENVER, COLORADO 80201

**Annual Banquet October 15, 1977**

*Henrici's*

Hilton Inn
I-70 at Peoria St.

**Cash Bar:** 6:00 P.M.

**Dinner:** 7:00 P.M.

DOOR PRIZES

Iceberg Lettuce Wedge

Chilled Tomato Juice

Baked Idaho Potato

YOUR CHOICE OF ONE OF THE FOLLOWING
**Broiled Spring Chicken**
One Half of a Succulent Pampered Bird Skillfully Pan Broiled, Pineapple Glazed
or
**Roast Sirloin of Beef**
This Traditional Henrici's Favorite is Old Style Salt Roasted with High Flame to Sear in its Natural Juices
DINNER WILL END WITH
Chocolate Mint Parfait

Coffee

Tea

Milk

**Program:**

Ed Gerlits made arrangements back in February for this year's Program. A very special treat is in store for all of us as we enjoy the "Titfield Thunderbolt". This is a full length feature film in color and sound depicting a small English village on a branch line railway. The ministry of railways wants to take out the tracks and replace the railway with bus service. The townfolk do not wish to lose their railway and petition the ministry to allow them an opportunity to run the railway themselves, thus, setting the stage for comedy and railroading excitement.

- - - - - - - - - - - - - - - - - - - - - - - - - - - - - - - - - - - - -

Please send_____ tickets @ $9.50 each.

My check is enclosed for $ _____.

PLEASE MARK YOUR SELECTION FOR YOUR CHOICE OF MAIN COURSE

Reserve _____ Beef     and/or     _____ Chicken Dinners

**RESERVATIONS MUST BE RECEIVED BY OCTOBER 12, 1977**

Make your check payable to:
ROCKY MOUNTAIN RAILROAD CLUB
BOX 2391 – DENVER, COLORADO 80201

October 15, 1977 - Flyer to advertise the Annual Banquet.

Laramie via the Dent Branch. Return was via the mainline. Roundtrip fare was $37.00 for adults and $30 for children, which included a box lunch. A number of photo run-bys were provided for this sold out trip. A windy day complicated some of the photo lines, with gusts as high as 66 mph in Cheyenne and 71 mph in Laramie. Car captains were assigned to each car of the train. These volunteers were responsible for passenger boarding, adherence to safety and anything else needed to make the trip run smoothly. At the photo stop at Carr, Car Captain Jim Ranniger experienced more than his share of frustration. The train was stopped headed in a northerly direction with passengers unloading on the east side. The wind was blowing mightily under the train. The car captains had to lean toward the train to maintain their footing. As one recalls, in those days train toilets dumped directly to the tracks. During this stop, some passenger flushed the toilet in the restroom immediately adjacent to the vestibule where Jim was standing (or leaning) on the ballast. Needless to say, Jim

1938-49
1950-59
1960-69
1970-79
1980-89
1990-99
2000-03
Color Extra

was drenched and added a specific aroma to his car during the remainder of the trip.

December – This year the Club erected two Christmas trees at Union Station, which were decorated by Amtrak employees using decorations provided by the Intermountain Chapter of NRHS.

December – Ed Haley retired from the U.S. Bureau of Reclamation after 36 years of service.

**1978** **Meetings at Christ Episcopal Church. Dues were raised to $6.00. Pres. Jim Trowbridge; V-P. Ed Gerlits; Secy. W. J. Gordon; Treas. Ardie Schoeninger; Ed. Darrell Arndt.**

February 25, 26 – Although not a Club sponsored activity, a number of members attended the 50th Anniversary of the Moffat Tunnel. Souvenir programs were provided and special guests included Edward Bollinger, Alexis McKinney and Robert W. Richardson.

March – The City of Littleton announced it is going to study the feasibility of lowering the railroad tracks that pass through the downtown area to eliminate congestion caused by the increased coal train traffic.

April 21 – Two buses took Club members to the Transportation Test Center in Pueblo. Fare was $10.00 not including dinner at Guiseppe's Old Depot Restaurant in Colorado Springs. The trip also visited the historic station in Pueblo.

May 6 – Morris Abbott, author and historian of the Manitou & Pikes Peak cog railway and long-time Club member died.

May 7 – Jack O. Riley long-time Club member and former President died.

May 13 – Workday at the Colorado Railroad Museum.

July 13 – Field trip via chartered bus to Cripple Creek for a buffet-style dinner and melodrama at the Imperial Hotel. Tickets ($11.00 per person) included a ride on the Cripple Creek & Victor Narrow Gauge Railroad.

July 15 – Mickey Hansen died. Mickey was the Road Foreman of Engines on the Colorado & Southern when he retired in 1965 and handled the throttle on all of the Club's trips over the C&S and CB&Q rails as well as on GW engine 51.

August 12 – Excursion on the Union Pacific behind engine 8444. This trip to Laramie was via the Dent Branch and Cheyenne with return to Denver for a fare of $39.00. A box lunch was provided and a number of photo stops were made to accommodate the riders.

July 15, 1978 - The Club lost a great friend when former Colorado & Southern Road Foreman of Engines, Mickey Hansen, died on this date. This photo of Mickey was taken at Pueblo on December 16, 1962. He was the engineer of locomotive 638 on its last trip to Trinidad for display, which was the finale for C&S steam south of Denver. **STANLEY HUTCHINSON PHOTO**

August 12, 1978 - Union Pacific 8444 waits at the signal at Forelle, WY for a westbound freight train before proceeding on the eastbound trip out of Laramie. **J. L. EHERNBERGER PHOTO.**

August 26 – Field trip hike on the Argentine Central near Silver Plume. For $5.00, members were treated to unlimited rides on the Georgetown, Breckenridge and Leadville Railroad. For a charge of $3.00 participants received a handout and map and a tasty meal provided by Ranniger's Roadbed Commissary. This was the first appearance of what was to become a much appreciated and anticipated tradition of Jim and Lil Ranniger's "ballastburgers."

September 8, 9, 10 – A second "Utah Fall Spectacular" trip was sponsored by the Club for $137.00. Travel was via Amtrak to Ogden. A side trip was taken on the Wasatch Mountain Railroad known as the *Heber Creeper*. Return to Denver was via the *Rio Grande Zephyr*.

October 7 – Herb O'Hanlon former President and long-time member died. Herb was President when D&IM car 25 was acquired.

October 14 – Annual Banquet was held at Henrici's Hilton Inn near Denver's Stapleton airport. Cost was $10.50 and the program was the movie "A Ticket to Tomahawk."

October 21 – Excursion on the Manitou & Pikes Peak Railway using diesel train 16. Photo stops were provided and the trip was limited to 80 people and sold out. A chartered bus was planned but canceled due to lack of interest. Members dined at Guiseppe's Old Deport Restaurant in Colorado Springs after the trip. Cost was $9.00 for adults and $4.00 for children.

November 15 – Charter member Jack Thode retired from the D&RGW after 42 years of service. Jack was the Chief Budget Officer and during his employment he arranged for many special inserts and items for the Newsletter from the railroad's files.

December 13 – Club members decorated a Christmas tree at Union Station in cooperation with the Intermountain Chapter of the NRHS and Amtrak. Refreshments and snacks were served.

## 1979

**Meetings at Christ Episcopal Church. Dues were $6.00. Pres. Ed Gerlits; V-P. Erwin Chaim; Secy. W. J. Gordon; Treas. Ardie Schoeninger; Ed. Darrell Arndt.**

Feb 24, 25 – First Glenwood Springs trip on the *Rio Grande Zephyr*. The trip was sold out. Members stayed at the Hotel Colorado while in Glenwood. Cost was $87.00 roundtrip and included a banquet where members watched "The Great Locomotive Chase."

February 28 – Long-time member and former officer George Trout died.

April – The Club raised the price of the *Memorial Edition Denver South Park & Pacific* book to $24.95.

May 5 – Workday at the Colorado Railroad Museum. Ranniger's Roadbed Commissary provided their famous "Cinderburgers" for lunch.

May 17 – The Club and the American Theater Organ Society hosted a concert at the Paramount Theater. Cost was $3.00.

June 9 – The Club held its monthly meeting on Saturday in the form of a dinner meeting held at Heritage Square, near Golden, with rides on the High Country Railroad. Cost was $8.50 for adults and $5.50 for children. Club members Stuart Anderson, Jim Ehernberger, Ed Gerlits, Dave Gross and Dan Peterson owned and operated the live steam line.

GLENWOOD SPRINGS / RIO GRANDE ZEPHYR
WEEKEND EXCURSION
OF THE
ROCKY MOUNTAIN RAILROAD CLUB
SATURDAY, FEBRUARY 24, 1979

DINNER
NEW YORK STRIP SIRLOIN STEAK
TOSSED GREEN SALAD
BAKED POTATO    VEGETABLE DU JOUR    ROLLS & BUTTER
SHERBET

PROGRAM
THE GREAT LOCOMOTIVE CHASE
STARRING FESS PARKER, JEFFREY HUNTER & JOHN LUPTON

FROM THE PAGES OF CIVIL WAR HISTORY COMES THIS EXCITING ACCOUNT OF ANDREW'S RAIDERS AND THEIR PLOT TO CRIPPLE THE CONFEDERACY'S VITAL RAILROAD SYSTEM BY DESTROYING ALL THE BRIDGES FROM BIG SHANTY, GEORGIA, TO CHATTANOOGA, TENNESSEE.

February 24, 1979 – Dinner invitation and menu on the first Glenwood Springs trip on the *Rio Grande Zephyr*. The trip was sold out.

June 30 – Field trip to Virginia Dale and a hike of the Denver, Laramie & Northwestern right of way, including a visit to the site of the Butte Royal Tunnel. First stop on the trip was a visit to the Ft. Collins Municipal Railway carbarn and an opportunity to see the restoration of Birney car 21. After completing the hike along the DL&NW, the group had a picnic lunch and then drove to Loveland to see the live steam Buckhorn Northern Railroad operated by Fred Lewis. A detailed map of the DL&NW grade northwest of Virginia Dale based on surveys conducted by Kenneth Jessen was given to each participant.

July 28 – Excursion on the Union Pacific behind engine 8444 from Denver to Sterling via the Dent Branch to LaSalle. The cost was $42.00 and included eight photo runbys. Meals were not provided for this trip. All departures and arrivals were on time.

Aug 18 – Field trip to Boreas Pass from Como to Breckenridge. The cost was $7.00 for adults and $3.00 for children. Dinner was at the Old Como Eating House where the group watched a slide presentation by Ed Haley depicting a train trip from Denver over the pass to Leadville. Trip leaders included Ed Haley, Dick Kindig and George Champion. Ed Haley prepared a detailed map of Boreas Pass for this trip that was given to all participants.

August – The newsletter stated, "The recent testing done by the Union Pacific's Challenger engine 3985 on display at Cheyenne revealed a leak in the superheater tube. The test was just that, a test, and there are no plans by the railroad to do any work on the engine."

Sept 6 to 9 – Trip on the Grand Canyon Railroad. Leaving Denver by bus, the members rode to Trinidad to catch the *Southwest Limited* to Flagstaff. Bus transportation was provided there for sightseeing near Flagstaff, Sedona and Williams. A dinner in Flagstaff included an informative talk on the proposed Grand Canyon Railroad passenger service. Roundtrip fare was $179 for double and $235 for singles and $85.00 for children.

October 6 – Annual Banquet was held at Henrici's Hilton Inn, Denver, and the price was $13.50. The movie "Emperor of the North" was shown.

October – Manitou & Pikes Peak cog railway locomotive

4 at the Colorado Railroad Museum was traded to the M&PP in Manitou Springs for their locomotive 1. It is hoped that engine 4 can be returned to service for steam powered excursions.

December 31 – The Club had over $28,880 in all accounts. There were 1040 members.

The 1979-1980 Club roster contained a photo insert with pictures of the Club's equipment. Included were photos of engine 20, business car 021 "Rico," car 25, Birney 22, caboose 0578, PCC car 3101, and the three live steamers 999, 4 and 210. This photo sheet was also reproduced as a stand-alone sheet.

# Scrapbook

The
**ROCKY MOUNTAIN RAILROAD CLUB**
Acknowledges
_____
for the contribution of $ _____ into the
Club's Equipment Restoration & Preservation fund.

DATE _____ _____ PRES.

**ROCKY MOUNTAIN RAILROAD CLUB**

| TIME PER MILE | MILES PER HOUR | | TIME PER MILE | MILES PER HOUR |
|---|---|---|---|---|
| 4:00 | 15.0 | | 1:02 | 58.1 |
| 3:00 | 20.0 | | 1:01 | 59.0 |
| 2:24 | 25.0 | | 1:00 | 60.0 |
| 2:00 | 30.0 | | 0:59 | 61.0 |
| 1:43 | 35.0 | | 0:58 | 62.1 |
| 1:30 | 40.0 | | 0:57 | 63.2 |
| 1:29 | 40.4 | | 0:56 | 64.3 |
| 1:28 | 40.9 | | 0:55 | 65.5 |
| 1:27 | 41.4 | | 0:54 | 66.7 |
| 1:26 | 41.9 | | 0:53 | 67.9 |
| 1:25 | 42.4 | | 0:52 | 69.2 |
| 1:24 | 42.9 | | 0:51 | 70.6 |
| 1:23 | 43.4 | | 0:50 | 72.0 |
| 1:22 | 43.9 | | 0:49 | 73.5 |
| 1:21 | 44.4 | | 0:48 | 75.0 |
| 1:20 | 45.0 | | 0:47 | 76.6 |
| 1:19 | 45.6 | | 0:46 | 78.3 |
| 1:18 | 46.2 | | 0:45 | 80.0 |
| 1:17 | 46.8 | | 0:44 | 81.8 |
| 1:16 | 47.4 | | 0:43 | 83.7 |
| 1:15 | 48.0 | | 0:42 | 85.7 |
| 1:14 | 48.6 | | | |
| 1:13 | 49.3 | | | |

**Rocky Mountain Railroad Club**
HIKE ON THE ARGENTINE CENTRAL RAILWAY
SILVERPLUME TO PAVILION POINT, COLORADO
AUGUST 26, 1978
LUNCH AT: RANNIGER'S ROADBED COMMISSARY

LUNCH

GRAYS PEAK ROUTE ARGENTINE CENTRAL RY.

№ 158

BALLOT TO BE USED IN THE ELECTION OF OFFICERS AND DIRECTORS FOR THE ROCKY MOUNTAIN RAILROAD CLUB IN 1978

NOTE: Write-in blanks may be used for names of candidates of your choice. Be sure person chosen is willing to run.

**PRESIDENT**
James R. Trowbridge

**VICE PRESIDENT AND PROGRAM CHAIRMAN**
Edward F. Gerlits

**SECRETARY AND EQUIPMENT CHAIRMAN**
William J. Gordon

**TREASURER**
Ardie J. Schoeninger

**DIRECTORS**
Vote for only three of the following persons. The three receiving the most votes will serve during 1978 and 1979.

Danny Abbott
Carl Carlson
George Lawrence
Steven McCormick
James Ranniger
Neal Reich

March 28, 1971- At Eastlake (milepost 13.8 on the Dent Branch), engine 8444 heads the Club's twelve-car train.
**R. H. KINDIG PHOTO**

September 5, 1971 – In a photo that could have been taken many years earlier, D&RGW engine 478 takes water at Needleton Tank on the Silverton Branch. **J. L. EHERNBERGER PHOTO**

September 1, 1972 – The Club's train operated on the Cumbres & Toltec and is shown waiting at Osier. Locomotive 484 displays white flags denoting an extra. **NEAL REICH PHOTO**

January 20, 1974 – UP 8444 passes a line of photographers, tender first. The engine could not be turned on the Laramie wye track and was operated backwards to Sherman. **PETE WEST PHOTO**

1938-49
1950-59
1960-69
1970-79
1980-89
1990-99
2000-03
Color Extra

June 15, 1975 – Club members were guests of Ralph McAllister many times during this decade. Ralph built this 2-8-8-2 mallet from scratch to operate on his 14 1/8" gauge scale railroad near Boulder. It weighed nearly ten tons fully loaded. **DARRELL ARNDT PHOTO**

September 12-14, 1975 – The Club's first "Utah Fall Spectacular" including an outing on the Salt Lake, Garfield & Western. Lettered for the defunct Saltair resort, engine DS-1 pulls the Club's three-car special on the flats west of Salt Lake City.
**PETE WEST PHOTO**

December 1976 – By popular demand, the Club publishes the *Memorial Edition Denver South Park & Pacific*. This reprint of the book originally published in 1948, reproduced the text and photos. It included full color paintings by Phil Ronfor and sold for $24.00.

# Chapter 5: 1980 - 1989

**1980** Club meetings were at Christ Episcopal Church. Dues were $6.00 a year. Pres. Ed Gerlits; V-P. Erwin Chaim; Secy. W. J. Gordon; Treas. Ardie Schoeninger; Ed. Neal Reich.

January – Four long-time members received Certificates of Merit from President, Ed Gerlits. They included Dick Kindig, Ed Haley, Bryant McFadden and Bill Gordon.

February 23, 24 - Annual trip to Glenwood Springs on the *Rio Grande Zephyr*. The trip was sold out and overnight accommodations were at the Hotel Colorado. The ticket included admission to the hot springs pool and a dinner Saturday evening.

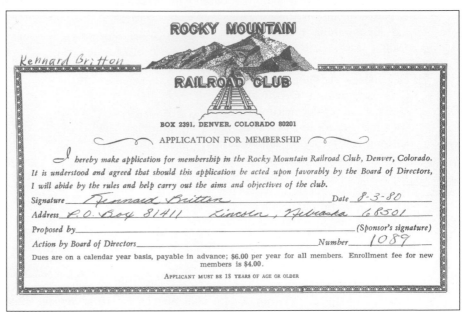

1980 - Membership application form required approval by the Board of Directors.

April 12 – Charles Ryland died.
Charles joined the Club in 1945 and suggested to "Mac" Poor that the Club might want to publish his book on the DSP&P. For many years Charlie printed the Club's embossed membership cards, trip flyers, tickets and rosters on his basement printing press.

June 22 – Trip to the High Country Railroad at Heritage Square. The $4.00 permitted unlimited rides and included lunch provided by Ranniger's Roadbed Commissary.

June 28 – Workday at the Colorado Railroad Museum. Ranniger's Roadbed Commissary again served lunch.

July 26 – Excursion on the Union Pacific behind engine 8444 from Denver to Sterling via the Dent Branch and LaSalle. The train was serviced in Ft. Morgan and Sterling. Over 440 riders took this trip which cost the Club $17,000. Individual tickets were $48.00, which did not include meals or beverages.

July – The Board of Directors authorized member Bill Gould to attempt to purchase Rio Grande Southern geese numbers 6 and 7 from a Mr. Brinkerhoff. Rumors were that he was going to scrap the geese. Although he did not sell them to the Club, he did sell them in 1982 to a man in Durango. Later, these geese were acquired by the Colorado Railroad Museum.

August 9 – Field trip to Central City and Blackhawk to explored the abandoned right of way of the Gilpin Tramway Company. More than 40 members participated, which included a train ride on the Colorado Central Railroad and food at Ranniger's Roadbed Commissary, all for $4.00.

September 13 – Trip on the Manitou & Pikes Peak Railway using steam engine 4 and wooden coach 104. This was the first Club trip using this engine, refurbished by the railroad after making a trade with the Colorado Railroad Museum. This was limited to 50 seats, first-come, first-served ticket orders. A second diesel-electric section accommodated twenty more members and guests. Near Minnehaha, riders were transferred to the diesel-electric coach for the remainder of the round trip. The trip also included a tour of the shops and was $10.00 for adults and $5.00 for children.

September 19, 20, 21 – Trip to Rock Springs, WY via the *San Francisco Zephyr*. The cost was $155 per person and included sightseeing in Atlantic City, South Pass City and various historical and industrial sites around Green River and Rock Springs.

October 4 – Club member (since 1948) Michael Koch died. Michael was the author of the well-known books on Shay locomotives and was a charter member of the "Eastern Division" of the Rocky Mountain Railroad Club.

October 11 – Annual Banquet was at Henrici's Hilton Inn in Denver. The cost was $13.00 and the program was viewing 2,000 feet of Otto Perry 16mm films.

December – Club auctioned two nearly complete sets of "signatures" (forming one book). Signatures are 16 or 32 pages of a book that form the sections of a book to be bound. The signatures were found in the Club archives and were from the *Pictorial Supplement to Denver South Park & Pacific*. One set was made available for a mail auction. Individual signatures, along with color 8x10 prints from the same book were sold at $0.25 each. More than $400 was raised with these auctions and the money was used to preserve and catalogue the memorabilia owned by the Club.

December – The Club honored Bob Griswold with a Certificate of Merit at the regular meeting. Bob was recognized for his work in mailing newsletters and many years of dedicated service to the Club. William Van Patten also received a Certificate of Merit for his work with publications, the newsletter and for service as a former officer.

December – Dues were raised to $12.00 per year, due to increased cost of operations. The projected annual budget for 1981 was $12,500. The Board decided to reprint three booklets published by the Club in the 1950s.

During this decade, members would find Bruce, Jim and Lil Ranniger serving meals from the Ranniger's "Silver Commissary."
**J. L. EHERNBERGER PHOTO**

lunches to about 125 people. On the train, guests coul[d] order from a menu "Dinner Aboard the Silve[r] Commissary" which included choices for condiment[s] on the "Cinderburger," chips, beans, cookie and lemon[-] ade. The menu clearly stated "N[o] tips permitted – our waiters are no[t] worth it." Erwin and Bobbie Chaim and Sam and Carrie Arnold were the waiters. The "Silver Commissary" was a cooking car with fluted sides and lettering that matched that found on the "Burlington Zephyrs." With the "Silver Commissary" in the middle, patrons would sit in cars on either end of the cooking car while they had their specially prepared meals served to them.

July – The Burlington Northern Railroad and Denver Center Cinema offered a full month's worth of railroad related films at

**1981**  **Meetings at Christ Episcopal Church and dues raised to $12.00. Pres. Jim Ranniger; V-P. Erwin Chaim; Secy. W. J. Gordon; Treas. Ardie Schoeninger; Ed. Neal Reich.**

January 17, 18 – Union Pacific volunteers completed most of the restoration of engine 3985. This was the first time in 23 years that the locomotive had been operated.

February 21, 22 – Club chartered two cars on the *Rio Grande Zephyr* for a trip to Glenwood Springs. More than 80 members participated in this trip that cost $109 per person. The cost included a room at the Hotel Colorado, an admission to the pool and a dinner. Westland Travel organized this trip on the Club's behalf.

May 30 – Club member Ralph McAllister hosted an open house for Club members in Boulder on his 14 1/8-inch gauge live steam railroad.

June – Club purchased a new public address system with a clip on microphone, a hand microphone, an amplifier and two speakers for use at meetings.

June 13 – Workday at the Colorado Railroad Museum.

June 21 – Trip to the High Country Railroad in Heritage Square with prices $5.00 for adults and $3.00 for children. Ranniger's Roadbed Commissary provided

June 21, 1980 - The "Silver Commissary" on the tracks of the High Country Railroad. **DARRELL ARNDT PHOTO**

For more than 15 years, field trips and workdays included lunch at Ranniger's Roadbed Commissary. **J. L. EHERNBERGER PHOTO**

September 26, 1981 - The Club sponsored an excursion on the Manitou & Pikes Peak Railway. The cog train is shown (left) as it approaches Mountain View with engine 4 shoving old wooden coach 104. The view (right) shows the diesel car 14 preparing to load passengers who rode one-way and returned on the steam train. **J. L. EHERNBERGER PHOTOS**

1938-49

1950-59

1960-69

1970-79

1980-89

1990-99

2000-03

Color Extra

the Denver Center for Performing Arts. U.S. and foreign films were shown throughout the month.

July 11 – Excursion on the Union Pacific behind engine 8444 on a trip from Denver to Sterling via the Dent Branch. Tickets cost $53.00, and the trip was sold out. Members were on their own in Sterling for lunch, but a map and handout provided suggested restaurants. Temperatures were in the 90s with clear skies. There were eight excellent photo run-bys. A unique opportunity was offered riders in that they could purchase "super fidelity" original master 33 1/3 LP or stereo cassette double sets of recorded sounds of steam locomotives 8444, 4449, 765 or 614. Original Master Recordings Company made this offer and a portion of the proceeds went to the Club.

August – Newsletter contained the first of a series of biographical sketches (written by Bob Griswold) of charter members. This one featured William Van Patten.

August 8 – Ed Haley led a Club field trip on the "Switzerland Trail," the Denver, Boulder & Western Railroad. Ranniger's Roadbed Commissary provided meals for members who paid $5.00 for tickets. Jack Morison provided much of the commentary. An eighteen-page flyer with photographs was provided to each guest.

September 4 to 7 – A number of members took a Club sponsored trip to the 32nd Annual Reunion of Old Settlers & Threshers Association in Mt. Pleasant, Iowa. Travel was via the *San Francisco Zephyr*. The cost was $225 not including any Amtrak sleeping accommodations.

September 26 – Trip on the Manitou & Pikes Peak cog railway using steam powered engine 4 and wooden coach 104. 80 members and friends paid $20.00 (adults) or $12.00 (children). The excursion was shortened due to a number of fires set by the 4. 50 members were entitled to ride the upbound steam train based on first-come, first served. The remaining 30 rode the diesel-electric.

All passengers participated in photo stops. At Mountain View everyone rode the diesel-electric to the top. Upon return to Mountain View, the 30 passengers from the diesel-electric who had ridden up to Mountain View rode down to Manitou on the steam train.

October – The newsletter contained a biographical sketch of Charter member Dick Kindig.

October 10 – Annual Banquet was held at Henrici's Hilton Inn in Denver. The price was $14.00 and the program a viewing of Otto Perry movies and a short newsreel presentation by Jim Ranniger.

November 10 – The Club held a member's auction at the regular meeting.

December 8 – Darrell Arndt received a Certificate of Merit for his work as former Newsletter Editor and his work on the equipment and trip committees. Treasurer Schoeninger reports that the Club spent $11,749 in 1981 with newsletter and postage costs the largest items ($6,720).

December – Club members cut a tree and took it to Union Station where it was decorated by Amtrak employees using decorations furnished by members of the Intermountain Chapter of the NRHS.

1982    **Meetings at Christ Episcopal Church. Dues remain $12.00. Pres. Jim Ranniger; V-P. Erwin Chaim; Secy. W. J. Gordon; Treas. Ardie Schoeninger; Ed. Neal Reich; Assoc. Ed. Steve McCormick.**

January 1 – The Colorado & Southern Railway Company ended 83 years of service when it was merged into the Burlington Northern system. Incorporated in on December 19, 1898, it comprised the holdings of the Union Pacific Denver & Gulf and the Denver Leadville & Gunnison companies. Grenville Dodge was the first Chairman of the Board.

February 14, 1982 - The Club's first Durango & Silverton Narrow Gauge Railroad trip shown near Rockwood carried more than 300 on a rare February excursion.
**J. L. EHERNBERGER COLLECTION**

ried Mayme Delaney, daughter of the owner of the famous Delaney's Saloon in Como, where George lived during the summer.

April 24, 25 – Ninety members and guests took the Club's annual trip to Glenwood Springs on the *Rio Grande Zephyr*. Accommodations were provided at the Hotel Colorado and the two dome coaches were sold out, as usual. Cost was $115.00, which included the train ticket, hotel room, admission to the Hot Springs pool and a Saturday evening dinner. Beginning with this trip, the Club produced a number of different style trip flyers that included brief histories of the train, Glenwood Springs, the Hotel Colorado and milepost guides along the D&RGW route. Also, a quiz was provided to those who wished to answer questions about scenes or history along the route. Prizes were given to the person with the most correct answers.

January – Newsletter contained a biographical sketch of Charter member Jack Thode.

February 13 – Bob Griswold arranged a side trip to Blanca for those going via bus to the Durango excursion. The stop at Blanca included a visit to the Southern San Luis Valley Railroad (Colorado's loneliest railroad) where photos were taken.

February 14 – Winter trip on the Durango & Silverton Narrow Gauge Railroad. Chartered buses were available to take members to Durango, although many drove themselves. Train tickets were $20.00 for adults and $12.00 for children to ride to Teft Siding and return. A special package that included the train, bus, lunch and hotel arrangements was available for between $114 and $177 depending on the hotel choices selected. More than 300 passengers rode the ten-car train pulled by engine 481. Owner Charles Bradshaw flew in from Florida to be the guest speaker at the Club's Sunday evening dinner. The movie "The Denver & Rio Grande" was also shown that night. Members were able to visit the yards in the evening for a night photography session.

April – Club made available three 200 foot Super-8mm reels of Otto Perry films. The films were produced in cooperation with Sunday River Productions. The price for Reel 1 was $33.05, Reel 2 was $30.95 and Reel 3 was $35.70. These prices to Club members were discounted 30% off the normal selling prices of $47.20, $44.20 and $51.00 respectively.

April 23 – Long-time member George Champion, Sr. died at age 98. George worked on the Colorado & Southern (including the last run of a rotary snowplow through the Alpine Tunnel) and on the Denver & Salt Lake. He mar-

May – Club established a policy that trip tickets would be made available to Club members (and family) only for the first 30 days of the sale. After that period, tickets would become available to the public if any remained.

May 15 – Workday at the Colorado Railroad Museum. Ranniger's Roadbed Commissary provided lunches to the volunteers who applied a fresh coat of paint to the "Rico."

May 30 – Steam-powered excursion on the Union Pacific behind engine 8444. The trip ran from Denver to Sterling via the Dent Branch and LaSalle. More than 430 riders enjoyed numerous photo stops. The price was $59.00. Sirens in downtown Denver welcomed the train back. It seems as if the Denver Fire Department had received several calls that a viaduct or Union Station was on fire. The railroad issued Train Order No. 5001 that stated ... "Passengers are requested to keep a close lookout for wild Indians, prairie fires, wagon trains and buffalo on the track, high water, total eclipse and anything that may effect (sic.) the movement of this train. Have a safe trip. Signed, J. W. McMullen, Trainmaster, UPRR."

June 20 – The High Country Railroad at Heritage Square near Golden hosted Club members at an open house.

August 14 – Field trip on the East side of Rollins Pass to Needles Eye Tunnel and Yankee Doodle Lake. Ranniger's Roadbed Commissary provided members lunch for a $6.00 ticket. Bill Gould's "Mobile Loco Sound Effects Co," provided a haunting accompaniment to a portion of the hike.

August – The Club provided all members a copy of the recently printed booklet containing three previously published monographs about *The Colorado Eastern Railroad, Steam Tramways of Denver* and the *Denver, Longmont and Northwestern Railroad.*

September 3 to 6 – Forty-one members participated in the Reno bound "Rail Ramble '82" to the Nevada State Railroad Museum via Amtrak's *San Francisco Zephyr.* Departure from Denver was at 12:30 p.m. with arrival in Evanston, WY at 9:00 p.m. Passengers could change to sleeping cars or remain in coach. Travel continued via the Lucin Cutoff to Reno. Three nights were spent in Reno with bus side trips to Donner Pass, Truckee, CA and Carson City, NV to visit the Nevada State Railroad Museum and the former Virginia & Truckee Railroad shops. Arrival back in Denver was on Labor Day at 6:05 p.m. by way of the *San Francisco Zephyr.*

September 25 – Club excursion on the Manitou & Pikes Peak cog railway. Seventy-six members rode the combined steam and diesel powered trip to the summit. Like last year's trip, fifty first-come, first-served tickets were sold for the steam portion (using engine 4) to Minnehaha with the balance of the riders aboard the diesel train. At Minnehaha, the "uphill fifty" boarded the diesel to the summit. Upon their return, the "downhill twenty-six" boarded the steam train to the bottom. Cost was $25.00.

October 9 – Annual Banquet was at Henrici's Hilton Inn. The price was $14.75 and Dick Kindig, who narrated three reels of Otto Perry films, provided the program. At this event, Club received a $1,000 donation from the National Narrow Gauge Convention to be used in the preservation of Otto Perry films.

October 23 – Charter member Arlington "Arl" Cuthbert died. Arl served as Treasurer and on the Board of Directors and was a regular at Club meetings and on excursions for many years.

December – Newsletter contained an article about Charter member Walker Edwards.

December 14 – President Ranniger presented Certificates of Merit to Bryant McFadden for his work on the Publications Committee, Bob Griswold for his work on the Newsletter Committee, and Neal Reich for his work as Newsletter Editor for the past three years.

December – Club members cut a tree and took it to Union Station where it was decorated by Amtrak employees using decorations furnished by the Intermountain Chapter of the NRHS.

## ROCKY MOUNTAIN RAILROAD CLUB

### ROCKY MOUNTAIN RAILROAD CLUB

BOX 2391
DENVER, COLORADO 80201

| TIME PER MILE | MILES PER HOUR | | TIME PER MILE | MILES PER HOUR |
|---|---|---|---|---|
| 4:00 | 15.0 | | 1:02 | 58.1 |
| 3:00 | 20.0 | | 1:01 | 59.0 |
| 2:24 | 25.0 | | 1:00 | 60.0 |
| 2:00 | 30.0 | | 0:59 | 61.0 |
| 1:43 | 35.0 | | 0:58 | 62.1 |
| 1:30 | 40.0 | | 0:57 | 63.2 |
| 1:29 | 40.4 | | 0:56 | 64.3 |
| 1:28 | 40.9 | | 0:55 | 65.5 |
| 1:27 | 41.4 | | 0:54 | 66.7 |
| 1:26 | 41.9 | | 0:53 | 67.9 |
| 1:25 | 42.4 | | 0:52 | 69.2 |
| 1:24 | 42.9 | | 0:51 | 70.6 |
| 1:23 | 43.4 | | 0:50 | 72.0 |
| 1:22 | 43.9 | | 0:49 | 73.5 |
| 1:21 | 44.4 | | 0:48 | 75.0 |
| 1:20 | 45.0 | | 0:47 | 76.6 |
| 1:19 | 45.6 | | 0:46 | 78.3 |
| 1:18 | 46.2 | | 0:45 | 80.0 |
| 1:17 | 46.8 | | 0:44 | 81.8 |
| 1:16 | 47.4 | | 0:43 | 83.7 |
| 1:15 | 48.0 | | 0:42 | 85.7 |
| 1:14 | 48.6 | | 0:41 | 87.8 |
| 1:13 | 49.3 | | 0:40 | 90.0 |
| 1:12 | 50.0 | | 0:39 | 92.3 |
| 1:11 | 50.7 | | 0:38 | 94.7 |
| 1:10 | 51.4 | | 0:37 | 97.3 |
| 1:09 | 52.2 | | 0:36 | 100.0 |
| 1:08 | 52.9 | | 0:35 | 102.9 |
| 1:07 | 53.7 | | 0:34 | 105.9 |
| 1:06 | 54.5 | | 0:33 | 109.1 |
| 1:05 | 55.4 | | 0:32 | 112.5 |
| 1:04 | 56.3 | | 0:31 | 116.1 |
| 1:03 | 57.1 | | 0:30 | 120.0 |

**1982**

| S M T W T F S | S M T W T F S | S M T W T F S |
|---|---|---|
| JANUARY | FEBRUARY | MARCH |
| APRIL | MAY | JUNE |
| JULY | AUGUST | SEPTEMBER |
| OCTOBER | NOVEMBER | DECEMBER |

1982 - New members and renewal memberships received a speed conversion table and calendar along with the Club's events listed on the back.

**1983**

**Meetings are still at Christ Episcopal Church and dues remain $12.00. Pres. Darrell Arndt; V-P. Erwin Chaim; Secy. W. J. Gordon; Treas. Ardie Schoeninger; Ed. Neal Reich (January) and Les Grenz beginning in February.**

February – The *Rail Report* sported a new masthead with the title in large font, bold letters.

February 16 – Bryant McFadden long-time member died. Bryant and his wife, Shirley (also a Club member), handled all the book shipments from their home. Thousands of books when first printed were stored in their garage, forcing their car to be parked outside for long periods of time. They typed the mailing labels and delivered books to the Post Office. Their efficiency and dedication to the Club cannot be forgotten.

February 17 to 22 – Thirty-nine members of the Club participated in a trip to California. Leaving Union Station by bus, they took the *Southwest Limited* from Trinidad to Los Angeles. While in Southern California, they visited Knott's Berry Farm, Long Beach, Los Angeles area rail sites. The return was on Amtrak's *Desert Wind* through Las Vegas including a visit to Hoover Dam and to Salt Lake City where they took the *Rio Grande Zephyr* to Denver. Price was $499 and up depending on accommodations.

April 23, 24 – The Club chartered two cars on the last run of the *Rio Grande Zephyr* for their annual trek to Glenwood Springs. The $113.00 fare included a room at the Hotel Colorado, admission to the pool and a

April 23-24, 1983 - Silver and black ticket for the last run of the Rio Grande Zephyr.

dinner. This was the last run of the *Rio Grande Zephyr*. Engine 5771 headed the train, accompanied by two B units, a steam generator car, a combine, a diner, three dome coaches, two flattop coaches, the "Silver Shop," then another dome coach, and "Silver Sky" on the end. The price included round trip train tickets, hotel room, admission to the Hot Springs pool, and dinner in the Hotel's Red Steer Room. Special tickets for the trip were printed on silver paper with bold black ink, in a style never used before by the Club.

May – The *Rocky Mountain Rail Report* masthead now combined the bold font heading with a drawing of engine 20 in RGS lettering. Gone is the drawing of D&SL engine 203 from the cover. This design would be virtually unchanged until 1998.

May 22 – Club workday at the Colorado Railroad Museum, with Ranniger's Roadbed Commissary in full operation.

May 29 – Excursion on the Union Pacific from Denver to Laramie over Sherman Hill and return. From Denver, motive power was a pair of GP40Xs to Speer (near Cheyenne), changing to engine 3985 (4-6-6-4) on its first public excursion. The twelve-car train included one baggage car, a dome car and ten coaches. The return from Speer was again behind diesel power. Seven photo run-bys were made. The fare was $75.00. Each trip handout during the UP trips in the 1980s included information on the trip, specifications for the Challenger or engine 844, a recent Club newsletter and a letter describing Club activities. Commemorative buttons were given to each rider for the trip.

June 6 – Former officer and long-time member Dan Peterson died.

May 29, 1983 - On the first public excursion behind Challenger 3985, the train is seen westbound at Dale Junction, WY. **STEVE PATTERSON PHOTO**

May 29, 1983 - Not all run-bys are perfect. A freight train blocked the view of the 3985 near the Hermosa Tunnel. **STEVE PATTERSON PHOTO**

June 18 – Rocky Mountain Railroad Club Day at the Colorado Railroad Museum. Engine 346 and the galloping goose operated.

June 19 – The High Country Railroad at Heritage Square hosted Club members this day. The cost was $7.00 for adults and $5.00 for children and lunch was provided by Ranniger's Roadbed Commissary.

August 13 – Despite rain and thundershowers, members took a field trip on the West side of Rollins Pass, originating at Winter Park. Ranniger's Roadbed Commissary provided lunch on the trip, which cost $6.00. Over the years, many members have added colorful memories to the Club's outings and one of these people was Sister Mary Borgia. Sister Mary resided at the Immaculate Conception Basilica and attended meetings regularly dressed in her long black robe with the white starched collar and rosary beads at her side. She also took as many of the Club's trips as she could, despite her advanced age. On this particular field trip, the rain and pea sized hail had intermittently pelted the participants all day. During the lunch stop, nearly 100 members waited in line for the food to cook, which it does more slowly at the 10,000 altitude. Sister Mary finally exhausted her patience as she approached the chief cook, Jim Ranniger. Her tongue-lashing included her thoughts of his ability to cook 1/2 pound ballast burgers any faster. Jim, looked her in the eye and said, "Sister, I'm in charge of the cooking today and you're in charge of the weather." Seconds later, a large bolt of lightning struck a tall pine tree a hundred yards away, brilliantly throwing splinters of wood all over and simultaneously deafening everyone with the clap of thunder. The expression on Sister Mary's face was indescribable. She never complained again about having to wait for food on future field trips. Unfortunately, at a later time Sister Mary Borgia was killed in an automobile accident when a Denver police car struck her as she crossed Colfax at Sherman, near the Basilica.

September 3, 4 – Two-day marathon in Southwestern, Colorado on the Cumbres & Toltec Scenic Railroad and the Durango & Silverton Narrow Gauge Railroad. Both days included many run-bys. The cost for the two-day trip was $65.00 for adults and $50.00 for children. The overnight stay (not included in the ticket price) was in Chama.

> September 3 – Leaving Chama at 7:00 a.m., over 300 members and friends rode nearly 11 1/2 hours on the Cumbres and Toltec Scenic Railroad (train powered by engine 488) the first day. Thirteen photo stops were provided and there were three meets with other trains.
>
> September 4 – On the second day, a like number rode more than 12 1/2 hours on the Durango & Silverton Narrow Gauge Railroad. Engines

476 and 478 provided power. Again, many photo stops were included and lunch was in Silverton. All four locomotives of the D&SNGRR were in Silverton (the Club's double-headed train and the two regular trains).

September 24 – "Moonbeam Special" (diesel powered) on the Manitou & Pikes Peak cog railway to the summit of Pikes Peak. Leaving before sunset, the trip provided an opportunity to view both the sunset and the moonrise over the plains. A sandwich buffet was included in the $17.00 price ($12.00 for children). As the train descended under a full moon, a fiddler/song leader led the passengers in a number of appropriate songs, including "Shine on Harvest Moon."

October 15 – Annual Banquet is held at the Hilton Inn near Stapleton Airport. The program was the movie "Von Ryan's Express." Dinner was $15.00.

October – The Club purchased over 12,000 feet of 16mm movie film from Irv August for $5,000.

November 8 – Long-time member and former Treasurer Ane Clint died. Ane also served as Secretary of the Colorado Railroad Historical Foundation (doing business as the Colorado Railroad Museum). Ane has been memorialized at the Museum by the creation of the Ane O. Clint Yard.

December 9 - Club members cut a tree and took it to Union Station where it was decorated by Amtrak employees using decorations furnished by the Intermountain Chapter of the NRHS.

**1984    Meetings are at Christ Episcopal Church and dues remain $12.00. Pres. Darrell Arndt; V-P. Erwin Chaim; Secy. W. J. Gordon; Treas. Ardie Schoeninger; Ed. Les Grenz for January; Jim Trowbridge becomes Editor in February.**

February – Jim Trowbridge became the Editor of the *Rocky Mountain Rail Report*, a position he would hold until January 1998.

February 25, 26 – Eighty-one members and friends rode a reserved "Superliner" car on the Amtrak *California Zephyr* for the Club's annual trip to Glenwood Springs. Fare included a blinding snowstorm upon arrival, as well as a room at the Hotel Colorado, admission to the pool and dinner in the hotel's "Devereux Room." Despite the change in operating companies, the Club was able to continue the tradition begun in 1979.

April 1 – The Club chartered a heavyweight, ex-Northern Pacific car (built in 1915) on the last *Ski Train* of this season. The fare was $15.00 for the train with additional side trips available in the Winter Park area for an added cost. The train consisted of locomotive

May 27, 1984 - Railfans shoot the action from a photo line on Sherman Hill. Professionals with movie cameras, complete with sound, compete for space in the line along with amateurs with pocket-sized point-and-shoot cameras. **R. W. ANDREWS PHOTO**

Much was done on the Birney 22 as well as other pieces of equipment.

May 27 – Sold-out excursion on the Union Pacific. Over 500 fans rode from Denver to Speer behind Centennial engine 6922. A stop was made in Greeley to pickup passengers, as needed. At Speer, engine 3985 took over for the trip over Sherman Hill and return. In Laramie, diesel GP30 number 844 switched the train for the return to Speer behind the 3985. Nine photo stops were made. The cost of the trip was $75.00.

June 1 – The first train was operated by the Georgetown Loop Railroad over the recently reconstructed High Bridge.

5771, steam generator car 253, locomotives 5762, 5763, baggage-coach 1230, coaches 1017, 1016, 1013, 1011, 1015, 1018, 1012 and 1014.

April – The Club proposed to the Colorado Railroad Museum that a large shed be erected at the Club's expense to protect Club equipment. Photos of models of the proposed structure were included in the April *Rocky Mountain Rail Report*. The Museum Board turned down the proposal.

April – Club authorized Bob Griswold to oversee the preparation of a book to commemorate the rebuilding of the Georgetown Loop.

May 5 – Club member R. H. Kindig was recognized by the Railway & Locomotive Historical Society when they presented him the Society's "Photography Award."

May 12 – Workday at the Colorado Railroad Museum. Ranniger's Roadbed Commissary provided lunch to all members working on Club equipment.

June 8 to 17 – Thirty-one members of the Club took a trip to Chicago ("Illinois in '84") via the *California Zephyr*. The events included visits to Galesburg Railroad Days, the Museum of Science and Industry,

June 1984 - Members pose in front of the *Pioneer Zephyr* at the Museum of Science and Industry in Chicago. **DARRELL ARNDT PHOTO**

Amtrak's Chicago maintenance facility, the Chicago, South Shore and South Bend Railroad, the East Troy Trolley Museum, Kalmbach Publishing Company's headquarters in Milwaukee, WI, the Illinois Railway Museum and to EMD's locomotive plant in La Grange. The purpose of the trip included presentation of a special plaque to the Museum of Science and Industry to commemorate the 50th anniversary of the first run of the *Pioneer Zephyr* to Denver.

August 18, 19 – Field trip to Cripple Creek led by Jack and Erma Morison. The Denver to Florence caravan included nearly 25 cars and visited many historic sites in the Cripple Creek and Victor area. Rides on the Cripple Creek & Victor Narrow Gauge Railroad were also included. Ranniger's Roadbed Commissary provided lunches on both days, which were hamburgers the first day, steaks the second day. A special treat on this hot weekend was ice cream on Saturday. Participants stayed at the Imperial Hotel where they enjoyed the famous melodrama.

August 25 – First Club trip over the Georgetown Loop Railroad was behind locomotive 40. The trip was limited to 155 tickets and sold out at $20.00 per person.

September 30 – D&RGW F unit 5771 made its last run from Pueblo to Denver prior to being stored at Burnham shops.

October 6 – Trip on the Manitou & Pikes Peak cog railway. Diesel-hydraulic powered railcar 24 was used on the trip which cost $18.00 for adults and $12.00 for children. Snow removal equipment was required to open the line prior to the trip because of a fast moving storm the night before.

October 13 – Annual Banquet was held at the Hilton Airport Inn. The program was the showing of selected footage of Irv August films. Cost was $16.00.

November – The Club sold the last of the remaining copies of the *Memorial Edition Denver South Park & Pacific* for $39.95 in the November *Rocky Mountain Rail Report*.

December 15 - Club members cut a tree and took it to Union Station where it was decorated by Amtrak employees using decorations furnished by the Intermountain Chapter of the NRHS. The "Travel by Train" sign was illuminated this evening for the first time in many years.

December 29 – The Ft. Collins Municipal Railway Society rolled out and operated car 21 for the first time on approximately 2,200 feet of re-laid track. Their car 21 was a sister car to the Birney "Safety Car" owned by the Club.

August 25, 1984 - The first Club excursion aboard the Georgetown Loop Railway on the newly reconstructed High Bridge. **J. L. EHERNBERGER PHOTO**

1985   **Meetings at Christ Episcopal Church. Dues remain $12.00. Pres. Keith Kirby; V-P. Erwin Chaim; Secy. W. J. Gordon; Treas. Ardie Scho-eninger; Ed. Jim Trowbridge.**

February 9, 10 – Fifty Club members and friends rode the *California Zephyr* on a reserved Superliner coach to Glenwood Springs for the Club's annual trip. The round trip fare of $125 (children $55.00) included overnight accommodations, admission to the Hot Springs pool and dinner at the Hotel Colorado's Devereux Room.

February – The Club leased an office in room 212 at Denver Union Station. The new "international" headquarters was a room 22'x12' painted bile green with a black linoleum floor and a single window. The Club's archives were located here. Not elegant, but functional.

March – Editor Trowbridge started a monthly column titled "Life in the Rocky Mountain Railroad Club" highlighting various members of the Club and their experiences.

March 31 – The Club chartered a heavyweight, ex-Northern Pacific car on the last *Ski Train* of this season. The fare was $15.00 for the train with additional side trips available in the Winter Park area for an additional

1938-49
1950-59
1960-69
1970-79
1980-89
1990-99
2000-03
Color Extra

fee. The train consisted of GP40-2 locomotives 3125 and 3122, steam generator car 253, baggage-coach 1230, coaches 1012, 1017, 1016, 1014, 1011, 1015, 1018 and 1013, in that order.

May – Due to budget considerations, the format of the newsletter was reduced to an eight-page edition.

May 11 – Workday at the Colorado Railroad Museum. Ranniger's Roadbed Commissary provided lunches.

May 20 to June 2 – Club sponsored an "Expo 86" trip from Denver to Seattle by air, then via coach to Vancouver where eight days were spent in British Columbia. Activities included a trip behind the "Royal Hudson," tours of Victoria, a trip on the *Dayliner* to Duncan, BC and sightseeing in both Seattle and Vancouver. Costs ranged between $1,355 and $2,515 depending on occupancy and accommodations and was limited to 46 participants.

May 26 – Another sold-out excursion on the Union Pacific. About 550 fans rode the fourteen-car train from Denver to Speer via the Greeley mainline behind Centennial engine 6936, where engine 3985 took over for the trip over Sherman Hill to Laramie and return. The round trip cost $75.00 and included nine run-bys.

June 16 – Over 120 members and friends enjoyed food from Ranniger's Roadbed Commissary at the High Country Railroad at Heritage Square. Cost was $7.00 for adults and $5.00 for children.

June 19 to July 4 – Thirty-two members participated in a Club sponsored trip to Europe. The thirteen-day trip included many train rides and visits to rail-related sites in France, Switzerland, Italy, Monaco and Germany.

June – Along with members of the Intermountain Chapter of the NRHS, Club members help relocate the famous Zephyr Monument in Glenwood Canyon to the Colorado Railroad Museum. First erected in 1950, the monument weighed 29 tons and was 8' by 14' by 14' tall.

August 10 – 11 – Rocky Mountain Railroad Club workday on the Cumbres & Toltec Scenic Railroad at Chama.

August 13 – In lieu of the regular meeting, the Club toured rail facilities at the Coors Brewery in Golden. Nearly 300 members and friends participated in this event.

August 17 – Field trip over Marshall Pass. Seventy-seven members and friends drove in a 33-car caravan from Mears Junction, to the summit of the pass and to Sargent. Ranniger's Roadbed Commissary provided lunch. Rich Dais was Trip Leader. Cost was $6.00.

December 14, 1985 - Club members supply the Christmas tree for Union Station and Amtrak employees decorated it for the twelveth year in a row. **DARRELL ARNDT PHOTO**

August 24 – Approximately 30 members met in Fort Collins for a Club sponsored outing on the Fort Collins Municipal Railway car 21. The cost was only $2.00 for a four-ride pass.

August 30 to September 3 – Thirty-two members rode the *California Zephyr* to Mt. Pleasant, IA for the 36th Annual Old Settlers and Threshers Reunion. Cost was $358, not including Amtrak bedroom charges or hotel rooms.

September 21, 22 – The Club hosted the "First Annual Farewell to Amtrak's *California Zephyr*" trip to Glenwood Springs. Members stayed at the Hotel Denver. Fare included two days swimming at the Hot Springs pool, steak dinner and cocktails and a Sunday brunch. This trip was planned because of the rumors of the potential demise of Amtrak.

October 12 – Annual Banquet was held at the Airport Hilton Inn. 115 members and guests paid $16.00 for dinner that evening. The program was a showing of selected Irv August 16mm film footage.

December 14 – For the twelfth year in a row, Club members cut a tree and took it to Union Station where it was decorated by Amtrak employees using decorations furnished by the Intermountain Chapter of the NRHS.

**1986**    **Meetings are at Christ Episcopal Church. Dues were raised to $15.00 (approximately 1100 members). Pres. Keith Kirby; V-P. Erwin Chaim; Secy. W. J. Gordon; Treas. Bert Bidwell; Ed. Jim Trowbridge.**

January – Plans were made to publish periodic historical stories of the Club by Club members in the *Rocky Mountain Rail Report*. This month was the beginning of printing the Club newsletter only on white paper. From 1960 to this time, newsletters were printed on colored paper with issues alternating colors throughout the year. The white or off-white paper also enhanced the photographs used in each issue.

February – Ardie Schoeninger and his wife Cyndi Trombly were appointed Co-Chairs of the Club's 50th Anniversary Celebration. Ardie received a lithograph of Otto Kuhler's "Desert Storm" at the February meeting in appreciation of his work as Treasurer.

February 11 – Philip Ronfor, artist for the original paintings used in the Club's *Denver South Park & Pacific* and the *Colorado Midland* books died.

February 22, 23 – Thirty-three members took the annual trip on the *California Zephyr* to Glenwood Springs. The round trip fare of $125 (children $55.00) includes overnight accommodations and a dinner at the Hotel Denver.

March 23 - The Club chartered a heavyweight, ex-Northern Pacific car on the last *Ski Train* of this season. The fare is $20.00 for the train with additional side trips available in the Winter Park area for an additional fee. The train consisted of locomotives 5507 and 5516, steam generator car 253, private car "Utah," private car "Colorado," baggage-coach 1230, coaches 1018, 1013, 1011, 1015, 1016, 1014, 1012 and 1017, in that order.

March – The Club established the Rocky Mountain Railroad Club Preservation Fund, the purpose of which is to provide funding to preserve railroad structures and artifacts (starting in Colorado) but not including rolling stock. This monthly drawing will provide funds for various future projects.

May – The *Rocky Mountain Rail Report* had the first of series of articles on the history of the Club. This one was written by Jack Thode (cardholder number 4).

May 21 to June 2 – Thirty-six members of the Club participated in "Expo 86" to Vancouver, Canada. Members spent three days enjoying railroading which included such notable engines as the "Royal Hudson" and UP engine 3985. The cost was between $1,350 and $1,750 and included Amtrak to Seattle, bus to Vancouver, ship to Seattle and return by rail or air.

May 24 – The Colorado Live Steamers hosted an open house. About 40 Club members enjoyed the trip to their facility in Waterton Canyon.

June 15 – The Club hosted a Father's Day outing on the Ft. Collins Municipal Railway car 21. Cost was $5.00. Members presented a donation of $1,000 to the Ft. Collins Municipal Railway out of the new Preservation Fund.

June – The Board approved an abridged edition of the *Pictorial Supplement to Denver South Park & Pacific*. This project was not a Club publication but instead was produced by Trowbridge Press and sold for $39.95.

June 28 – Workday at the Colorado Railroad Museum (rescheduled from May due to rain and snow).

July 12 – More than 40 members and friends went on a field trip to Tie Siding, WY. The outing included hikes to the site of the Dale Creek Bridge, the Ames Monument and the town of Sherman. Ranniger's Roadbed Commissary provided lunches. Cost was $7.50. Carl Carlson, Jack Morison and Jim Ranniger

1938-49

1950-59

1960-69

1970-79

1980-89

1990-99

2000-03

Color Extra

were trip leaders. As is not uncommon, this was a rather windy day and as the Commissary crew was setting up the tent, a gust of wind picked up the tent and also picked up Erma Morison who attempted to restrain it. Fortunately she was not hurt, only her pride bruised. The tent was not torn but lunch was served without benefit of shelter.

July 16 – Marguerite Jenks, age 94, died. Marguerite was an early member of the Club, having joined in 1948. As Ed Haley recalled, because it was difficult to get passengers for Club trips, Ed advertised in the Colorado Mountain Club's bulletin board. Ten to twelve women of that organization became regular riders. Marguerite was one of the first women to join the Rocky Mountain Railroad Club.

August 9, 10 – Over seventy-five members took a driving field trip to the Alpine Tunnel. Beginning in Salida, they drove to Hancock by way of St. Elmo. From Hancock, they hiked to the East Portal. After spending the night in Salida, they drove over Monarch Pass to Pitkin and to the West Portal. Cost was $10.00 not including hotel. Rich Dais and Tom Lawry led the trip. Jim Ranniger's Roadbed Commissary provided gourmet lunches before the group headed home.

August 29, 30, 31 – Nineteen Club members took a Club sponsored trip to Omaha on the *California Zephyr* to visit the Union Pacific Historical Museum, the Western Heritage Museum, the Strategic Air Command Museum and other Omaha area sites. The round trip cost was approximately $350, depending on Amtrak accommodations.

September 6 – The Club chartered a special train on the Cadillac & Lake City Railroad from Falcon to Limon and return. The trip on the three-car train cost $26.00 per person and included a box lunch and six photo stops. Locomotive 2509, a CF7, was former AT&SF GP7 rebuilt by the railroad in 1977 at the Cleburne shops. The 5-bedroom/Buffet lounge observation car number 551 "Mountain View" was built by Budd in 1949 and served on the New York Central, the Canadian Pacific and the Algoma Central. The "Silver Pine" (number 100) was a former *California Zephyr* sleeping car rebuilt by the railroad as a 48-passenger coach. The third car number 301 "Smoky Hill River" was a heavy weight

coach built for the CB&Q in 1912 and rebuilt into a combine car for CB&Q commuter service. Total cost of the trip for the Club was $1,590 and signing the contract for the railroad was Joe Minnich, who in 2000 would become the Club's Trip Committee Chair.

September – The Club donated $200 to the Como Roundhouse; $100 to the Colorado Historical Society for work on the CB&Q station in Fleming, CO; and $100 to the town of Victor to help preserve the Florence & Cripple Creek/Alta Vista Depot. All donations were from the Preservation Fund.

October 11 – Annual Banquet was held at the Sheraton Greystone Castle in Northglenn. The program was planned to be a showing of the movie "The Titfield Thunderbolt." However, a malfunction of the projector used by the previous group to show the movie, resulted in all three reels of the movie being damaged. The substitute movie was "The Great Train Robbery" with Sean Connery. Cost was $16.00.

October 19, 1986 - Club chartered private open platform car "Caritas," seen here at Glenwood Springs, for an excursion on the *California Zephyr* from Denver to Salt Lake City. **DARRELL ARNDT PHOTO**

October 17, 18, 19 – Club chartered the private open platform car "Caritas" for an excursion on the *California Zephyr* from Denver to Salt Lake City. The car also provided transportation to the Great Salt Lake over the Salt Lake, Garfield & Western Railway on Saturday. The cost of the trip was $399 per person, double occupancy. Had adding the "Caritas" necessitated the use of another locomotive, each fare would have increased by $112.

November – The *Rocky Mountain Rail Report* featured an article by Irv August about the Club's September 18, 1948 excursion to the Black Canyon of the Gunnison.

**1987**  **Meetings at Christ Episcopal Church. Dues were $15.00. Pres. John Dillavou; V-P. Rich Dais; Secy. W. J. Gordon; Treas. Bert Bidwell; Ed. Jim Trowbridge.**

February 7 – Limited to sixty, Club members took a tour of Union Station. Cost was $1.00 and a second tour was scheduled for April.

March 28 – The Club chartered the "Silver Sky" (the vista dome lounge observation car) on the *Ski Train*. GP40-2 3116 and GP30 3017 powered this train. Fifty-two Club members paid $67.00 for this experience. This seven-car train was the last *Ski Train* of the season and the railroad retired the ex-Northern Pacific heavy-weight cars following this trip. Eight of these cars were sold in September of this year to the Napa Valley Wine Train in California.

April 4 – A second Union Station tour was sponsored by the Club again limited to 60 members and guests.

April – The Club made a donation of $1,000 to the Rollins Pass Restoration Association from the Preservation Fund and becomes a lifetime member of this group.

May 2, 3 – Approximately 20 Club members spent the weekend in Fleming, restoring and painting the former CB&Q station. The Preservation Fund donated $500 for this event.

May 9 – Trip on the Manitou & Pikes Peak cog railway in railcar 16. This charter trip cost $16.00 for adults and $8.00 for children and included a souvenir booklet and passage through a number of cuts in snow drifts left over from a storm the previous week.

May 24 – The Club sold all 250 seats on a ten-car excursion on the Union Pacific. Fans left Denver on a rainy day behind diesel power for Cheyenne. Challenger 3985 made the run over Sherman Hill to Laramie and return. Diesel power was used on the trip back to Denver. A total of twelve run-bys were made. Ticket cost was $165.00. In an interview conducted in 1988, Jack Morison recalls that he and his son Chuck went to Cheyenne the night before the trip, camping overnight near the station. The next morning, a carload of people from Connecticut pulled up and Jack asked them if they were there for the trip. They replied that they did not have tickets but were hoping there would be cancellations. Soon a second car from California pulled up and these people said exactly the same thing. Both vehicles had driven from the far ends of each coast in hopes of getting a seat on the sold out train.

May 30 – Workday at the Colorado Railroad Museum.

June – A number of Club members took a trip to the eastern United States on a "Preserved Rail Heritage Tour." The trip cost was between $1,600 and $2,000 depending on accommodations and included visits to museums, sites and rail lines in Pennsylvania, Maryland and Washington, D.C. Fourteen nights were included along with an Amtrak daylight trip on Horseshoe Curve in Pennsylvania.

June – The Board decided not to reprint *Rails Around Gold Hill* or *Colorado Midland* as proposed by Trowbridge Press.

June – The Board of Directors authorized the purchase of a Macintosh Plus computer, with an ImageWriter printer and accessories all for $2,605.

June 21 – The Club hosted a Father's Day outing on the High Country Railroad at Heritage Square. More than 90 members and guests had lunch at Ranniger's Roadbed Commissary and enjoyed unlimited rides on the trains. Cost was $7.00.

July 4 – The Blackhawk & Central City Narrow Gauge Railroad was dedicated.

July 25 – Club members participated in a Preservation Work Day at Victor on the former Florence & Cripple Creek Railroad's Alta Vista Depot.

August 22, 23 – Field trip on the Colorado Midland to Hagerman Tunnel. More than 55 members and friends enjoyed gourmet steak sandwiches and Baskin-Robbins ice cream provided by Ranniger's Roadbed Commissary. Fog and rain added to the enjoyment of

September 6, 1986 - The Club's drumhead adorns the "Mountain View" seen here at Limon on a unique excursion on the Cadillac & Lake City Railroad. **DARRELL ARNDT PHOTO**

1938-49

1950-59

1960-69

1970-79

1980-89

1990-99

2000-03

Color Extra

September 19, 1987 - The Cadillac & Lake City had picked up a boxcar in revenue service during the Club's excursion. **R. W. ANDREWS PHOTO**

the hikers. Members were responsible for their own overnight accommodations in Leadville. Cost was $13.00.

September 19 – Four-car excursion train on the Cadillac and Lake City Railroad. Eighty-five members were treated to mixed freight revenue operations on the 122-mile trip from Falcon to Limon and return. The cost was $29.00 and included a BBQ lunch, numerous run-bys and beverage service. The total cost of this trip to the Club was $1,900. The consist was the same as the 1986 trip, except that Café car 101 was added. This car was originally a 16-section drawing room sleeper built for the Pullman Company and sold to the Great Northern in 1957 where it was converted to a lunch counter car assigned to maintenance service.

October 10 – Annual Banquet was at the Greystone Castle in Northglenn. The program was a showing of the classic 1935 movie "Silver Streak." Ticket cost was $16.00.

November – The *Rocky Mountain Rail Report* unveiled the 50th Anniversary logo designed by Howard Fogg. The 50th Anniversary slogan "Silver Rails & Golden Memories" was submitted by Dave Goss and would be used in future anniversary activities.

November – Regular monthly meeting time was changed from 7:45 to 7:30 p.m.

December – Publication of 1,000 50th Anniversary Commemorative black and white calendars containing 26 photos of trips taken by Club members over the years. The calendar sold for $6.00 plus $1.50 for first class shipping.

December 28 – The Internal Revenue Service notified the Club that its application for a 501(c)3 exemption was denied. The IRS noted several reasons including:

" 1) an organization that operates exclusively for one or more exempt purposes (which in the Club's application was stated to be "educational") may be granted the exemption; 2) the term "educational" means that instruction or training of the individual takes place for the purpose of improving or developing his capabilities, or the instruction of the public on subjects useful to the individual or beneficial to the community; 3) that the presence of a single non-educational purpose, if substantial in nature, will destroy an exemption regardless of the number of truly educational purposes; 4) the Club's long history of operating excursions without scheduling educational seminars, but instead which appear to be pleasure and social outings; 5) therefore indicate the primary focus of the trips feature free time with non-501(c)3 enticements; 6) therefore the Club is not operated for educational purposes and does not qualify for this exemption."

December – Working with the Intermountain Chapter of the NRHS, Club members placed twenty artificial Christmas trees in Union Station instead of the single tree as had been the past practice.

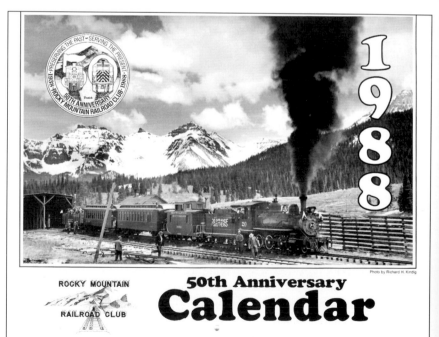

As part of the "Golden Anniversary" celebration, commemorative calendars with photos taken exclusively by members depicted trips during the Club's five decades and were sold for $6.00. They are now collector's items.

**1988** Meetings at Christ Episcopal Church. Dues are still $15.00 plus a $4.00 fee for new members. Pres. John Dillavou; V-P. Rich Dais; Secy. W. J. Gordon; Treas. Bert Bidwell; Ed. Jim Trowbridge.

January – Club commissioned a 50th Anniversary belt buckle that sold for $10.00. The Club also commissioned a special 50th Anniversary Commemorative plate ($24.95).

Logo (above) and belt buckle (left) commemorated the Rocky Mountain Railroad Club's 50th Anniversary.

March 26 – Club chartered a first-class parlor car on the *Ski Train*. Limited to only 39 passengers, the fare was $48.00 per person.

March – The Club authorized purchase of a brass HOn3 model of engine 20 made by Sunset Models. Raffle tickets to win the model were sold for $2.00 each or ten chances for $18.00.

April 11 – City of Denver issued a proclamation honoring the Club's "50 years of commitment to preserving the rich and significant history of the railroad in Denver and the West."

April 12 – Date proclaimed as "Rocky Mountain Railroad Club Day" by the State of Colorado. Governor Romer issued an acknowledgement of the Club's contributions to the preservation of railroad history and the education of the public on the roles the railroads played in the development of the State of Colorado.

April 16 – Fiftieth Anniversary Banquet was held in the Grand Ballroom of the Brown Palace Hotel with more than 357 members and guests. Cost is $20.00 per person. Special menus and souvenir 50th anniversary HO scale cabooses were given to each attendee. The theme was "Silver Rails and Golden Memories," presented in a multi-media format by Darrell Arndt, Jack Morison and Ron Ruhoff.

May 14 – Workday at the Colorado Railroad Museum.

June 17 – Members attend a special open house hosted by the Denver Society of Model Railroaders in the basement of Union Station.

June 18 – Excursion on the Union Pacific behind engine 3985. Centennial unit 6936 took the train from Denver to Cheyenne where the 3985 took over for the run over Sherman Hill to Laramie and return. Ten cars carried more than 340 passengers who paid $190.00 each for the excursion. Unlike previous years, there was no stop in Greeley for passengers. Six photo stops were provided.

June 19 – Excursion on the Georgetown Loop Railroad using engine 40. Numerous run-bys and lunch were included. The handout included numerous photos, maps and a brief history of this line. Cost was $25.00 per ticket.

June 20 – Excursion on the Manitou and Pikes Peak cog railway. The three and a half-hour trip began at noon and was via a diesel-hydraulic cog train. The train fare was $18 and for an additional $9.50 one could enjoy an evening of western entertainment and a chuck wagon dinner at the Flying W Ranch.

June 21 – Club members took both a hiking/driving field trip of the historic Cripple Creek mining district and enjoy riding the 2-foot gauge Cripple Creek & Victor Narrow Gauge Railroad. Tickets were $8.00.

June 21 – Excursion on the Cadillac and Lake City Railroad from Falcon to Limon. Photo run-bys and a lunch were included. Ticket cost was $30. This was the

April 16, 1988 - Ticket to the 50th Anniversary Banquet at the Brown Palace Hotel, Denver, where 357 members and guests attended.

Club's last trip on the C&LC, which ceased operations in January 1990.

June 23 – Special mixed 21-car passenger and freight on the Cumbres & Toltec Scenic Railroad. Leaving Chama for Big Horn wye and return, the passengers enjoyed lunch at Osier. The train included eleven freight cars ahead of the coaches. Engines 488 (in road service) and 489 (helper) were used. Ticket cost was $60.

June 24 – Field trip from Chama to Durango along the abandoned right of way of the old narrow gauge D&RGW. An optional dinner was available for $16 that evening.

June 25 – Double-headed excursion on the Durango & Silverton Narrow Gauge Railroad. Engine 476 was one of the engines used. Cost was $60. It is interesting to note that the ticket for the trip included two stubs for the

meals or accommodations, but did provide for daily field guides and an informational brochure.

July – Club published the first printing of the *Georgetown and The Loop* book for pre-publication price of $24.50 and $27.50 thereafter. This printing was 1500 copies.

August 13 – Excursion on the Great Western Railway between Loveland, Longmont and near Eaton and return. Diesel locomotive 703 provided power to the four-car train. Lunch was provided by Ranniger's Roadbed Commissary in a Johnstown park where the Gold Nugget Brass Band provided music. Price was $25.00 for adults and $15.00 for children. Several lucky members received cab rides in engine 703. Five photo run-bys were provided. On August 22, the *Rocky Mountain News Lifestyles* section carried an article about this trip, including a number of photographs.

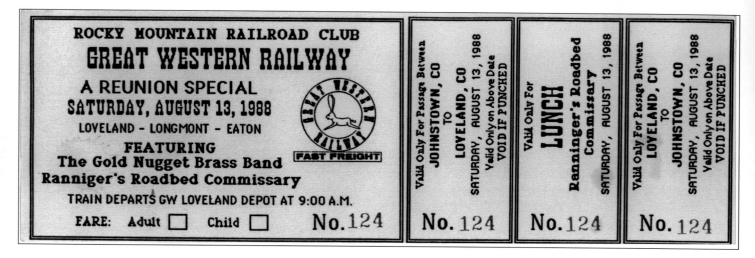

Durango-Silverton and return passage dated June 25th, but the main body of the ticket was dated June 19th.

June 26 to July 1 – Special field trips including along the Rio Grande Southern from Durango to Mancos to Dolores to Rico, Lizard Head Pass to Telluride (overnight). The next day was from Lizard Head Pass to Trout Lake to Placerville or Dallas Divide to Ouray (overnight). The next day was spent exploring the three Otto Mears lines in the Silverton area (overnight in Ouray). From Ouray the group went to Montrose to Cimarron to Morrow Lake and a boat ride to the Curecanti Needle and then to Gunnison (overnight). Next the group went from Gunnison to Crested Butte via Baldwin and Ohio Pass back to Gunnison (overnight). The last day was from Gunnison to Sargents and over Marshall Pass and back to Denver. More than 100 people participated in these trips and the convoy numbered up to 55 vehicles. The entire trip was planned and arranged by Cyndi Trombly, Ardie Schoeninger, Rich Dais, Tom and Cathy Lawry and Zona Stephens. Cost for these seven days was $25, which did not include

August 13, 14 – Colorado Live Steamers invited Club members to a free open house at the Waterton Canyon location.

September 1 to 5 – Excursion via bus to Trinidad, staying overnight and boarding the *Southwest Chief* on September 2 for a trip to Flagstaff. The next two days were spent touring the Navajo – Hopi lands of Arizona with trips to the Verde Valley, Jerome, Sedona, Oak Creek Canyon, and the South Rim of the Grand Canyon. Return was via the *Southwest Chief* to Trinidad and by bus coach to Denver. The five-day trip was $395.00 per person/double occupancy and thirty-seven members and guests took this trip.

September – The Board authorized $13,000 each for preservation of D&IM car 25 and RGS engine 20.

October 15 – In conjunction with several other organizations, Club members participated at "A Railroad Night at the Historic Paramount Theatre." Besides music on the Dual Wurlitzer Consoles, the Buster

December 12, 1988 - Car 25 on its way from the Colorado Railroad Museum to its new home at the Denver Federal Center. **DARRELL ARNDT PHOTO**

1938-49

1950-59

1960-69

1970-79

1980-89

1990-99

2000-03

Color Extra

article written by Irv August on his trip to Salida in September 1941.

February 10 – The Durango roundhouse on the D&SNG RR was destroyed by fire.

February 18 – Open house at the Denver Federal Center to see D&IM car 25.

March 18 – The Club chartered a coach on the *Ski Train*. Tickets cost $26.00 and the trip was sold out.

March 20 – Charter member Rollin Cordill died. Rollin served as President and in other leadership roles during his tenure and was an active model railroader.

Keaton film "Our Hospitality" was shown. Cost is $7.00, with tickets at the door for $8.00.

October 29 – Special guests who participated in the planning and execution of the 50th Anniversary activities were invited to a "Fiftieth Finale Get-together" aboard the private car "Cedar Rapids" at Union Station.

December 6 – Club executed an agreement with the General Services Administration to lease Building 78 at the Denver Federal Center to use it for storage and restoration of car 25. The cost was $140 per month.

December 10 – Traditional Trim-the-Tree night at Denver Union Station, sponsored by the Intermountain Chapter of the NRHS assisted by the Club and station employees.

December 12 – Car 25 was moved from the Colorado Railroad Museum to Building 78 at the Denver Federal Center. This location provided a heated space with rails and room for restoration work.

December 13 – Ardie Schoeninger and Cyndi Trombly were recognized for their outstanding work in planning and organizing the 50th Anniversary celebration.

**1989**    **Meetings at Christ Episcopal Church and dues remain $15.00. Pres. John Dillavou; V-P. Carl Carlson; Secy. W. J. Gordon; Treas. Bert Bidwell; Ed. Jim Trowbridge.**

January 7, 8 – Author Clive Cussler searched Kiowa Creek for the Kansas Pacific's lost locomotive 51. An article in the March *Rocky Mountain Rail Report* added light on the subject.

February – The *Rocky Mountain Rail Report* contained an

April 3 – Long-time Club member "Olie" Larsen died. Olie helped erect catenary at the Museum for trolley operations there. He is also remembered as Superintendent Transmission Lines for Public Service Company of Colorado. During winter, at times, "Olie" snow-shoed over Argentine Pass to inspect transmission lines.

April 22 – Three members participated in painting the inside of the Comanche Crossing Historical Society caboose in Strasburg.

April 29, 30 – Annual trip to Glenwood Springs on the *California Zephyr*. The cost was $129.00 and included accommodations at the Hotel Colorado and fees for the Hot Springs pool.

May 13 – Workday at the Colorado Railroad Museum.

June 17 – Excursion behind Union Pacific engine 3985 from Cheyenne to Laramie over Sherman Hill. Cost was $165 and the seven-car train was sold out (270 passengers) at a price of $165.00 per passenger. This was the last trip behind the 3985 before it was converted to oil. Trip cost to the Club was $30,000. Eleven photo run-bys were provided.

June 18 – Sunday trip on the Wyoming Colorado Railroad from Laramie to Walden, with lunch on the way at Fox Park. Buses return 65 members and guests to Laramie. This was the Club's only excursion to Walden. Cost is $65.00. Passengers could remain overnight in Walden, on their own, and secure passage back to Laramie on Monday on the regular public train. The two locomotives were former Alaska Railroad F units, and the train included two ex-D&RGW Rio Grande Zephyr dome cars, ex-Southern Railway streamlined coaches, and the ex-Great Northern streamlined lounge observation car "Appekunny Mountain."

June 29 to July 14 – A number of Club members participated in a Club-sponsored trip on a 3,200 mile trip across Canada. The fare of approximately $2,200 included airfare to Vancouver, rail transportation across British Columbia, Banff, Jasper, Ottawa and Montreal, hotel accommodations, sleeping car accommodations on VIA Rail, and return airfare to Denver.

July 22 – Outing on the Fort Collins Municipal Railway on car 21. Thirty-six members rode the trip, which cost $5.00 for families or $2.50 for single.

July – Club authorized publication of the second printing of the *Georgetown and The Loop* book. 1,000 copies were printed.

August 12 – The Colorado Live Steamers hosted Club members at an open house at their Waterton Canyon facility.

August 19 – Field trip and hike along the Argentine Central abandoned roadbed. Ranniger's Roadbed Commissary provided the hot food. Cost was $8.00.

September 2, 3, 4 – The Club sponsored a Labor Day

excursion to St. Louis. Organized by Alpine World Travel, the four-day trip included round trip airfare, two nights accommodations, tours of the Anheuser-Busch Brewery, a day-long visit to the National Transportation Museum and a dinner cruise on the "President" riverboat. The total fare for this trip was $509.

September 30 – Charter member William Lee Van Patten died. He held a number of offices, served on newsletter committees for many years and was a skilled model railroader.

October 7, 8 – Club members drove to North Platte to visit rail sites there. Although a visit to the shops facility was not possible, members enjoyed visiting the museum at Cody Park, night photography sessions at display locomotive 3977 and general photography along the busy Union Pacific mainline. The cost was $6.00.

October 14 – Annual Banquet was at the Denver Athletic Club. One hundred and sixty-seven members and guests pay $20.00 each for dinner. The program, arranged by Erwin Chaim is a showing of the movie "Titfield Thunderbolt."

# S c r a p b o o k

May 29, 1983 - Badge for the Memorial Day Club excursion on the Union Pacific from Denver to Laramie over Sherman Hill.

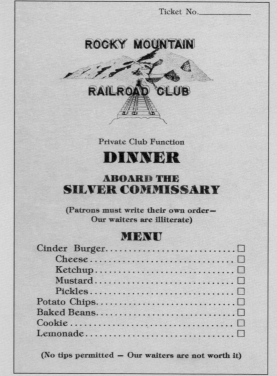

Guests could select food items using the menu provided by Ranniger's "Silver Commissary" which operated exclusively on the High Country Railroad.

June 21, 1981- A favorite attraction on any outing on the High Country Railroad was the "Silver Commissary." This "dining car" was staffed by the Rannigers and other volunteers, providing gourmet "Cinderburgers" and other treats from a menu provided to all riders. **PETE WEST PHOTO**

September 4 – 7, 1981 – The Club sponsored four trips to the annual reunion of the Old Settlers & Threshers Association in Mt. Pleasant, Iowa. This steam engine and others like it were featured along with antique vehicles, trolley cars and good food. **PETE WEST PHOTO**

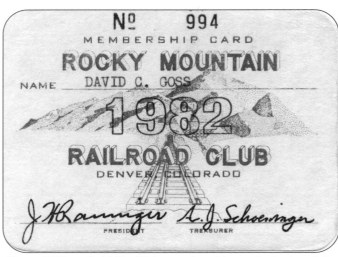

September 26, 1981 – For three years, 1980, 1981 and 1982, steam locomotive 4 provided power for a wooden coach on excursions on the M&PP. At Mountain View, passengers on the diesel train and steam train exchanged seats so each could experience the other's style of transportation. **PETE WEST PHOTO**

From 1955 until 1999, Club membership cards featured the year on the card in embossed, raised type. During the same period each card was individually lettered or typed with the member's name and sequential number. Beginning in 2000, the raised type printing technique was no longer used and blank membership cards were produced without the raised numbers. Starting in 2001, names and numbers were printed on the blank card using a computer.

1938-49
1950-59
1960-69
1970-79
1980-89
1990-99
2000-03
Color Extra

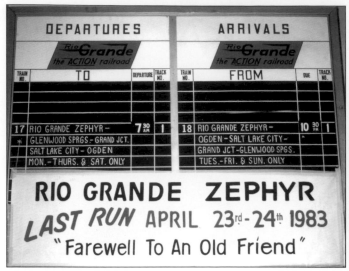

April 23-24, 1983 – This sign in Union Station bids farewell to the Rio Grande Zephyr. Diesel locomotive 5771 (now located at the Colorado Railroad Museum) powered the last run of this Colorado icon to Grand Junction and back. **R. J. FRYML PHOTO**

December 14, 1985 – For the twelfth year in a row, dedicated Club members cut down a tree, drug it through snow, at times hip-deep, to be set up and decorated at Denver Union Station.
**DARRELL ARNDT PHOTO**

May 24, 1986 – Erwin Chaim seems to be enjoying his ride on a miniature train operated by a member of the Colorado Live Steamers at their Waterton Canyon facility. **DARRELL ARNDT PHOTO**

May 2-3, 1987 – Club volunteers repaint the former CB&Q station in Fleming. Throughout the years, many Club members have volunteered thousands of hours in similar service projects around Colorado. **DARRELL ARNDT PHOTO**

# Chapter 6: 1990 - 1999

**1990**  **Meetings at Christ Episcopal Church and dues remain $15.00 – Pres. Dave Salter; V-P. Joe Priselac; Secy. W. J. Gordon; Treas. Bert Bidwell; Ed. Jim Trowbridge.**

March 2 – The Rocky Mountain Railroad Historical Foundation was incorporated.

March 9 – The Bylaws of the Historical Foundation were issued.

February 9 – Cadillac and Lake City Railway ceased operations.

February – Durango & Silverton Narrow Gauge Railroad opened its new roundhouse, one year after the fire had destroyed the previous building.

March 17 – Annual *Ski Train* trip to Winter Park on a reserved coach. Tickets were $28.00 per person.

May 8 – Past President John Dillavou was presented with a framed print of Howard Fogg's "California Zephyr" (commissioned for the book *Portrait of a Silver Lady*) in recognition of John's three years as Club President, including during the 50th Anniversary celebration.

May 12 – To celebrate the fortieth anniversary of the end of Denver Tramway Company trolley operations (June 3, 1950), a Denver Tramway historical tour on bus 119 was sold out. Forty Club members toured historic railroad and street railway locations in Denver, Arvada, Leyden and Golden (lunch). The trip included a visit to the restoration activities of car 25 at the Denver Federal Center.

May 23 – Jack Thode received the prestigious Fred A. and Jane R. Stindt Photography Award from the Railway and Locomotive Historical Society. Jack was presented the award in part for his editorial work on the two-volume work *George L. Beam and the Denver & Rio Grande*.

May 24 to 28 – Forty-three members and guests took a bus to Trinidad to catch Amtrak's *Southwest Chief* to Flagstaff for three nights and return. While in Flagstaff, members took a bus to Williams to ride the Grand Canyon Railroad and to enjoy "Williams Days." They rode behind engine 29, a 2-8-0, to the Grand Canyon and back, returning to Flagstaff Sunday afternoon. Return to Denver was via the *Southwest Chief* to Trinidad and bus to Denver.

The Rocky Mountain Railroad Club
*presents*
**The Southwest and The Grand Canyon**
*via*
**The Route of The "Super Chief"**
*aboard*
**The Amtrak "Southwest Chief"**
**The Grand Canyon Railway**

**Memorial Day Weekend May 24-28, 1990**

Return with us again for a bit of the flavor of the Southwest—the days of Fred Harvey, the Santa Fe Super Chiefs, The Indian Detours, and the Santa Fe branch line to the Grand Canyon.

On Thursday evening, May 24, we will board our deluxe motor coach for a relaxing twilight trip to Trinidad, Colorado for our overnight stay at the Holiday Inn. Friday morning we board the "Southwest Chief" for a spectacular trip over historic Raton Pass and then an all day journey across the ranch and desert lands and Indian country of New Mexico and Arizona. We arrive at Flagstaff in the evening where we will be overnight at the beautiful Flagstaff Howard Johnson Hotel.

On Saturday we will have an early departure by motor coach for a short trip to Williams. We will arrive in time to see the early train departure of the Grand Canyon Railway. A complimentary continental breakfast follows in the former Santa Fe depot and Harvey House Hotel, The Fray Marcos, which has been beautifully restored. A tour of the Railway's facilities will precede our departure for the Grand Canyon. Our 64 mile journey to the Canyon behind an early 1900's steam train faithfully restored to mint condition will feature 3% grades and 1200 feet elevation changes. Our stay at the Grand Canyon will be at the Quality Inn in Tusayan, 9 miles south of Grand Canyon Village.

At the Grand Canyon, everyone will have the opportunity to plan their own time—canyon rim tours, hiking, or just relaxing with easy-access shuttle service to our Inn. On Sunday afternoon we will reboard the Grand Canyon Railway for the scenic return trip to Williams and then on to Flagstaff for a relaxing evening at the Howard Johnson Hotel.

**Amtrak's**

May 24-28 – Advertising flyer for the *Southwest Chief* and the Grand Canyon excursion which was enjoyed by 43 members and guests.

June 2 – Field trip to Palmer Lake for photography and a hike along the former Santa Fe grade. Cost was $2.00 and more than 30 members and guests attended.

June 6 – The Internal Revenue Service granted a 501(c)3 designation to the Historical Foundation.

June 16 – Workday at the Colorado Railroad Museum.

July 21 – Trip on the Leadville, Colorado and Southern Railroad. Fifty-eight members and guests paid $14.50 each for adults and $8.50 for children for the trip.

August 4 – Excursion on car 1977 of the Platte Valley Trolley from Confluence Park to Sheridan Boulevard and return. Cost was $5.00 for adults and $2.50 for children. Nearly sixty members participated.

August 11 – Field trip to Boreas Pass. More than eighty members drove from Breckenridge to the summit of the pass and on to Como. Trip leader was Rich Dais.

May 12, 1990 - Denver Tramway Company bus 119 provided transportation for the Club's historic tour of Denver, including this stop along the Platte Valley trolley line west of Federal Blvd.
**DARRELL ARNDT PHOTO**

February – The *Rocky Mountain Rail Report* contained an article by Irv August describing his exploration of the Alpine Tunnel on October 2, 1948, along with several other Club members. It was on this outing that Irv, Les Logue, Everett Rohrer and Ed Haley cut a six-foot long piece of 40-pound rail near the approach to the Alpine Tunnel station. The rail was later cut into 100 pieces. Persons who had purchased the *Denver South Park & Pacific* book received a piece of that DSP&P rail.

March 8 – Long-time Club member Stan Morgan died. When the Club outgrew its space in the Rio Grande Building at 1531 Stout St., Stan arranged for meetings to be held at the City and County Building, Room 101.

August 17, 18, 19 – Club members were invited to a free open house of the Colorado Live Steamers at their site near Waterton Canyon.

August – The Club transferred title of car 25 to the Rocky Mountain Railroad Historical Foundation.

October 6 – Diesel powered "Moonlight Train" on the Manitou & Pikes Peak cog railway. More than 150 members and guests rode. Cost was $21.00 for adults and $14.00 for children.

October 13 – Annual Banquet was at Denver Athletic Club. Cost was $20.00 per person. The program was a slide presentation on "Railroading in New Mexico" by Club member John Lucas and his wife, Marcia, of Los Alamos, NM.

October – Prints (16" x 20") of a painting by Club member Joe Priselac of car 25 were made available to members and friends for $10.00. Proceeds from the sale of the prints went to the restoration of car 25.

November 13 – Jack and Erma Morison received a Certificate of Appreciation for many years of volunteer work with the Club, especially on the Newsletter Mailing Committee. It is estimated that Erma cleaned house 168 times, preparing goodies for each meeting. Together, they served seven years, attended 84 committee meetings and carried more than 94,500 newsletters to the Post Office.

March 24 – The Club chartered a car on the *Ski Train*. Cost was $28.00 and side trips were available in Winter Park at added cost.

May 4 to 12 – Thirty-five members took "Railfair '91" which was a trip to the California State Railroad Museum and other sites. Travel was via the *California Zephyr* to Sacramento to visit the museum. The trip included stops in Napa Valley, Fisherman's Wharf in San Francisco, and rail travel on the *Coast Starlight* to Los Angeles on the private dome-observation car "Native Son." Sightseeing in the Long Beach area included the Spruce Goose and the Queen Mary. Members took the *Desert Wind*, via Las Vegas, to Salt Lake City where they changed to the *California Zephyr* to return to Denver. Costs ranged from $1,200 to $2,500 depending on accommodations.

June 8 – Twenty members took the *Twilight Limited* from Limon to Arriba on the Kyle Railroad. Cost was $12.95 for adults and $7.95 for children on the non-exclusive trip.

June 15 – Workday at the Colorado Railroad Museum.

June 28 – Several Club officers helped celebrate the 100th Anniversary of the Manitou & Pikes Peak cog railway in Manitou Springs. Dignitaries and guests enjoyed cake and festivities.

June – Charter member Ed Calahan died.

July 13 – Trip on chartered car 21 on the Ft. Collins Municipal Railway. The cost was $5.00 for families. Participants took picnic lunches.

**1991**    **Meetings at Christ Episcopal Church and dues were $15.00. Pres. Dave Salter; V-P. Joe Priselac; Secy. W. J. Gordon; Treas. Bert Bidwell; Ed. Jim Trowbridge.**

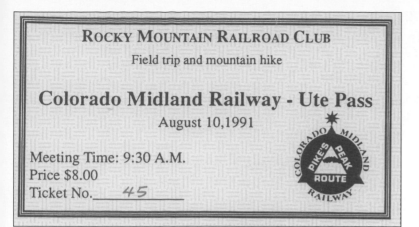

August 10, 1991 - Ticket and guide for field trip and lunch to explore the abandoned tunnels along the route to Ute Pass.

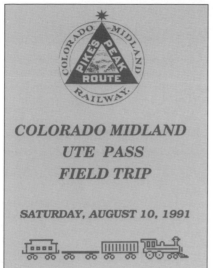

COLORADO MIDLAND
UTE PASS
FIELD TRIP

SATURDAY, AUGUST 10, 1991

August 10 – Over 110 members and guests enjoyed a field trip on the Colorado Midland railroad grade above Manitou Springs. Ranniger's Roadbed Commissary provided lunch to the hikers who explored the abandoned tunnels along the route to Ute Pass. Cost was $8.00. Rich Dais, Tom and Cathy Lowry were trip leaders.

September 1 – Double-headed mixed freight and passenger train (22 cars total) on the Cumbres and Toltec Scenic Railroad. The trip ($75.00) was from Chama to Big Horn wye and back behind locomotives 487 and 489. Eleven photo run-bys were provided. One hundred and forty members and guests enjoyed the trip, which included lunch at Osier and a snack. Passengers arranged their own hotel accommodations. It was forty years earlier, to the day, that the Club rode the Rio Grande Southern, and in remembrance of that occasion, the drumhead for this trip read "Rio Grande Southern."

September 2 – An optional trip on the Durango & Silverton was available for $38 for adults and $19 for children (19 members rode).

September – Bob Richardson, founder of the Colorado Railroad Museum and visionary who purchased engine 346 for $800, retired from the museum. At age 81, Bob moved to Pennsylvania.

September 10 – Club member Jim Ehernberger on behalf of and as President of the Union Pacific Historical Society, donated $200 to the Club for equipment restoration (in appreciation of Club's assistance on the UPHS May 18-19 excursion between Salt Lake and Cheyenne).

October 5 – The Club chartered car 1977 on the Platte Valley Trolley for a round trip from Confluence Park to Sheridan Boulevard and back. Sixty members paid $5.00 ($2.50 for children) for the outing.

October 11 – Approximately 125 members enjoyed the Annual Banquet at the Denver Athletic Club. Irv August showed movies of early Club trips. Cost was $20.00.

October 28 – Bert Bidwell, the man instrumental in establishing the Rocky Mountain Railroad Historical Foundation died. Bert had served as Treasurer since 1985.

November – In the *Rocky Mountain Rail Report,* Irv August wrote an article describing the mounting of the Club's bronze plaque on the Westall Monument in 1962. Unfortunately, vandals removed the plaque just months after it was installed.

**1992**  **Meetings at Christ Episcopal Church and dues $15.00. Pres. Joe Priselac; V-P. Frank Stapleton, Jr.; Secy. W. J. Gordon; Treas. Larry Lombard; Ed. Jim Trowbridge.**

March 21 – A tour limited to 36 members visited the Burlington Northern shop facilities in Denver. Members who wanted to take the trip had their names drawn. The tour cost was $2.00 and lasted nearly four hours.

April – The *Rocky Mountain Rail Report* contained the 1991 balance sheet from the Treasurer. The Club's financial assets amounted to $84,776. Revenues for the fiscal year ending October 31, 1990 were $50,659 with expenditures of $48,927. The Foundation's assets amounted to $5,260, with revenue of $2,050 and expenditures of $369.

May 30 – Club members took a tour of the Colorado Railroad Museum and had a picnic, all for $5.00. Thirty-five members participated.

June 6 – Workday at the Colorado Railroad Museum.

June 28 – Second Club trip on the Wyoming Colorado Railroad. The $30.00 fare included a round trip from Laramie to Fox Park, WY in coach class. For $42.00, members could ride in the first class car. Diesel units 1510 and 1512 (FP7s formerly of the Alaska Railroad) pulled the train, which made a number of photo run-bys.

July 18 – *The Denver Post* re-established the tradition of running a special train from Denver to Cheyenne and

1938-49
1950-59
1960-69
1970-79
1980-89
1990-99
2000-03
Color Extra

back for Frontier Days. The cost for riding the Union Pacific 18-car train was $100 per person. Although this was not a Club-sponsored trip, a number of members rode this train.

July 25 – Trip on the Georgetown Loop Railroad behind Shay locomotive 14. The $25.00 ($21.00 for children) cost included a visit to the shops at Silver Plume and a picnic lunch.

July – The *Rocky Mountain Rail Report* contained an article by Irv August about a hike on the abandoned grade of the Moffat Road in August 1952. Members "Mac" Poor, Jack Thode, Dan Peterson, Les Logue and Jack Riley joined Irv on the trip. Heavy rains didn't dampen their enthusiasm. Jack Thode added a footnote to this trip in the September *Rocky Mountain Rail Report*.

July – The Board conducted a two-page questionnaire of members in a survey on Club activities. The results were published in 1994.

August 15 – Members were invited to an open house at the Colorado Live Steamers facility near Waterton Canyon.

August 22 – Carl Carlson led nearly 90 members and guests on a field trip on the Colorado Midland route from Divide to Trout Creek Pass. The trip was $10.00 and included lunch by Ranniger's Roadbed Commissary. Also included was a special visit to Eleven-Mile Reservoir Dam. The Club was the first group to vist the dam since it was built in 1931.

September 4 to 8 – Twenty Club members took the *California Zephyr* to the Old Settlers and Threshers Reunion in Mt. Pleasant, IA. A round-trip ticket cost $325, plus Amtrak accommodations. Side trips by motor coach were provided to Nauvoo, IL, Hannibal, MO and other locations in the Mississippi River Valley.

September 19 – Charter member Forest Crossen died. Holder of membership card number 1 upon his death, Forest was a former President and well-known author. Best known for his book, *The Switzerland Trail of America*, he wrote more than a dozen booklets titled *Western Yesterdays*. He also contributed to national publications such as *Trains*, *True West*, *Field and Stream*, and many others.

September 25 – The second printing of the *Georgetown and The Loop* book was sold out.

September 27 – The High County Railroad at Heritage Square ended operations. Built and operated by five Club members (Stuart Anderson, Jim Ehernberger, Ed Gerlits, Dave Gross and Dan Peterson), the 1.5-mile, two-foot gauge steam railroad operated successfully for 21 years. The original owners decided to retire from the railroad business and pursue other interests. The road hosted many Club members and guests at numerous outings.

October 24 – Annual Banquet was at the Denver Athletic Club. Nearly 170 members and guests attended this dinner at $25.00 a person. The program was entitled "Rio Grande – Scenic Line of the World."

November 14 – An open house was held at the Denver Federal Center for Denver & Intermountain car 25. More than 60 members and guests attended.

November 16 – A special open house for Federal Center employees to view car 25 drew more than 90 people.

November – The Board authorized the transfer of over 50,000 feet of 16mm Otto Perry films on to 1 inch video masters at Wickerworks Video Productions.

**THE ROCKY MOUNTAIN RAILROAD CLUB**
PRESENTS
**THE OLD THRESHERS REUNION IN MT. PLEASANT, IOWA**
**LABOR DAY WEEKEND SEPTEMBER 4-8, 1992**

Plan now to join the Rocky Mountain Railroad Club on an exciting Labor Day Excursion to the Midwest Old Threshers Reunion in Mt. Pleasant, Iowa. Established in 1950, this is the largest show of it's type. It will feature over 100 operating engines, 300 antique tractors, 800 gasoline engines, antique cars and trucks, operating electric trolleys and steam trains. In addition you will find Iowa's latest working craft show, top name Country/Western entertainers and the finest in homemade farm food.

After a relaxing overnight trip aboard Amtrak's California Zephyr, we will arrive in Burlington, Iowa. A motor coach will immediately take us to the fair where we will spend the rest of the day. In the evening we will return to our accommodations in Burlington. Sunday will be spent again enjoying the sights, sounds and food at the fair. Late Sunday afternoon we will return to Burlington. There we will board the riverboat Emerald Lady for a dinner cruise on the Mississippi River.

September 4-8, 1992 - Flyer announcing the Club's excursion via the *California Zephyr* to the Old Threshers Reunion in Mt. Pleasant, Iowa.

November – The Board authorized a third printing of 1,000 copies of the *Georgetown and The Loop* book, to be sold for $39.95. Estimated cost of printing was $10,000.

**1993**  **Meetings at Christ Episcopal Church and dues were raised to $20.00 for members and $10.00 for spouses. Pres. Joe Priselac; V-P. Roger Callender; Secy. W. J. Gordon; Treas. Larry Lombard; Ed. Jim Trowbridge.**

January 30 – The Club chartered a car on the *Ski Train* to Winter Park and return. Cost was $25.00 and no side trips were offered this year.

February 23 – Ralph McAllister, who hosted numerous open houses on his live steam railroad in Boulder died at age 87.

April – The *Rocky Mountain Rail Report* contained an article by Irv August about Irv and three other Club members who rode the D&RGW *San Juan* from Alamosa to Durango in late December, 1949. Irv served as "fireman" on the Durango to Alamosa leg. The entire trip from Denver to Alamosa, Durango and return totaled over 900 miles, all behind steam.

May – The *Rocky Mountain Rail Report* contained another article by Irv August, on Tomichi Pass. Irv recalled a 1952 hiking trip with Club member Les Logue along the abandoned grade of the Denver, South Park & Pacific.

May 11 – Club announced to members that the "tentative" date for completion of the restoration of car 25 would be the spring of 1994.

May 15 – The Club sponsored a 40th Anniversary trip on the Union Pacific behind engine 3985 (renumbered for this trip as 3967 with smoke lifters added - also known as elephant ears). It was forty years ago that elephant-eared 3967 hosted the Club's first UP excursion behind a Challenger class locomotive. The trip sold out quickly with more than 500 fans on the fifteen-car special running from Denver to Laramie and return. Eleven Club members on this trip had ridden the first trip in 1953. Cost was $155.00 per person. Club member and

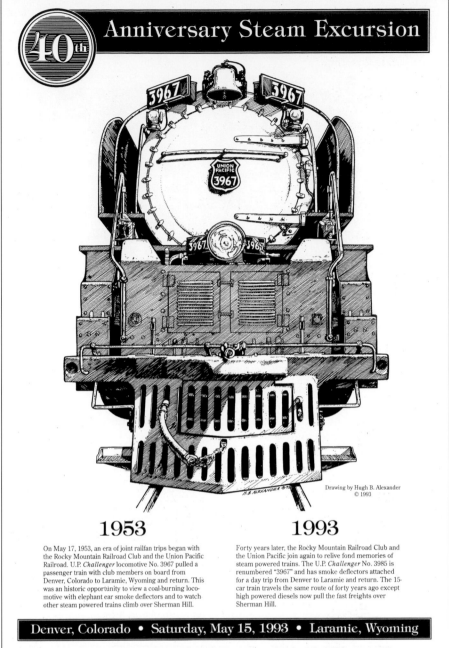

## 40th Anniversary Steam Excursion

### 1953

On May 17, 1953, an era of joint railfan trips began with the Rocky Mountain Railroad Club and the Union Pacific Railroad. U.P. *Challenger* locomotive No. 3967 pulled a passenger train with club members on board from Denver, Colorado to Laramie, Wyoming and return. This was an historic opportunity to view a coal-burning locomotive with elephant ear smoke deflectors and to watch other steam powered trains climb over Sherman Hill.

### 1993

Forty years later, the Rocky Mountain Railroad Club and the Union Pacific join again to relive fond memories of steam powered trains. The U.P. *Challenger* No. 3985 is renumbered "3967" and has smoke deflectors attached for a day trip from Denver to Laramie and return. The 15-car train travels the same route of forty years ago except high powered diesels now pull the fast freights over Sherman Hill.

Drawing by Hugh B. Alexander
© 1993

**Denver, Colorado • Saturday, May 15, 1993 • Laramie, Wyoming**

Rocky Mountain Railroad Club • P.O. Box 2391 • Denver, Colorado 80201 • (303) 431-4354

Club member and illustrator Hugh Alexander created many high-quality special tickets and flyers during his tenure on the Trip Committee. This original pen and ink drawing announced the Club's 40th Anniversary trip behind Union Pacific Challenger 3985, renumbered as 3967 for this excursion. Signed, numbered copies of this poster were sold as a fund raiser.

artist, Hugh Alexander did a special pen and ink poster board sketch of the front of 3967 especially for this excursion. The numbered and signed copies were used as fund raisers to promote the trip.

May 21 – The Club "discovered" a piece of long forgotten equipment at the Colorado Railroad Museum. A motor car obtained through the efforts of deceased member "Olie" Larsen was found to belong to the Club and was in poor condition at the museum. Plans for restoration were initiated.

1938-49
1950-59
1960-69
1970-79
1980-89
1990-99
2000-03
Color Extra

June 5, 1993 - More than eighty members and guests rode the Comanche Crossing & Eastern Railroad near Strasburg in conjunction with a visit to the Uhrich Locomotive Works. **DARRELL ARNDT PHOTO**

October – Irv August wrote an article in the *Rocky Mountain Rail Report* on early Club trips in 1949, 1952 and 1961.

October 1 to 9 – Forty Club members took a trip on the Copper Canyon Railroad. Airfare from Denver to Tucson and return was included as well as hotel rooms and meals in the $1,375 price. Traveling in three private cars (two sleepers and a diner/lounge car) the trip originated in Tucson where they rode the bus to Nogales, Mexico to take the train. Motor-coach side trips to various rail facilities were included at Empalme, Guaymas and La Junta. Return was by the same route in reverse.

October 16 – Annual Banquet was at the Denver Athletic Club. Cost was $25.00. The program was the first example of the Otto Perry films on video format.

June 5 – Over eighty members and guests visited the Uhrich Locomotive Works and rode the Comanche Crossing & Eastern Railroad near Strasburg. The cost was $10 and included unlimited rides on the 5-inch scale live steam railroad.

June 12 – Workday at the Colorado Railroad Museum. Efforts focused working on the "Rico."

July 10 – Fifty members and guests took a driving field trip led by author Jim Jones exploring the abandoned route of the Denver and New Orleans Railroad. The trip went from Connors to Parker to Elbert to Falcon and concluded in Colorado Springs. The cost was $2.00. Jim was asked in 2001 to conduct this trip again, but declined since many of the sites and locations cannot be found anymore due to the tremendous growth in the metro-area.

August 21 – Over eighty members and friends took a driving field trip to the D&RGW Tennessee Pass line including a visit to the tunnel at the summit. Ranniger's Roadbed Commissary provided lunches. Cost was $8.00. Cathy and Tom Lawry and Rich Dais led the trip.

August 22 – Trip on the Leadville, Colorado and Southern Railroad. Fares were $18.50 for adults and $9.75 for children.

August – RTD received its first light rail car.

December 4 – In an open house jointly sponsored by the Club, the Intermountain Chapter of the NRHS, Denver Rail Heritage and the Colorado Railroad Museum, nearly 250 visitors toured the new light rail facilities at 7th and Mariposa St.

**1994**  **Meetings at Christ Episcopal Church. Dues at $20.00 and membership approximately 1000. Pres. Roger Callender; V-P. Sherm Conners; Secy. W. J. Gordon; Treas. Larry Lombard; Ed. Jim Trowbridge.**

January to July – Results of the 1992 survey were covered in six issues of the *Rocky Mountain Rail Report*. The survey dealt with issues concerning the future of the Club, trips, activities and general suggestions.

February – The *Rocky Mountain Rail Report* contained an article by long time member Chuck Powell on his trip from Los Angeles to Denver and around the narrow gauge circle in 1948.

April 30 – The Club, the Intermountain Chapter of the NRHS, Denver Rail Heritage and the Colorado Railroad Museum sponsored a special excursion for members and guests only on the RTD light rail line from the Mariposa Shops to Colfax and back. Cost was $2.00. More than 500 rode this day, of which 304 were Club members and guests.

May 6 to 14 – Forty-four Club members took a trip to the Golden Spike Ceremony near Ogden, UT. Members rode the bus to Cheyenne where they boarded a special Union Pacific train behind engine

Buttons were given to all riders on the Club's inaugural RTD light rail excursion.

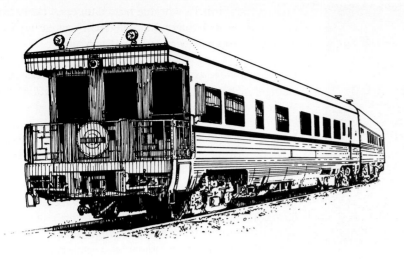

August 29, 1994 - Artwork used to advertise the trip to Grand Junction in a private car owned by Philip Anschutz. **HUGH ALEXANDER ILLUSTRATION**

3985 for the trip to Utah. The train had originated in Omaha. Club members rode in the reserved UP dome car "Columbine," one of 22 cars on the train. Special events in Utah included the re-enactment of the Golden Spike Ceremony (witnessed by between 8,000 and 12,000 people), a tour of the Bingham Copper Mine and visits to sites around Salt Lake City. Members returned to Denver via the *California Zephyr*.

May 28 – Field trip to Lakeside Park for a behind-the-scenes look at the amusement park railroad. Twenty members helped the railroad celebrate its 86th birthday. Cost was $5.00. The Club drumhead was displayed on the rear of a double-headed steam powered train on this 22" gauge line, pulled by engines 17 and 18.

June 25, 26 – Workdays at the Colorado Railroad Museum. Twenty members enjoyed the 100-plus degree days.

July – The *Rocky Mountain Rail Report* contained an article by Irv August recalling a 1949 field trip to the Busk-Ivanhoe Tunnel on the old Colorado Midland Route.

July 21 to 31 – Trip to Chicago that largely duplicated the events of the Club's trip in 1984 to sites in and around the Chicago area. Besides the Museum of Science and Industry, members visited the METRA's shops (former Rock Island "Rocket House"), Illinois Railroad Museum, the Fox River Trolley Museum, the East Troy Railway Museum, Kalmbach Publishing Company, and the Experimental Aviation Association air show in Oshkosh, WI. The trip commemorated the 60th anniversary of the *Pioneer Zephyr* and the 10th anniversary of the Club's previous trip to the Chicago area.

August 20 – More than 70 members and guests took a field trip to Sherman Hill. Led by Jack Morison,

Jim Ranniger, Carl Carlson and Jim Ehernberger the group visited the Ames Monument, the former site of the Dale Creek Bridge, and other historic sites on the Union Pacific. The cost was $8.00 and included Ranniger's Roadbed Commissary. This was the last run of the commissary that had operated since 1978. Organized and planned by Jim and Lil, with assistance from other Club members, the food prepared at every outing was noteworthy and accompanied by much good cheer.

August 29 – Club members were able to buy tickets for an exclusive trip on the D&RGW in one of Philip Anschutz's private cars. Members rode the private car attached to the *California Zephyr* to Grand Junction and then returned via the *California Zephyr* in coaches. Cost was $295.00 per person.

September 17 – In a jointly hosted celebration, the Club, the Intermountain Chapter of the NRHS, Denver Rail Heritage and the Colorado Railroad Museum dedicated a 3,000-pound pink granite marker at the light rail station at Broadway and I-25. The inscription states "Trolleys of the Past – Light Rail of the Future." Over 400 fans and members rode the trains that day to inaugurate service from Broadway to 30th Avenue. Cost was $5.00.

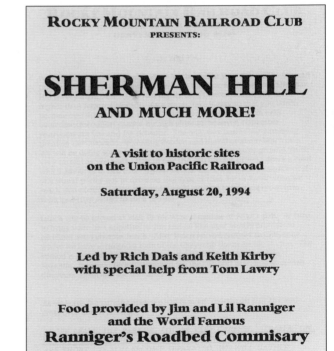

**ROCKY MOUNTAIN RAILROAD CLUB**
PRESENTS:

# SHERMAN HILL
## AND MUCH MORE!

A visit to historic sites
on the Union Pacific Railroad

**Saturday, August 20, 1994**

**Led by Rich Dais and Keith Kirby
with special help from Tom Lawry**

Food provided by Jim and Lil Ranniger
and the World Famous
**Ranniger's Roadbed Commisary**

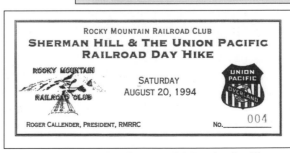

ROCKY MOUNTAIN RAILROAD CLUB
**SHERMAN HILL & THE UNION PACIFIC
RAILROAD DAY HIKE**

ROCKY MOUNTAIN
RAILROAD CLUB

SATURDAY
AUGUST 20, 1994

UNION PACIFIC
OVERLAND

ROGER CALLENDER, PRESIDENT, RMRRC          No._____ 004

LUNCH TICKET
ROCKY MOUNTAIN RAILROAD CLUB
SHERMAN HILL & THE UNION PACIFIC
RAILROAD DAY HIKE
AUGUST 20, 1994
No._____ 004

August 20, 1994 - Brochure and ticket for the Sherman Hill field trip.

1938-49
1950-59
1960-69
1970-79
1980-89
1990-99
2000-03
Color Extra

October 8, 1994 - The Club's special train heads to the peak on the Manitou & Pikes Peak cog railway. **HUGH ALEXANDER PHOTO**

October 8 – Diesel-powered trip on the Manitou & Pikes Peak cog railway. The clear day, following a fall snowstorm, made for excellent photos during several run-bys. The two-car chartered train included diesel locomotive 9 and coach 12. Sister Mary Borgia had an attack of altitude sickness and was airlifted off the mountain to a Colorado Springs hotel. Dinner was at Guiseppe's Depot Restaurant after the trip (and Sister Mary recovered fully and quickly). Cost was $25.00 per person.

October 15 – Annual Banquet was at the Denver Athletic Club. Columnist Dick Kreck of *The Denver Post* was the guest speaker talking about the Cheyenne Frontier Days Train, from inception to modern times. More than 100 members and guests paid $25.00 for dinner and to see a number of lifetime members receive special brass membership cards. These individuals all held membership numbers 1 through 10.

November 5 – R. W. ("Mac") McSpadden of the Denver Union Terminal Railway conducted tours of Union Station for Club members. A portion of the $6.00 ticket ($4.00) was donated to the Denver Society of Model Railroaders and the Platte Valley HO Club.

November 9 – The Club held its first "Video Potpourri Night." Similar in format to the slide potpourris of the past, this program presented videos by Club members.

November 26 – The Club's Birney car 22 from the Ft. Collins Municipal Railway was taken to Colorado Springs where it was leased to the Pike's Peak Historical Street Railway Foundation. The fifteen-year lease included restoration of the car and future operation.

**1995**   **Meetings at Christ Episcopal Church. Dues were $20.00. Pres. Michael Johnson; V-P. Roger Callender; Secy. W. J. Gordon; Treas. Ardie Schoeninger; Ed. Jim Trowbridge.**

January 14 – Jim Trowbridge hosted an open house on his Colorado & Western Railway HOn3 gauge layout. More than 140 members and guests attended.

February 5 – Thirty-eight members and guests rode in a chartered car (the "Pyramid Peak") on the *Ski Train* to Winter Park.

March – The *Rocky Mountain Rail Report* contained a definition of associate membership; spouses and children of regular members.

May – The Board approved the publication of Bob Griswold's new book, *David Moffat's Denver, Northwestern and Pacific — The Moffat Road*. It was to be the first of a multi-volume work on this railroad.

June 3, 4 – Workday and Rocky Mountain Railroad Club Day at the Colorado Railroad Museum. Lunch was included in the $4.50 price.

June – The *Rocky Mountain Rail Report* contained a request from Chuck Albi, Executive Director of the Colorado Railroad Museum. Chuck was seeking trip flyers, handouts, and other Club memorabilia, primarily from before 1963 to fill out the Museum's files.

June 17 – Ninety-four members and guests visited the Uhrich Locomotive Works and rode the Comanche Crossing & Eastern Railroad near Strasburg. The cost was $13.00 and included unlimited rides on the 5-inch scale live steam railroad.

July 15, 16 – Twenty-four members took an exclusive ride in coach on Amtrak's *California Zephyr* to Grand Junction. The next day they returned via the *California Zephyr*, in the private car "Kansas" owned by Philip Anschutz. Cost was $299.

July 22 – The Club chartered one coach on the *The Denver Post* Cheyenne Frontier Days train from Denver to Cheyenne and return. Forty-four members rode behind the train pulled by Union Pacific Challenger 3985 and Centennial unit 6936. Cost was $175.00 per person.

August 15 – Field trip to Como, King City and Leavick along the Denver, South Park & Pacific. The trip included hiking, lectures by the trip guides and caravaning by car to several points. Rich Dais, Keith Kirby and Tom and Cathy Lawry led more than 100 members.

August – The August issue of *Trains* magazine included an article by Club Member Watson Warriner titled "Journey to Destiny."

September 29 to October 8 – A number of Club members took the *Southwestern Chief* from Trinidad to Flagstaff, AZ. From there a bus tour was arranged to the

Grand Canyon Railroad, the Verde Canyon Railroad (from Clarkdale to Perkinsville, AZ on the former Arizona Central Railroad) and on the Santa Fe Southern Railway (from Santa Fe to Lamy, NM).

October 14 – Annual Banquet was at the Regency Hotel. Cost was $18.00. The speaker was Margaret Coel, who presented a program on "Goin' Railroading," the same title as her book.

November 4 – R. W. McSpadden of the Denver Union Terminal Railway offered another tour of Union Station. Approximately 40 members attended.

November – The Wyoming Colorado Scenic Railroad announced it will shut down permanently. High maintenance costs and a short operating season were identified as the reasons.

December 1, 2, 3 – More than 100 members and guests

December 2, 1995 - Engine 473 powers the Durango and Silverton Narrow Gauge Railroad train at Tall Timber. **HUGH ALEXANDER PHOTO**

enjoyed a trip on the Durango and Silverton Narrow Gauge Railroad, behind steam locomotive 473 to Cascade and return (on December 2). Tours of the yards and shop facilities were available. The round trip was by motor coach. The route from Denver to Durango was via LaVeta Pass and Wolf Creek Pass. The return was via Montrose, Ouray, Cimarron, Monarch Pass and through South Park. Costs ranged from $65 to $179, depending on the package selected. On Saturday evening, Jim Ehernberger presented a multi-projector slide program on railroad folklore songs.

December – Members Jack Thode, Ed Haley, Ed Gerlits, Bob Griswold and Chuck Albi were featured in a video program sponsored by KRMA-TV titled "Railroad Memories – Rocky Mountain Legacy." The program contained their recollections and was available for $24.95 from the TV station.

**1996**  **Meetings at Christ Episcopal Church. Dues are $20.00. President Michael Johnson; V-P. Roger Cal-lender; Secy. W. J. Gordon; Treas. Ardie Schoeninger; Ed. Jim Trowbridge.**

March 17 – A tour limited to forty members was sold out as Club members visit the Rader Rail Car facility in East Denver. The cost was $4.00 and members saw part of the 18-car Marlboro train under construction as well as two cars for Princess Cruises. Most impressive was the way Rader used a tow truck to maneuver the rail cars on steerable bogies around the facility.

March 31 – Twenty-eight members took the *Ski Train* to Winter Park. The last train of this season was headed by Southern Pacific diesel unit 9738. The cost was $35.00.

---

The Rocky Mountain Railroad Club
*presents*

**THE DURANGO & SILVERTON NARROW GAUGE RAILROAD**

SPECIAL EXCURSION TRAIN

**WINTER IN THE SAN JUAN MOUNTAINS**
**DECEMBER 1-3, 1995**

In this age of jet transportation and high speed railways, riding the *Durango & Silverton Narrow Gauge Railroad* in the Colorado's San Juan Mountains is an experience of stepping back into time. Each season of the year paints a different picture of the magnificent scenery through which the railroad travels. Many have ridden the railroad in the summer season, but few have experienced winter in the San Juans.

The *Durango & Silverton* branch of the *Denver & Rio Grande Western Railroad* dates back to 1882 with trains operating to Silverton year round, weather conditions permitting. In the early 1950's the train evolved into a summer only tourist operation. With the *Rio Grande's* of sale the line to Mr. Charles Bradshaw in 1981, winter trips once again became a reality. On February 14, 1982 the *Rocky Mountain Railroad Club* sponsored the first winter excursion on the line.

Since Colorado winter weather conditions are somewhat unpredictable, our trip from Denver will include deluxe motor coach to Durango and return. Each coach will have a knowledgeable club member who will narrate and point out the historical and scenic features en route.

Our route to Durango on Friday, December 1 will be along the front range on I-25 to Walsenburg, over 9,382 foot La Veta Pass across the historic San Luis Valley, over 10,857 foot Wolf Creek Pass to Pagosa Springs and into Durango.

Aboard our private excursion train on Saturday, December 2 we leave Durango, the "Narrow Gauge Capital of the World" and travel through the beautiful Animas River Valley. As we climb along the mountainsides the track comes out on a narrow ledge hundreds of feet above the awesome depths of the Animas River Gorge. Our route continues along the river ringed by 12,000 - 14,000 foot peaks. North of Durango we reach the Cascade Wye which is our terminus and the northern limit of operations during the winter months. A number of photo runbys will be made at selected locations. All of our passengers cars will be heated. In addition, our consist will have two open gondola cars for photography and a concession car. Upon return to Durango, a tour of the yards and shop facilities will be made available for those who would like to see behind the scenes operations.

*D&SNG engine #481 train in a snowy winter setting from the RMRRC 1982 excursion.*
*Photos: Jim Trowbridge*

Our return trip from Durango on Sunday, December 3 will be anything anti-climactic. We will travel Highway 550, the spectacular "Million Dollar Highway," over Red Mountain Pass to Silverton and on to Ouray, the "Little Switzerland of America." From Montrose we will travel east over Cerro Summit and across the beautiful Gunnison River Valley. A stop will be made at Cimarron to view a historic narrow gauge exhibit.

Advertising flyer for the December 1-3, 1995 excursion

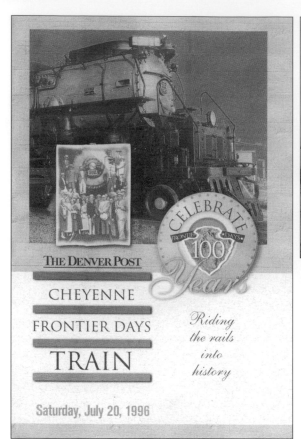

July 20, 1996 - (Left) *The Denver Post* provided a brochure aboard this excursion celebrating 100 years of the Cheyenne Frontier Days. The Club chartered the coach "City of Salina" for 44 members. Union Pacific engine 3985 and Centennial engine 6936 powered the train from Denver to Cheyenne and on the return the railroad doubleheaded the train back to Denver using engines 844 and 3985. **HUGH ALEXANDER PHOTO**

April 20 – One bus load of 46 members visited the Coors rail facilities in Golden. The trip was limited and sold out quickly at a cost of $10.00. An optional visit to the brewery was available after the Club's tour.

April – The Club lost its lease at Denver Union Station due to reconstruction activities on the second floor of the station. Club records and book inventory were moved to a new location at 2701 Alcott St., which became known as World Headquarters (WHQ).

May 18 – Forty-four members and friends took a tour of historic Denver Tramway sites in the Denver area, on vintage Denver Tramway bus 119. This bus broke down and had to be replaced early in the trip. The tour also included a stop at the Denver Federal Center to see car 25 where the replacement bus had a flat tire. RTD sent a tow truck and another bus to allow completion of the trip. Prior to the trip, the Club presented Ed Haley a plaque which stated "To Ed Haley – For his profound knowledge, advice and tireless help. In gratitude from the Rocky Mountain Railroad Club."

June 1, 2 – Workdays at the Colorado Railroad Museum.

June 15 – More than 40 members attended a Club sponsored outing to Ft. Collins to ride the Ft. Collins Municipal Railway car 21. Additionally, members visited a private zoo and rode the Timnath Northwestern Narrow Gauge Railroad, an 18" live steam railroad. This railroad was taken up shortly after the Club's visit.

July 20 – The Club chartered the coach "City of Salina" for 44 members on *The Denver Post* Cheyenne Frontier Days train. Union Pacific engine 3985 and Centennial engine 6936 powered the train. Included in the $200 fare was a BBQ, parade and rodeo, as well as a light meal during the return trip. There were 29 cars on this train, which celebrated the 100th anniversary of Frontier Days. In a surprise move, the railroad doubleheaded the train back to Denver using engine 844 and 3985.

July – Board approved the publication of the second railroad book by Bob Griswold, the *Denver and Salt Lake Railroad*. Approximately $20,000 was authorized to print 1,500 copies.

August 24 – Field trip to the Western Mining Museum and the Colorado Springs and Manitou Traction Company in the Roswell Trolley Barn in Colorado Springs. Members saw restoration work on the Club's Birney car 22 and looked at PCC car 3101 stored at the facility.

September 29 to October 12 – Twenty-eight Club members took an extended rail sojourn in Great Britain. Cost for the trip from Denver to St. Louis to London and return was approximately $2,500 to $3,000 depending on accommodations.

October 1 – Club member Howard Fogg, well-known painter and illustrator died. Howard did a number of illustrations for the Club.

October 12 – Annual Banquet was at the Regency Hotel Denver. Cost was $19.00 and Jim Ehernberger presented the program on the Club's 1995 excursion on the Durango & Silverton Narrow Gauge Railroad. Attendance totaled 110 members and guests.

October – Distribution of the *Denver and Salt Lake Railroad* book began (Price $39.95).

November – Club made available a limited number of mint condition, dust jackets from Morris Cafky's *Colorado Midland*. Each dust jacket was $12.00 plus $1.50 for shipping. Also, a reproduction of the Santa Fe poster "Chico" was available for $6.00 and $1.50 for shipping.

December 12 – W. J. "Bill" Gordon, just re-elected Club Secretary died suddenly. Bill served in many leadership positions and was Club Secretary since 1970. He had attended the first Club meeting in 1938 with his father Roscoe.

**1997**     **Meetings at Christ Episcopal Church and dues remain $20.00. Pres. Jimmy Blouch; ; V-P. Walter Weart; Secy. Carolyn Blouch; Treas. Dave Goss; Ed. Jim Trowbridge.**

February 8 – Long-time member John Maxwell died. John was a member of the Club in the1940s and held membership card number 4 at the time of his death. A former president and leader in the Club, John was an active member until 1996. Among his many talents, John was known for meticulously detailed drawings of locomotives, rolling stock, facilities and equipment from the D&RGW, other railroads of Colorado and railroads in other parts of the United States. He also had an extensive collection of photographs.

February 21 – Long-time member Carl Carlson died. Carl was a former President, Board member and active on many committees. He and his wife, Mary, had shared the role of Treasurer and Membership Chair.

March 5 – Long-time member Ed Haley died. Besides being a former President, Ed served many years in leadership positions, most notably as Trip Committee Chair for nearly 25 years. He designed the Club's logo, early stationery and was responsible for creation of the Club's drumhead or tailplate. He was deeply involved in the publication of the *Pictorial Supplement to Denver South Park & Pacific* book. Ed was responsible for all the Club's early narrow gauge excursions as well as those on the Union Pacific, the Colorado and Southern and other roads until he stepped down as Trip Committee Chair in 1972. He held membership card number 5 at the time of his death.

March 23 – The Club chartered one car on the *Ski Train* to Winter Park. Thirty-five members took the trip, which cost $35.00.

April – Elitch Gardens removed the 100-foot turntable at the former site of the Colorado & Southern roundhouse. The turntable was donated to the Cumbres & Toltec Scenic Railroad in Chama, NM.

June 14, 15 – Workdays at the Colorado Railroad Museum.

June – Marlboro announced cancellation of its promotional train. Rader Rail Car plans for demolition of the partially completed cars.

June – Club bought ceiling fans which were installed in Barnes Hall of Christ Episcopal Church.

July 8 – In a special meeting, the board discussed with Newsletter Editor Jim Trowbridge, the Board's decision to reformat the *Rocky Mountain Rail Report* to an eight-page publication that could be prepared using desktop publishing techniques. This would allow more timely news preparation and lower the costs of production and postage. Jim agreed that he did not have the capability to make these changes.

July – Club established a website "www.rockymtnr-rclub.org" thanks to the efforts of member Chris Wolf of Ft. Collins.

July 19 – Club reserved a special coach on the Cheyenne Frontier Days train. Limited to 44 seats, the $210 ticket included the train, breakfast, the parade, a private BBQ luncheon, the Frontier Days Museum, seats for the rodeo and a light supper during the return to Denver. Steam locomotive 844 and Centennial unit 6936 double-headed the 25-car train.

September 13, 1997 - A special mixed freight excursion behind engine 40 on the Georgetown Loop Railroad provided 68 members and guests numerous photo runby opportunities. **HUGH ALEXANDER PHOTO**

July – Club formed a committee to plan the upcoming Sixtieth Anniversary of the Club to be celebrated in 1998.

August 9, 10 – Excursion to Glenwood Springs on the *Ski Train*. Cost was $39.00 not including overnight hotel accommodations.

August 30 – Long-time member Charles Max died. Author of a book titled *Teenage Hobo* in the 1930s, Charlie served as a President, was active in equipment restoration activities and was a skilled modeler.

September – The *Rocky Mountain Rail Report* contained a nostalgic recollection of early Club trips written by Cornelius Hauck.

September 13 – Special mixed freight excursion behind engine 40 on the Georgetown Loop Railroad. Sixty-eight members and guests paid $50 for this photographer's special that included many run-bys and photo opportunities. The six-car special provided many run-bys during this day filled with the Aspen gold of the season. Cars included D&RGW flat car 6742 (which was a former boxcar cut down for pipe hauling to Farmington), White Pass & Yukon tank car 59, C&S boxcar 8311, Georgetown, Breckenridge & Leadville gondolas 1163 and 1036 and the 1902 Hammond Car Company coach 34, the "Tahoe."

October 18 – Annual Banquet was at the Arvada Center. Ron Ruhoff gave a multi-media program "Adventure Trails on Colorado Rails" and dinner was $22.00. Ninety-six members and guests attended.

November – Jim Trowbridge stepped down as newsletter editor, with his last issue to be January 1998.

December 10 – The Colorado State Historical Society added car 25 to the State Register of Historic Properties.

December – The Treasurer reports that Club revenue in 1997 was $61,027 with expenses of $56,791. Total assets in checking, interest bearing accounts and all other Club accounts amounted to $51,536.

**1998** Meetings at Christ Episcopal Church and dues remain $20.00 for members and $10.00 for associates. Pres. Jimmy Blouch; V-P. Walter Weart; Secy. Carolyn Blouch; Treas. Dave Goss; Ed. Bruce Nall.

This was the Club's Sixtieth Anniversary. A special committee planned activities throughout the year. Each month's newsletter featured an article written by Dave Goss that included recollections of Club activities. Special memorabilia were also offered throughout the year.

January 13 – President Blouch presented plaques of special recognition to former newsletter Editor (for fourteen years) Jim Trowbridge, former Membership Chair (for four years) Linda Johnson and former Trip Committee Chair (for thirteen years) Bud Lehrer.

January 28 – Charter member and former President, Everett Rohrer died. A former fireman on the Union Pacific, Everett was well known for his ownership of

COLORADO HISTORICAL SOCIETY

This is to certify that

## DENVER & INTERMOUNTAIN RAILROAD INTERURBAN # 25

has been included in the

# State Register of Historic Properties

by the
## COLORADO HISTORICAL SOCIETY
under provisions of the
Colorado Revised Statutes, Article 80.1
Register of Historic Places

*December 10, 1997*

Date Listed

*Georgianna Contiguglia*
President, Colorado Historical Society

December 10, 1997 - Certificate recognizing the placement of the Denver & Intermountain Railroad interurban car 25 on the State Register of Historic Properties.

ex-Great Western locomotive 75 and other rail equipment.

January 29 – Charter member Walker Edwards died. Walker served on the Board of Directors, and was an active member who had ridden the first passenger train through the Moffat Tunnel, and the last train from Leadville and the last streetcar in Denver. He held membership card number 1 at the time of his death.

February – The *Rocky Mountain Rail Report* featured a special masthead for this year only, depicting the joint importance of steam and diesel motive power in Rocky Mountain railroading. Hugh Alexander, Club member and a talented artist, designed the special anniversary logo.

February – With the permission of the DUT, the Club issued a reproduction of the Denver Union Terminal Railway Co. Timetable No. 107, dated February 20, 1938 to indicate trains using Union Station in Denver sixty years earlier.

April 19 – Tour of the light rail facilities at the RTD shops, rides on the line on cars 110 and 117 and a visit to car 25 at the Denver Federal Center. Eighty-eight members and guests participated and the cost was $15.00. Lunch was provided by car 25 volunteers at the Federal Center.

April 30 – Caboose Hobbies hosted a special night for Club members whose dues were paid in full. Unique discounts were offered to members who attended in person or shopped via the Internet. Caboose Hobbies celebrated its sixtieth anniversary this year as well.

April – Club made available a commemorative HO scale box car marking the Club's 60th Anniversary. Kits were $13.95 and assembled cars $22.95. Members were given a 25% discount.

June 13, 14 – Workdays at the Colorado Railroad Museum.

June 21 – The Club, along with the Intermountain Chapter of the NRHS and the Organ Historic Society, sponsored a showing of the movie "White Desert" at the Paramount Theater. This silent movie was filmed on the Denver and Salt Lake Railroad. Price was $10.00.

**1938–1998**
**ROCKY MOUNTAIN RAILROAD CLUB**

The Club's Special 60th Anniversary logo, designed by Hugh Alexander, recognized the diversity of interests and the changing railroad scene in America.

added at Osier as a helper on the return segment to Cumbres Pass. Sixty members paid $175.00, which included many run-bys. The C&TS authentically lettered the train as Rio Grande equipment for this trip.

August 8 – A "do-it-yourself" tour where members met at the Great Western Railroad shops in Loveland. After seeing many operations there, they were given directions for other sites in the area to visit, including Ft. Collins and Longmont. Twenty-three members partook of this no-cost field trip.

August 13 – Long-time member Francis Rizzari died. A noted historian, he held membership card number 11 at the time of his death and was known for his work with members Richard Ronzio and Charles Ryland who reprinted *Crofutt's Grip Sack Guide of Colorado – 1885* edition. He was particularly active in Club work in the 1950s.

August 22 – Excursion on the Manitou & Pikes Peak cog railway. Seventy-five members and guests rode the train powered by diesel-electric unit 16. The cost was $35.00 and included run-bys and a visit to the shops.

July 12 – Long-time member Chuck DeSellem died. Chuck and his wife Ginny spent many hours and years serving on the Newsletter Mailing Committee. Chuck is ever remembered for his sense of humor and tireless smile.

July 25, 26 – Special train on the Cumbres & Toltec Scenic Railroad between Chama and Antonito. Engine 463 was used as the road power. Engine 489 was

July 26, 1998 – Authentically lettered for the D&RGW this trip, the Club's C&TS special is shown on a photo run-by west of Osier. **HUGH ALEXANDER PHOTO**

1938-49

1950-59

1960-69

1970-79

1980-89

1990-99

2000-03

Color Extra

October 17, 1998 - Annual Banquet ticket.

DENVER & RIO GRANDE WESTERN RAILROAD

October 17, 1998 - Annual Banquet menu and program was a replica of a Denver Rio Grande and Western Railway menu from the 1930's provided by the Colorado Railroad Museum.

September 12 – The Club made a unique visit to the Cyprus Amax Henderson Mine. Forty-six members (limited to that number) were given an extensive tour of the mine's operations and watched the remote controlled railroad operate. The cost was $30.00.

September 14 – Members were invited to an open house at the Granite Mountain Railway (HO scale) in Longmont.

September 19 – The Club and Foundation sponsored an open house at the Denver Federal Center to show car 25.

September 26 – Former officer and member since 1955, Mike Blecha died. Mike served on trip committees and as Club Secretary.

October 10 – A planned Georgetown Loop trip was can-celled due to removal of the steam locomotive that had been requested for the trip.

October 17 – Annual Banquet was at the Arvada Center. Cost was $23.00 and over 130 members and guests attended. Bob Griswold and Neal Miller were given special recognitions for their work in the Club. Jim Ehernberger presented the program "Smoke and Steam." A special souvenir menu was created resembling a menu used on the D&RGW. Artwork for the menu was provided by the Colorado Railroad Museum.

October 24 – Club members with an expertise in photography provided a night photo clinic at the Colorado Railroad Museum for other Club members who wished to try nighttime techniques. A $5.00 donation was made to the Museum for each attendee. The Equipment Committee provided special lighting on engine 20 and smoke coming out of the stack. Number 20, the business car "Rico" and RGS caboose 0404 were spotted at "No Agua" tank for this special session.

November 2 – Warren "Rusty" Bailey who held membership card number 4 died.

December 5 – A special photographers' mixed freight and passenger train was created by the Durango & Silverton Railroad expressly for the Club's use on this trip. Authentically lettered and numbered D&RGW, the all-freight (and two coaches) train was pulled by engine 478 (with spark arrestor removed and "dog house" added), resembling very closely the Club's excursion in 1956. Eighty-nine members paid $150.00 to ride this train which included many run-bys. A limited number of caboose seats were sold for $200.00 each. Visitors came from as far away as England, Germany, Canada and Japan. The train included two flat cars, three boxcars, long caboose 0505 (with kerosene marker lamps installed), combine 212 and coaches 312 and 327.

December – The Treasurer reported that revenue in 1998 was $91,167 and expenses were $63,600. All cash and financial accounts totaled $78,702 at the end of the year.

**1999** **Meetings at Christ Episcopal Church and dues remain $20.00. Pres. Jimmy Blouch; V-P. Wally Weart through March; Don Zielesch through December; Secy. Carolyn Blouch; Treas. Dave Goss; Ed. Bruce Nall.**

January – The *Rocky Mountain Rail Report* featured a new front page, with a pen and ink rendition of RGS engine 20 created by Steve Cross.

February 6 – The Club, jointly with the Intermountain Chapter of the NRHS, sponsored a field trip by bus to former sites of the Midland Terminal Railroad. This was the 50th anniversary, to the day, of the Club's trip in 1949. This trip sold out and cost $30.00. Two members, Morris Cafky and Bob Griswold, were recognized for having ridden on the original trip in 1949.

March 9 – Carl Hewett died. Carl was the founder and person who convinced a group of railroad enthusiasts to form the Club in 1938 to meet periodically to share their experiences about railroading. Carl became the Club's first President. His prose in early newsletters was reminiscent of Lucius Beebe's writings.

March – The Union Pacific Railroad provided a $10,000 grant to the Foundation for restoration of car 25.

March 21 – The Colorado Railroad Museum dedicated D&RGW diesel F unit 5771, which had been recently restored, and celebrated the 50th Anniversary of the *California Zephyr*.

April – The *Rocky Mountain Rail Report* recognized ten members who reached their fifty-year memberships this year (R. W. Richardson, Carl Helfin, J. C. Thode, Bob Griswold, Lillian Stewart, Donald Duke, Ralph Vance, Chuck Powell, G. W. Pool, Jack Pfeifer, Cornelius Hauck, Stanwood Griffith and Emil Schmutzler).

April 17 – Club celebrated the 100th birthday of locomotive 20 at the Colorado Railroad Museum. Built in 1899 for the Florence and Cripple Creek Railroad as number 20, the locomotive served many years in Colorado, ending up on the Rio Grande Southern. The Club purchased locomotive 20 in 1952. A special pamphlet was issued in commemoration of this event.

April 24 – Two buses took more than 90 members and guests to the Union Pacific steam shops in Cheyenne as well as to the Wyoming Transportation Museum and other sites around the city. Cost was $35.00.

September 11-12, 1999 – Club members help relocate a pedestrian crossing at the West Portal of the Alpine Tunnel as part of a service project **ROBERT E. WILSON PHOTO**

1938-49
1950-59
1960-69
1970-79
1980-89
1990-99
2000-03
Color Extra

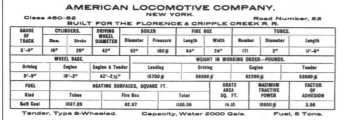

| GAUGE OF TRACK | CYLINDERS. | | DRIVING WHEEL DIAMETER | BOILER | | FIRE BOX | | TUBES. | | |
|---|---|---|---|---|---|---|---|---|---|---|
| | Diam. | Stroke | | Diameter | Pressure | Length | Width | Number | Diameter | Length |
| 3'-0" | 16" | 20" | 42" | 52" | 180 # | 84" | 24" | 171 | 2" | 11'-8" |

AMERICAN LOCOMOTIVE COMPANY, NEW YORK.
Class 460-52   Road Number, 52
BUILT FOR THE FLORENCE & CRIPPLE CREEK R. R.

| WHEEL BASE. | | | | WEIGHT IN WORKING ORDER—POUNDS. | | | |
|---|---|---|---|---|---|---|---|
| Driving | Engine | Engine & Tender | | Leading | Driving | | Tender |
| 9'-9" | 18'-2" | 42'-2½" | | 15700 # | 66500 # | 82200 # | 53500 # |

| FUEL | | HEATING SURFACES, SQUARE FT. | | | GRATE AREA SQ. FT. | MAXIMUM TRACTIVE POWER | FACTOR OF ADHESION |
|---|---|---|---|---|---|---|---|
| Kind | Tubes | | Fire Box | Total | | | |
| Soft Coal | 1037.09 | | 92.97 | 1130.06 | 14.10 | 18650 # | 3.56 |

Tender, Type 8-Wheeled.     Capacity, Water 2000 Gals.     Fuel, 5 Tons.

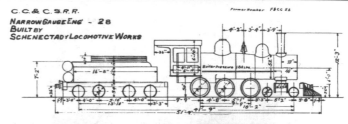

C. C. & C. S. R. R.
Former Number F&CC 52
NARROW GAUGE ENG' - 28
BUILT BY
SCHENECTADY LOCOMOTIVE WORKS

No. 5007   1899
SCHENECTADY LOCOMOTIVE WORKS
WM. D. ELLIS   A. J. PITKIN
PREST.   GEN. MGR.

Equipment Purchase Certificate
ROCKY MOUNTAIN RAILROAD CLUB
No. 101
J. L. EHRENBERGER

April 17, 1999 - In celebration of Engine No. 20's 100th anniversary at the Colorado Railroad Museum, the Club issued this special commemorative pamphlet.

May 14, 15, 16 - Motorcoach tour of the Powder River Basin. Twenty-eight members paid $92.00 including hotel rooms. They followed the joint lines in Wyoming and made visits to Bill, Gillette and the Belle Ayr Mine.

June 5 – Trip on the Canon City & Royal Gorge Railroad. Ninety-eight members and guests enjoyed the chartered coaches on the noon train and the trip through the magnificent canyon. Cost was $24.00.

June 19 – Trip to the Henderson Mine. This bus trip was sold out at $30.00 per person and gave members a chance to see the last operations before installation of the belt conveyor system.

July 10, 11 – Workdays at the Colorado Railroad Museum.

August 21, 22 – A planned trip on the Cumbres & Toltec Scenic Railroad was cancelled due to poor advance ticket sales.

August – The third printing of *Georgetown and The Loop* book was sold out.

September 11 – The official rollout of car 25 at the Denver Federal Center. It was announced that restoration was now 75% complete. More than 150 visitors participated.

September 11, 12 – A group of 14 Club members participated in a two-day service project at the West Portal of the Alpine Tunnel. Assisting the US Forest Service, members painted, laid rail and helped install a pedestrian bridge. Overnight accommodations were at the Pitkin Hotel (a hostel) with wooden bunk beds and lots of space. Cost was a $30.00 donation for which each member received a commemorative belt buckle.

September 18 – More than sixty members and guests took the Club excursion on the Leadville, Colorado & Southern Railroad. Cost was $22.50 (Children $12.50).

October 16 – Annual Banquet was at the Arvada Center. Erwin and Bobbie Chaim provided a multimedia music and slide presentation. More than 100 members and guests attended. The cost was $26.00.

December 14 – At the Club's regular meeting Lil and Jim Ranniger were recognized for providing exemplary food service on Ranniger's Roadbed Commis-

sary since 1978. Members of the Equipment Committee were recognized for their volunteer efforts and given Certificates of Appreciation. Jimmy Blouch was presented a framed R. H. Kindig photo in recognition for his three years service as President. Carolyn Blouch received a Pendleton wool blanket with an UP Overland Route logo on it for her service as Secretary for three years.

# Scrapbook

April 19, 1998 - Ticket and flyer for the Club's RTD Light Rail Fantrip.

September 13, 1997 - The excursion ticket for the mixed freight special on the Georgetown Loop.

July 25 - 26, 1998 - Excursion ticket.

1938-49

1950-59

1960-69

1970-79

1980-89

1990-99

2000-03

Color Extra

Flyer announcing the Club's 40th anniversary trip behind engine 3985 (right) and button given to all riders (above).

May 14 - 16, 1999 - Powder River Basin ticket and trip advertising flyer.

May 14, 1993 – A spotless engine 3985 leads an equally immaculate string of cars southbound at Platteville as it dead-heads equipment to be used on the Club's 40th Union Pacific Anniversary special. The temporarily added smoke-lifters and this engine renumbered as 3967 for the next day's trip would recall the Club's first excursion behind a Challenger class locomotive on May 17, 1953.
**J. L. EHERNBERGER PHOTO**

December 2, 1995 – Durango & Silverton engine 473 leads the Club's special returning from Cascade as the late afternoon sun highlights the train near Rockwood.
**J. L. EHERNBERGER PHOTO**

September 12, 1998 – In a most unusual trip, the Club chartered a bus to the Henderson Mine above Empire. This was one of the last opportunities to photograph the rail operations as they would be suspended the next year and replaced by a conveyor system. The following year's trip was one of the most unusual "last runs" that members witnessed. **STEVE MASON PHOTO**

1938-49

1950-59

1960-69

1970-79

1980-89

1990-99

2000-03

Color Extra

October 24, 1998 – A special "Photographer's Night" at the Colorado Railroad Museum provided the opportunity for professionals and amateurs to compose unusual and nostalgic photos. D&RGW locomotive 346 is captured emerging from a forest in this scene.
**J. L. EHERNBERGER PHOTO**

December 5, 1998 – Snow flakes the size of half-dollars nearly obscure Durango & Silverton Narrow Gauge Railroad locomotive 478 at Tacoma. The authentically lettered "freight special" attracted riders from Europe, Japan, Canada and many of the eastern United States.
**J. L. EHERNBERGER PHOTO**

April 17, 1999 – In conjunction with the celebration of the 100th Anniversary of RGS engine 20, Club members provided "smoke" in the stack giving the impression the locomotive was under steam. **DARRELL ARNDT PHOTO**

May 15, 1999 – Club members, guests and their motor coach are dwarfed by a 250 ton truck at the Belle Ayr Mine, part of the Club's first trip to the Powder River Basin in Wyoming. **STEVE MASON PHOTO**

September 11, 1999 – Pride of the Rocky Mountain Railroad Club and Foundation, car 25 made its official roll-out at the Denver Federal Center. More than 150 visitors celebrated this special event. Darrell Arndt, advocate, cheerleader and unwavering task master for the restoration is wearing the baseball cap and striding away from the car. **J. L. EHERNBERGER PHOTO**

1938-49
1950-59
1960-69
1970-79
1980-89
1990-99
2000-03
Color Extra

September 18, 1999 – More than sixty members and guests enjoyed an excursion on the Leadville, Colorado & Southern. A stop a French Gulch Tank provided riders an opportunity to enjoy the scenery and photograph the train high above Leadville on the former C&S Climax Branch. **J. L. EHERNBERGER PHOTO**

During the late 1990s, volunteers worked diligently almost every weekend on the interior and exterior restoration of car 25. (Left, Interior) **PHOTOGRAPHER UNKNOWN.** (Above) Exterior of car 25.
© **PHOTO BY BRUCE NALL**

# Chapter 7: 2000 - 2003

**2000**    **Meetings at Christ Episcopal Church and dues raised to $25.00 for regular members, $12.00 for associates and a new category of sustaining members was created at $40.00. Fifteen dollars of sustaining member dues were placed in the Equipment Fund. Pres. Dave Goss; V-P. Steve Mason; Secy. Jim Ehernberger; Treas. Fran Minnich; Ed. Bruce Nall.**

January – The Club received a Certificate of Appreciation from the U.S Department of Agriculture for the Club's participation in the 1999 "Passport in Time" program at the Alpine Tunnel Historic District.

March 12 – Officers and Directors met at the Colorado Railroad Museum for a strategic planning session. To better define the future of the Club, five questions were addressed: 1) What are our values? 2) Who are our customers? 3) What do we do well? 4) What could we do better? and 5) What are the outside influences? As a result, four areas of focus were identified and tentative strategies proposed: 1) Membership; 2) Publicity and Promotion; 3) Education/Outreach, and 4) Preservation.

May 12 – The Colorado State Historical Society approved inclusion of RGS locomotive 20 on the State Register of Historic Properties and forwarded a request for the engine to be placed on the National Register of Historic Places.

May 13 – Second annual tour to the Union Pacific steam shops in Cheyenne. Two buses carried 90 members and guests who paid $35.00 each for this tour that was much the same as last year's.

June – The summer 2000 issue of *Classic Trains* magazine had a feature length article on Dick Kindig and his photography. Fifty-nine years after the first article about Dick appeared in *Trains* magazine, he was again recognized for his photographs of western steam railroading.

June 21 – Board of Directors decided not to proceed with the publication of what would be Bob Griswold's third volume on the Denver & Salt Lake Railroad.

June 24 – More than 100 members rode double-headed steam trains at the Tiny Town Railroad. This was the Club's first trip to Tiny Town. The cost was $6.00 for adults and $2.00 for children and included unlimited rides and entrance to the park.

June 24 – For the first time since March 15, 1953, car 25 moved freely using its own traction motors. Electrical generation was provided by a track mounted generator. More than $1,300.00 was raised for the Foundation from the sale of books and merchandise at this open house.

July 2 – The Club, along with the Intermountain Chapter of the NRHS, the Denver Rail Heritage Society and the Colorado Railroad Museum, hosted the first passenger excursion (in cars 102 and 128) on new extension of the light rail system, from Broadway to Mineral Avenue. More than 400 riders participated and each paid $15.00 for unlimited rides all day on the entire system. One bewildered non-member joined the group, thinking this was the first day of regular service. "I couldn't understand why everyone had to have a camera to ride the train," he said in an Australian accent.

July 11 – The Club's regular meeting was held at the Bronco practice facility off Arapahoe Road. More than 115 members and guests enjoyed the video program on Chinese steam railways presented by Dave Gross.

August 12 – As a Club service project, sixteen Club members assisted US Forest Service volunteers on Kenosha Pass at the interpretive display. Work included

First railfan excursion to Mineral Ave. on RTD's Light Rail. Sunday July 2, 2000

June 24, 2000 - More than 100 members and guests enjoyed a full day of riding double-headed steam trains on the Tiny Town Railroad. This was the Club's first trip to Tiny Town and the price included food and unlimited rides.
**STEVE MASON PHOTO**

(Left) July 2, 2000 - Key ring for the first railfan excursion to Mineral Ave. on RTD Light Rail.

spreading ballast, replacing ties and installing a switch stand, all at 10,000 feet.

September 9 – Club members were invited to an open house hosted by Colorado Live Steamers at their new facility near Byers. Cost was $5.00, which included a donation to the group. Approximately thirty members and guests attended.

September 10 – Open house at the Denver Federal Center for car 25. Passengers were able to ride along the short length of track and return to a time when the car was fresh from the factory. The quality of the volunteers' work was impressive.

September 30 – As a follow up to the August 12 service project, twelve members returned to Kenosha Pass to assist again in redistributing nearly a hundred linear yards of ballast by hand.

September – The Club's Board issued a notebook containing policies, guidelines and procedures to help provide continuity between administrations.

October 8 – A special open house to view car 25 was provided for the Woeber family reunion. The Woeber Company built car 25 in 1911.

October 14 – Annual Banquet was at the Arvada Center. More than 100 members paid $28.00 for this dinner. Former President Dave Salter presented a slide program of his photography titled "Colorful Trains of the 50s." Dave's work would be featured in the *Classic Trains* magazine issue of Spring 2002.

October 17 – The Board authorized publication of *A Century of Passenger Trains ... And Then Some*, by Jack Thode (edited by Jim Ehernberger). Fifteen hundred copies would be produced at an approximate cost of $16,842 not including advertising and shipping.

October – The Club began accepting credit cards for all trips, merchandise, dues, etc.

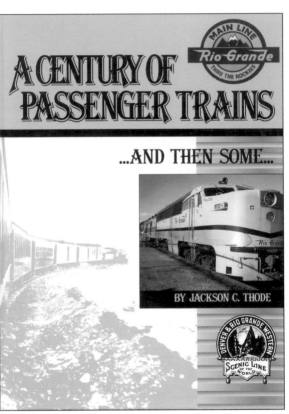

October 17, 2000 – The Board authorizes publication of *A Century of Passenger Trains ... And Then Some,* by Jackson C. Thode.

November 11 – Members were invited to an open house at the HO scale Granite Mountain Railway in Longmont.

December 6 – Several Club members participated as volunteers for the KRMA TV station fundraiser.

December 11 – Dave Gross who served as director for four years and as Chair of the Video Committee as well as an integral part of the Foundation was given a gift and Certificate of Achievement. Jim Ehernberger was recognized for his long service to the Club as well as for his work in overseeing the printing of Jack Thode's *A Century of Passenger Trains...And Then Some*. Steve Mason was recognized for his service as Vice President and Chair of the Equipment Committee. Hugh Alexander, who served many years and as Chair on the Trip Committee; Bruce Nall, Editor of the *Rocky Mountain Rail Report* and Chip Sherman, whose photos and news items add much to the newsletter were all given gifts and recognition for their work. Members of the Equipment Committee were given Certificates of Appreciation and recognition as well.

December 14 – RGS locomotive 20 was placed on the National Register of Historic Places.

December 31 – At the close of the Club's business year, total assets were valued at $475,320, which included the appraised value of Club equipment. Cash assets amounted to $75,770. During the year, the Club received $49,084 in income and expended $47,047.

**2001    Meetings at Christ Episcopal Church. Dues remained the same. Pres. Dave Goss; V-P. Mike Gailus; Secy. Frend John Miner; Treas. Fran Minnich; Ed. Bruce Nall.**

January – The Club published *A Century of Passenger Trains ... And Then Some*. This book was a significantly revised edition of the original book *A Century of Passenger Trains* that was published in 1972. Jim Ehernberger, working with Jack Thode, reset the format, added many new photos and text as well as updated the text through 1983. The book sold for $39.95 with a $5.00 pre-publication discount valid until March 31. Publishing costs were slightly over $16,000 for the book with some additional costs related to advertising. By the end of July, all the costs of publishing had been recovered as total income from the sales of the book were over $17,000.

COLORADO
HISTORICAL
SOCIETY

This is to certify that

### DENVER & RIO GRANDE WESTERN RAILROAD CABOOSE NO.0578

has been included in the

## State Register of Historic Properties

by the

**COLORADO HISTORICAL SOCIETY**
under provisions of the
Colorado Revised Statutes, Article 80.1
Register of Historic Places

*Georgianna Conteguglia*

*May 16, 2001*
Date Listed

President, Colorado Historical Society

May 16, 2001 - Announcement of the placement of the Club's Denver & Rio Grande Western Railroad caboose 0578 in the State Register of historic properties.

January – Members and associates whose dues were paid this year, received a metal nametag holder.

February – The *Rocky Mountain Rail Report* contained an article about long-time member Herb Votaw. He had built five highly detailed, superbly crafted, museum quality scale steam locomotives by hand.

February 17 – Car 25 celebrated its 90th birthday with an open house at the Denver Federal Center. More than fifty members and guests enjoyed cake and refreshments.

May – The May issue of the *Rocky Mountain Rail Report* was the 500th issue of the Club's newsletter.

May 5 – Third annual Union Pacific steam shops tour to Cheyenne was held. More than 90 members and guests rode two chartered buses to enjoy the same format tour as was provided last year. This day was also Cinco de Mayo in Cheyenne which added to the festivities.

May 16 – The Club's caboose 0578 received State Register of Historic Properties designation from the State Review Board.

May – The MOPAC (Merged Organization Process And Coordination) committee was formed to evaluate the

issues surrounding a proposed merger of the Club and the Historical Foundation.

June 9 – BBQ picnic and open house at the Colorado Railroad Museum. One hundred and eight members and friends paid $9.99 ($6.95 for children) for lunch.

July 13, 14, 15 – Workdays at the Colorado Railroad Museum.

July 17 – The Board decided to enter into negotiations with Boston Mills Press to publish a portion of the J. Foster Adams collection of photographs in conjunction with the Mid-Continent Chapter of the NRHS in Wisconsin.

July 22 – First Union Pacific steam powered excursion behind engine 3985 since 1993. More than 340 Club members and guests paid $94.50 for coach seating or $119.50 for dome seats from Denver to Cheyenne. This train was the Cheyenne Frontier Days "Denver Post" train on the preceding day. The return to Denver was via chartered buses. Cost to the Club for this trip was $26,635 (which included meals, advertising, train and buses). The revenue taken in was $32,696 for a profit of over $6,000. The train included a concession car (the "Sherman Hill"), baggage car, six coaches, three dome-coaches and a parlor-observation dome car.

August 27 – A planned trip on the Durango & Silverton Railroad was cancelled due to low ticket sales. It would have cost $77.50, and only 34 tickets were sold as compared to 135 needed to break even.

September 15 – The Foundation hosted a Volunteer Appreciation Day at the Denver Federal Center to honor the volunteers involved in the restoration of car 25. Approximately 80 members and guests attended.

September 29 – A planned day trip to Pueblo to visit the Pueblo Railfest was cancelled due to lack of ticket sales ($27.50) that would have included bus transportation.

October 13 – Annual Banquet at the Arvada Center. Jim Ehernberger, and Dave and Jean Gross presented a program on railroads of Cuba. Cost was $30.00 and 108 members and guests attended. Jim Ehernberger was recognized for his long time volunteer work with the Club and with other organizations. The Club made a $250 donation in Jim's name to the Wyoming Transportation Museum in Cheyenne. A certificate presented to Jim stated: "This award is given in recognition of a lifelong commitment to the goals and mission of the Club. Because of your extraordinary contributions to Club publications, willingness to coordinate special field trips and excursions, and outstanding leadership, we are truly grateful."

October 15 to 24 – Member Jim Ehernberger traveled to

Germany as the guest of German Public Television to assist in a documentary film on Union Pacific Big Boy locomotives. The November edition of *Modell Eisen Bahner* used eleven photos from his collection in an article on "Big Boy – Der Letzte Gigant" (The Last Giant).

October 16 – The MOPAC was dissolved and the decision was made not to pursue merger at this time but to instead develop long range plans to guide the organizations.

October 20 – Several Club members attended the annual membership meeting of the Pikes Peak Historical Street Railway Foundation in Colorado Springs. The members witnessed and photographed the Foundation's progress on restoring the Club's Ft. Collins Municipal Railway Birney car 22.

November 17 – The Jefferson County Historical Commission inducted RGS locomotive 20 into the county's "Hall of Fame." In that engine 20 resides in the county this award was made to recognize the historical significance of the locomotive and its placement on the National Register of Historic Places last December. A raised lettered bronze plaque, which stated "This Property Has Been Placed on the National Register of Historic Places by the United States Department of the Interior" was presented to the Club.

November 20 – The Board revisited the decision to negotiate with Boston Mills Press on the publication of J. Foster Adams photos. Instead, the Board decided to proceed with the publication of a new book featuring Adams' western photos without the assistance of either Boston Mills or the Mid-Continent Chapter of the NRHS.

December 11 – The Club presented President Dave Goss a framed photo and a gift certificate for his service as President during the last two years. Chip Sherman and Bruce Nall were presented monetary gifts for their continuing contributions to the *Rocky Mountain Rail Report*.

December 14 – Long-time member Ralph Vance died in an accident when responding to a fire while in the service of the Elk Creek Volunteer Fire Department. A member for more than

fifty years, Ralph held membership card number 16 and was very active on the Equipment Committee.

December – *The Rocky Mountain Rail Report* contained a lengthy description of the induction of engine 20 into the Jefferson County Hall of Fame, and included a pen and ink drawing by member Ruth Koons who was asked by the Commission to provide the drawing for the induction ceremony.

December – The Jefferson County Historical Commission featured car 25 in an article in the annual publication *Historically Jeffco*. Also included in this issue were articles on RGS engine 20 and caboose 0578, both owned by the Club.

December – The Club made blue denim shirts with the Club's logo over the pocket available to members for $20.00.

## Rio Grande Southern Railroad Steam Engine No. 20

Engine 20 is a rare surviving example of a narrow gauge, ten-wheeler steam locomotive. It is an important example of nineteenth century engineering and the only remaining old Schenectady Locomotive Works steam engine in Colorado. Only three narrow gauge 4-6-0 engines exist in the state. They are D&RGW No. 168 displayed in Colorado Springs, D&RGW No. 169 on display in Alamosa and Rio Grande Southern Engine No. 20, the largest and most powerful, on display in Golden. It has served Colorado residents and visitors to this state for over 100 years, first hauling passengers and freight in the central front range, then in the southwest mountains during the historic development and decline of gold and silver mining. It operated on three important railroads, each of which are no longer in existence, but remain a significant part of Colorado's growth and prosperity. Engine 20, on display for 6 years in Alamosa County and now for 44 years in Jefferson County, remains available for education and enjoyment due to the dedication, contributions and efforts of railroad enthusiasts from Colorado, all other states and many other nations. RGS #20 is owned and maintained by the Rocky Mountain Railroad Club and displayed at the Colorado Railroad Museum in recognition of Colorado's history and to benefit current and future generations of our citizens.
Engine 20 was listed on the National Register of Historic Places on December 14, 2000.

November 17, 2001 - Pen and ink sketch done by member Ruth Koons for the induction of RGS locomotive 20 into the Jefferson County Hall of Fame.

Meetings at Christ Episcopal Church. Dues remained the same. Pres. Mike Gailus; V-P. Steve Mason; Secy. Frend John Miner; Treas. Fran Minnich until March and Frend John Miner through December; Ed. Bruce Nall.

January 15 – The Board of Directors voted to participate in a restoration project at Union Station wherein organizations could contribute funds to purchase paver stones for use on the walls of the main entrance. The Club decided to purchase a paver with its logo for donation.

February 15 – The review committee of the Colorado Historical Society recommended placement of the Club's caboose 0578 on the National Register of Historic Places.

February 19 – Lucian Sprague and Jerre Moriarty (Lucian's sister) were each given a lifetime membership in the Club because of their donation of the films of the Uintah Railway made between 1925 and 1930.

February – Member Dave Salter was honored as one of *Classic Trains* magazine's "Great Photographers" in the Spring 2002 issue. Dave's color photographs of post World War II railroads in the South were featured in this magazine.

March 22 – The Club's live steam locomotive 999 was moved from the Colorado Railroad Museum to the City of Edgewater Historical Museum. The Club and city officials arranged for a 10-year loan for this locomotive to be displayed on the second floor of City Hall.

March 23 – The Club's "World Headquarters" was moved from 2701 Alcott to a storage facility located at 1699 S. Broadway, Unit 800. This fire-protected, air conditioned facility provides space for the Club's less valuable archives. Original films and other assets are stored at the Public Service Company corporate archives. The landlords of the Alcott property wanted to raise the Club's rent by 108% and insisted on a five-year lease.

April 13 – Fran Minnich stepped down as Club Treasurer as she and her husband Joe (who had served as Trip Committee Chair for the last two years) moved to Ohio. Fran had been managing Club membership, all financial and credit card transactions, and most ticket sales. The Board decided it would be appropriate to hire a part-time

bookkeeper to perform many of the activities she performed. Membership was handed off to Club volunteers.

May 4 – The Club's third tour of the Union Pacific Cheyenne shops and a ride on Fort Collins trolley 21. Sixty-one members and guests rode the buses, the tickets for which were $39.00. Lunch was not provided but time to eat at local restaurants was scheduled.

June 15 – Members enjoyed a BBQ lunch catered by Bennett's and spent a day at the Colorado Railroad Museum. Cost was $9.95 for adults and $6.95 for children.

June 15, 2002 – Colorado Railroad Museum hosted the second annual Club picnic where members and guests feasted on barbecue.
**CHARLES MOFFAT PHOTO**

July 21 – Club excursion behind Union Pacific locomotive 3985. The one-way trip to Cheyenne was the return leg of the railroad's trip for the Cheyenne Frontier Day special operated on July 20. Motor coaches took the riders back to Denver after a BBQ lunch at the Terry Bison Ranch. Cost for the trip was $99.50 for coach seats, $129.50 for parlor car seats and $134.50 for dome seats. Approximately 450 seats were sold, of which only 136 were to Club members. Approximately 313 responded to a special mailing list purchased from Kalmbach Publishing of its *Model Railroader* magazine subscribers in the states surrounding Colorado. Forty new

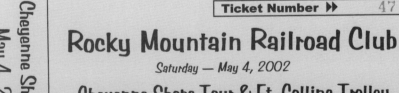

Cheyenne Shops Tour
May 4, 2002

| Ticket Number ▶▶ | 47 |

**Rocky Mountain Railroad Club**

Saturday — May 4, 2002

**Cheyenne Shops Tour & Ft. Collins Trolley**

TOUR BUSSES LEAVING RTD PARK-N-RIDE (I-25 & Broadway) at 8:00am
(Loading begins at 7:30am)

**PUNCH INDICATES** ▶▶ **BUS #1** ☐ **— OR — BUS #2** ☒

Ft. Collins Trolley
May 4, 2002

1938-49
1950-59
1960-69
1970-79
1980-89
1990-99
2000-03
Color Extra

members joined as a result of the trip and mailing. Gross revenue for the trip was $48,931 with a net profit of approximately $5,000. The twelve-car train included the concession car "Sherman Hill," a baggage car, four dome-coaches, five 5400-series flat top coaches, and a parlor-observation dome car.

July 27, 28 – Workdays at the Colorado Railroad Museum.

August 3 – Charter member Jackson Thode who held membership card number 2, died. Jack provided sixty-four years of leadership, inspiration and commitment to the Club. Author of many publications, his most recent book *A Century of Passenger Trains...And Then Some* was published by the Club in 2001. Jack was considered by many to be the foremost authority on Colorado railroads, especially the Denver & Rio Grande. Dr. Tom Noel and other notables eulogized Colorado's "Railroader Emeritus" at the memorial service.

September 26 – Long-time Club member Newell Melcher who held membership card 34 died.

September 27, 28, 29 – A planned motor coach trip to Nebraska, including Crawford Hill, was cancelled due to a lack of sufficient advance sales to cover the expected cost. Despite extensive advertising, only 20 of the 32 needed to break even pre-registered. However, approximately 25 new members joined at a special $6.00 rate (for the remainder of 2002) that was advertised in the trip announcement flyer.

September 28 – Approximately 100 persons, mostly non-members, attended the roll-out of car 25 at the Denver Federal Center. More than $750 was collected in sales and donations.

Fall 2002 – Member Jim Ehernberger's photo of Colorado & Southern locomotive 806 was the cover photo of this issue of *Classic Trains* magazine. This issue contained a lengthy article on the final days of steam on the C&S, including trips operated by the Club in the 1960's.

October 11 to 14, 18 to 20 – Thomas the Tank Engine made a guest appearance at the Colorado Railroad

October 11, 2002 - Thomas the Tank Engine at the Colorado Railroad Museum.
© PHOTO BY BRUCE NALL

Museum. Club volunteers assisted throughout these two weekends, and the Club provided coloring pages, handouts and other information to visitors.

October 12 – More than 100 members and guests enjoyed the food and camaraderie at the Arvada Center for the Annual Banquet. Members of the Union Pacific steam crew were special guests and Bob Krieger, engineer, presented the program.

October 17 – The Board decided "Select Image Photograph" would publish the *Rocky Mountain Rail Report* for another year. Costs for the printing, photography, folding, collating and stapling averages $1,100 a month for 1,000 copies.

October 30 – Long-time member Joe R. Thompson died. He was a well known photographer whose works were published by Lucius Beebe, *Trains* magazine and many other publications.

October – The Club mailed out a survey along with renewal notices to obtain feedback from members on trips, focus, and interests.

November 3 – Long-time member (membership card number 6 in 2002) Morris Cafky died. Morris was a renowned and respected scholar who had written many books and articles, including *Rails Around Gold Hill* published by the Club in 1955 and the *Colorado Midland* published by the Club in 1965.

November 21 – The Board selected Trains Unlimited Tours (owned and operated by Club member Chris Skow) to become the Club's official tour operator for all trips except those specifically hosted by the Trip Committee. This partnership would allow better publicity, planning and overall support for trips conducted outside the immediate geographical region. The Board also selected the logo to be used for the 65th Anniversary during 2003.

December 10 – Annual Meeting with election of Officers and Directors as well as recognition of volunteers and departing Officers and Directors. The program was a slide program of Christmas card images set to music and presented by Erwin and Bobbie Chaim. This annual program has become a recent and greatly anticipated tradition. Cake and punch followed.

December 19 – The Board of Directors decided to loan the original oil painting "Thunder at Hagerman Trestle" by Phil Ronfor, that had been in Morris Cafky's possession for years, to the Colorado Railroad Museum for display.

December – The Club purchased a television with a combination DVD and VCR player for use at future train shows. Cost was less than $250.

December 31 – The income for 2002 was $99,998.79 and the expenses for the year were $99,057.73 for a net income of $941.06. During 2002 the Foundation received over $2,400 in donations and merchandise sales.

December 2002 – During 2002 twelve Club members donated more that 700 hours of their time in restoration and preservation activities on the Club's equipment displayed at the Colorado Railroad Museum. Fifty percent of the time was given by Bob Tully and Denny Haefele, with additional time provided by Duane Fields, Ken Gow, Bill Haefele, David Rudd, Roger Sherman, Russ and Sue Stuska, Mark and Matt Toman and Mona Tully. There may have been other volunteers whose names were not recorded, but the work of every volunteer is much appreciated.

February and March – In a two-part story in the *Rocky Mountain Rail Report,* Jim Ehernberger recounted his experiences as a fifteen-year-old when making a multi-day trip in 1952 to Silverton. Jim's adventure included bus and rail trips and stops in Salida, Gunnison, Montrose, Silverton, Durango and Alamosa.

February 6 – Past President (1967-68), former newsletter editor and long-time member Ed Schneider died.

February 8 – Member Barry Smith arranged and conducted a space-limited (to nine members) tour of the BNSF tower located at 38th Avenue in Denver.

**65**

*years*

**1938-2003**

**ROCKY MOUNTAIN RAILROAD CLUB**

*-Preserving Colorado Railroad History Since 1938-*

Logo designed by Steve Mason to commemorate the Club's 65th anniversary.

**2003**    **Meetings at Christ Episcopal Church. Dues remained the same. Pres. Mike Gailus; V-P. Steve Mason; Secy. and Treas. Frend John Miner; Ed. Bruce Nall.**

Beginning in January, Trains Unlimited became the "Official" Club tour operator. As part of this arrangement, Club members were offered special discounts for any of the sixteen trips planned by TUT during 2003. For each member who signed up, TUT paid the Club $50. Tours were throughout North America with international trips planned to Cuba, South America and China.

January 22 – Caboose Hobbies hosted a Rocky Mountain Railroad Club night. Forty-two members attended and received discounts. Caboose Hobbies grossed over $3,000.

January 23 – At the regular Club Board meeting, a decision was made to publish a brief narrative history of the Club and Foundation (the book the reader is holding), covering a sixty-five year chronology of the Club's activities, events and publications, beginning in 1938 and continuing through 2003. Cost for 1000 copies of the book was estimated to be approximately $5,500. The Board also gave approval to the United States Geological Survey to use map information originally prepared by Ed Haley for the Club for an historical map of Colorado that the USGS is preparing.

February 1 – Club members visited the Colorado Rail Car shop in Ft. Lupton. The open house at this manufacturing facility attracted 107 members. There was no fee for this field trip.

March – The Club decided to sponsor a photo contest for members and non-members. Black and white, slides or color photos would be eligible with the winner to receive a copy of Otto Perry's "San Juan Express" in DVD. The winning non-member would receive a year's membership in the Club. Winners would be announced at the Club's Annual Banquet in October.

March 31 – Long-time member Dick Kremers died. Dick epitomized the faithful and uncomplaining volunteers who put many long hours in working on the restoration of car 25. He worked almost every Saturday beginning in 1988 until the last few months before his death.

April 8 – In recognition of his work for the Club over the years, specifically his photographic gift to members handed out at December meetings, this meeting was declared "Neal Miller Night." It was also Neal's eightieth birthday.

April 11 – The Club hosted a trip on the Canon City & Royal Gorge Railroad leaving from Canon City to Parkdale and return. Cost was $50 for members, $55 for non-members and $25 for children. Diesel locomotive 403 and another F unit (both former C&NW engines) headed the ten-car train. A special feature of this trip was a drawing for two cab rides in each direction, from the adult fare-paying passengers. Box lunches were provided on board and a shop tour following the trip was also included in the price of each ticket. With 102 participants, the Club netted more than $1,300 on this trip.

1938-49

1950-59

1960-69

1970-79

1980-89

1990-99

2000-03

Color Extra

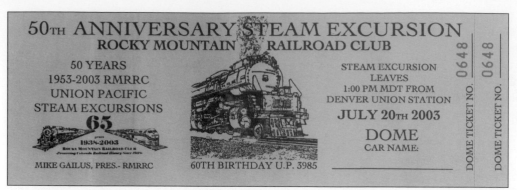

July 20, 2003 - Souvenir ticket and button given each rider of the Club's 50th Anniversary trip behind Challenger 3985, numbered as 3967 for this trip only.

May – The Board evaluated whether or not to hire a General Manager, either part-time or full time. In June, the decision was made not to do so.

May 17 – The Club conducted its fourth annual Union Pacific Cheyenne shops tour for members and guests. A chartered coach took approximately 50 members and guests to Ft. Collins where participants rode restored Birney car 21, sister to the Club's Birney car 22. The group then continued to Cheyenne to visit the UP steam shops and see the progress on the rebuilding of Northern 844. After lunch (not included) a photo stop was made in Holliday Park in Cheyenne to see Big Boy 4004. The return to Denver completed the trip. Members paid $46 and non-members paid $51 for each ticket on this trip.

June – The Club distributed the 2003 roster to all members. This 32-page publication included a color cover, black and white photos of Club equipment, advertising and other graphics. The 65th anniversary logo, designed by Steve Mason, was on the back cover.

June 14 – The Club held its Third Annual Picnic at Tiny Town. The $15.00 ticket for adults and $10.00 for children allowed participants unlimited rides on the railroad, tours of the roundhouse, the "long house" and unlimited food at the concession. In an achievement of superb planning, the Club realized a profit of $1.05 after all expenses were deducted.

June 26 – In support of a fundraising effort to assist in preservation of Denver Union Station, the Club purchased a 12" x 12" brick paver (Number 1) for $500 that was placed along with other pavers at the entrance of the station at 17th and Wynkoop St. The campaign allowed organizations and individuals to contribute between $75 (for a 4" by 8" brick) and $1,500 (for a 24" by 24" granite block).

July 14 – Trains Unlimited gave the Club seven tickets on Amtrak train 5, the *California Zephyr* to be used for

July 20, 2003 - Locomotive 3967 with an extra tender and diesel SD70M 3930 lead the Club's 50th Anniversary Steam Excursion from Denver to Cheyene. **DAVE GOSS PHOTO**

one way passage on this date between Denver and Helper, UT. The $20 ticket was one-third the normal price and available on a first-come, first-served basis.

July 20 – More than 370 passengers rode the Club's 50th UP Anniversary trip behind Challenger 3985 (renumbered as 3967). The Club's first UP mainline steam trip was May 17, 1953, pulled by Challenger 3967. Locomotive 3985 celebrated its sixtieth birthday this year, having been built in 1943. This year's trip included diesel power supplied by UP SD70M, 3930 (with a commemorative banner on the fireman's side) and 17 cars. A brief but intense shower at the first photo stop did not dampen the spirits but did result in brisk sales of T-shirts from the "Sherman Hill," concession car. Three more photo run-bys were included with the terminus of the trip at the Terry Bison Ranch, where dinner was served. Riders were from 29 states, the District of Columbia, Canada, Australia, England and Japan. Nine busses returned passengers to Denver by 9:30 p.m.

July 27 – The Club and Foundation each had tables at the Mile High Railfair held at the Jefferson County Fairgrounds.

August 23, 24 – Club members worked both days at the Colorado Railroad Museum to perform many restoration tasks on the "Rico" and engine 20. Refreshments were provided.

September 13, 2003 – (Right) Club hosted an open house to show the progess of car 25 restoration. (Below) A wheel-mounted auxiliary generator powered car 25 as it traversed a short section of track. **DARRELL ARNDT PHOTOS**

September 27, 2003 – Volunteers paint and prepare for further restoration of former Colorado and Southern caboose 10600 in Bailey.
**PAT MAURO PHOTO**

September 13 – Club hosted an open house at the Denver Federal Center so visitors could see the restoration progress on car 25. Special tickets were given to "riders" as car 25 traversed a short section of track powered by a wheel-mounted auxiliary generator.

September 27, 28 – Club members worked on a service project on former Colorado & Southern caboose 10600 in Bailey, organized by member Pat Mauro. Work

included preparation of the caboose for additional restoration and some painting. On Sunday, volunteers met at Kenosha Pass to work on the switch at the tail of the wye as a project for the US Forest Service.

September 27 – Club members were invited to join the Intermountain Chapter of the NRHS on their annual *Pea Vine Flyer* excursion on the San Luis Central Railroad in Monte Vista. Cost was $25 and members were required to provide their own transportation and overnight accommodations.

October 9, 10 – Twenty-seven Club members and guests participated on a Trains Unlimited Tours and Club sponsored "Rio Grande Photo Freight" trip on the Cumbres & Toltec Scenic Railroad. Visitors from as far away as Great Britain and Texas joined in this well-organized and managed outing.

October 25 – Annual Banquet was held at the Arvada Center. More than 110 members and guests were entertained by Mel Patrick who presented a multi-media slide show. As announced earlier in the year, the Board of Directors and guests judged entries for the Club's 2003 photo contest. The winners were David Henker (member) and Norm Havran (non-member). Both winning photos were published in the November *Rocky Mountain Rail Report*.

November – The Club made available 5 by 7 inch boxed Christmas cards featuring a color reproduction of Philip Ronfor's painting "Thunder at Hagerman Trestle." The set of ten cards cost $10.00 per box, plus shipping.

November 11– The Club authorized Jim Ehernberger to negotiate with Jack Wolff in Cheyenne to begin making copy negatives of each image in the J. Foster Adams photograph collection. A number of the original nitrate negatives have begun to deteriorate badly and would be lost entirely.

Volunteers spend many hours each year repairing, restoring and preserving RGS engine 20, the "Rico" and other Club equipment at The Colorado Railroad Museum
**ROGER SHERMAN PHOTO**

Tully and other Club volunteers. A set of four drawings depicting engine 20, a generic passenger car, caboose 0578 and railroad signs were given to children. During 2003, a small but dedicated cadre of Club members again logged more than 700 hours of volunteer time at the museum performing preservation and restoration on Club equipment.

December 14 – At the Club's Annual Meeting, a revision to the Articles of Incorporation was approved which changed the makeup of the Board of Directors from "...eleven members composed of the president, the secretary, the treasurer, the immediate past president and six additional directors..." to a new composition of "...the officers of the corporation called for in the bylaws and six additional directors..." This streamlined board should enable a closer working relationship on both Club and Foundation activities.

Since the mid-1990s Chip Sherman has been a regular contributor to the Club's monthly newsletter *Rocky Mountain Rail Report*. The Club is fortunate having someone of his caliber keeping us informed of current operations along the railroad scene. Chip has become one of the more prolific published railroad photographers in Colorado during modern times. His efforts recording modern scenes is preserving an era of railroading that will one day seem as important to future generations, as the steam locomotive era did to those past generations who experienced that type of motive power.

December – The Foundation made available a twelve-month, 2004 calendar and a 55-minute video titled *The Cars That Built Our Cities* which was an historic study of streetcars and interurbans. Sale of both items helped enable the continued restoration of car 25.

December – More than 1,100 visitors toured the "Rico" during Santa Claus Days at the Colorado Railroad Museum. Free refreshments were provided by Bob and Mona

December 31 – Club ended the year with a net profit of $886.02. Gross income was $110,337.86 and expenses were $109,451.84. The Foundation had a net loss of $1,382.07 after expenses of $13,087.82 and income of $11,705.75 that was due to ongoing preservation and restoration costs.

December 31 – Members renewing their 2004 dues received a pocket calendar card with an image of car 25 on one side and a 2004 calendar on the other.

J. Foster Adams photographed Union Pacific engine 4206 at Rieth, Oregon on October 10, 1921. This rare class of locomotive was built in 1889 by Schenectady (division of the American Locomotive Works) for the Oregon Railroad and Navigation Company and it was scrapped in August 1927. In November 2003, the Club authorized making copy negatives of the photographers' images to save the rapidly-deteriorating collection.
**J. FOSTER ADAMS PHOTO - RMRR CLUB ARCHIVES**

**65**
1938-2003
ROCKY MOUNTAIN RAILROAD CLUB
*Preserving Colorado Railroad History Since 1930s*

Saturday,
**June 14, 2003**
Steam Up at
8:00 AM

Mike Gailus, pres.
RMRRC

Go West on
Hampden Ave.
US 285
From C 470
3 3/4 Miles
Turn left onto
South Turkey Creek
Road
(Jeffco CR 122)
And go south
3/4 mile to
Tiny Town
Park on left side
(east)

**Tiny Town &
Railroad**

**One Adult
Ticket**
Ticket No.

0121

Souvenir tickets issued for the Club's tour of the
Union Pacific Cheyenne Shops and Ft. Collins
Trolley trip (left) and for the 50th Anniversary
special behind Union Pacific Challenger 3985
(renumbered as 3967 for this trip).

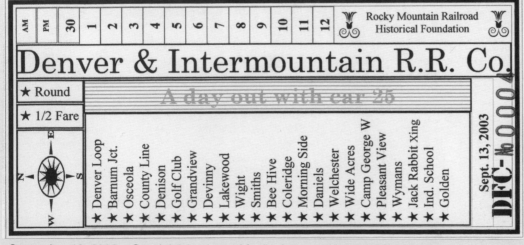

September 13, 2003 – Special ticket issued for "a day out with car 25."

1938-49
1950-59
1960-69
1970-79
1980-89
1990-99
2000-03
Color Extra

July 2, 2000 – President Mike Gailus (right) and Trip Committee Chair Steve Mason (left) hold the club's famous drumhead in front of RTD light rail car 113 prior to the Club's first excursion on the new extension from Broadway Station to Mineral Avenue. **DARRELL ARNDT PHOTO**

April 27, 2003 – Dedicated volunteers have spent countless hours working on the Club equipment over the years. Caboose 0578 is now on the State Register of Historic Properties by the Colorado Historical Society and it has been placed on the National Register of Historic Places. Obviously in this view, restoration work had been completed along with a fresh coat of paint and detailed lettering was appropriately applied. **BOB TULLY PHOTO**

Darrell Arndt and Tom Peyton take a break from car 25 restoration activities in this undated photo taken at the Denver Federal Center. **ROBERT E. WILSON PHOTO**

April 11, 2003 – The Club hosted a trip on the *Canon City* & *Royal Gorge Railroad* from Canon City to Parkdale and return. Four lucky riders were upgraded to cab rides as the result of a surprise drawing. **DARRELL ARNDT PHOTO**

September 28, 2003 – Eleven enthusiastic, but tired members participated in a service project at the interpretive display on Kenosha Pass. They worked on the switch at the tail of the wye at this location, more than 10,000 feet above sea level. **STEVE MASON PHOTO**

1938-49

1950-59

1960-69

1970-79

1980-89

1990-99

**2000-03**

Color Extra

# 2003 Photo Contest Winners

March 8, 2003 – UP 5933 photographed westbound, east of Rock River, WY. **DAVE HENKER PHOTO (MEMBER)**

May 26, 2003 – RGS Galloping Goose 5 displayed at Dolores. **NORM HAVRAN PHOTO (NON-MEMBER)**

# Color Photo Extra

Like many freight and passenger trains, this book has an extra section. This Photo Extra has been added in order to accommodate a few more photos that had to make this trip. Included are some color photographs of the Club's most memorable people, activities and trips. The memories on these few pages may further enrich your understanding of the rich tradition and heritage of the Rocky Mountain Railroad Club.

1938-49

1950-59

1960-69

1970-79

1980-89

1990-99

2000-03

Color Extra

August 4, 1940 - M&PP locomotive 6 at Windy Point on this year's summer excursion. **R. H. KINDIG PHOTO**

February 6, 1949 – The Club's drumhead adorns the rear of the last passenger train on the Midland Terminal Railway seen waiting at Midland. **R. H. KINDIG PHOTO**

September, 1952 – Sample "Salvage Share" certificate given to each Club member who supported the acquisition of former RGS locomotive 20.

February 22, 1954 – Dick Kindig and Ed Haley take a breather while placing builder plates on locomotive 20 at the Narrow Gauge Museum in Alamosa. **PHOTOGRAPHER UNIDENTIFIED**

September 25, 1955 – One of the Club's "Fall Foliage" excursions catches the morning light while sitting on three-rail track in Alamosa. **E. J. HALEY PHOTO**

March 11, 1956 – First of the class, but the last to operate, was UP engine 9000 (4-12-2) waiting at the Cheyenne station for its return trip to Denver on a frigid day. **E. J. HALEY PHOTO**

September 15, 1957 – Union Pacific engine 535 takes water at Fox Park, WY.  The venerable 1903 Baldwin steam locomotive seems out-dated when compared to the modern Studebaker in the foreground.  **E. J. HALEY PHOTO**

August 24, 1958 – C&S engine 646 makes a photo run-by at Church's Lake on an event filled trip over the CB&Q from Denver to Lyons via Lafayette, Erie and Longmont and back to Denver.
**J. L. EHERNBERGER PHOTO**

April 8, 1959 – C&S engine 809 awaits departure to Golden for the Club's Annual Dinner on a snowy April evening.  The train would not return until after midnight.
**E. J. HALEY PHOTO**

1938-49

1950-59

1960-69

1970-79

1980-89

1990-99

2000-02

Color Extra

July 19, 1959 – C&S engine 900 is southbound on this excursion that operated from Denver to Ft. Collins to Rex to Cheyenne and back to Denver. **E. J. HALEY PHOTO**

October 25, 1959 – The tender of C&S locomotive 647 is replenished by the Lyons Fire Department on this trip that ran from Denver to Burns Junction to Longmont to Lyons and back to Denver on a beautiful summer day. **E. J. HALEY PHOTO**

December 16, 1962 – This scene shows the difficulty of refueling a steam locomotive on its last run in a city where only diesels operate. C&S engine 638 takes coal in Pueblo. **E. J. HALEY PHOTO**

December 16, 1962 - The late afternoon sun seems to bid a poignant farewell to C&S locomotive 638 on the the last run of any C&S steam engine as it nears Trinidad.
**E. J. HALEY PHOTO**

May 2, 1965 – Lettered and painted for its role in the movie "Cat Ballou," former GW locomotive 51 operated on the D&RGW to the Moffat Tunnel and return.
**J. L. EHERNBERGER PHOTO**

May 30, 1965 – This scene near Needleton could have been repeated on many of the Club's Memorial Day excursions, as D&RGW engine 476 thunders past on a photo run-by. **J. L. EHERNBERGER PHOTO**

1938-49
1950-59
1960-69
1970-79
1980-89
1990-99
2000-03
Color Extra

October 19, 1969 – Colorado Central Narrow Gauge engine 44 made an awesome display of smoke on a cool, crisp fall morning. **J. L. EHERNBERGER PHOTO**

January 20, 1974 – One of the many remarkable photos taken of Union Pacific engine 8444 on the Club's excursion from Denver to Laramie and return. **DARRELL ARNDT PHOTO**

March 28, 1987 – The Club chartered the vista dome lounge observation car "Silver Sky" for this trip to Winter Park on the *Ski Train*. **DARRELL ARNDT PHOTO**

May 15, 1993 – Challenger 3985 carries the numbers 3967 for the Club's 40th Union Pacific Anniversary trip. More than 500 passengers rode this train. **HUGH ALEXANDER PHOTO**

October 24, 1998 – This nostalgic photo captured a bygone era as Club members participated in a special night photo clinic at the Colorado Railroad Museum.
**© PHOTO BY BRUCE NALL**

1938-49
1950-59
1960-69
1970-79
1980-89
1990-99
2000-03
Color Extra

The painting used on the cover of this book and seen here is titled "Photo Stop, 1947" by artist Philip A. Ronfor. It includes depictions of prominent Club members who are serious photographers impatiently waiting for the opportunity to take a perfect picture. The scene is typical of the contrast between the observer studying the locomotive's running gear in great detail and the photographers' fears that the lighting and background mood to be captured will be lost by this delay. This dichotomy is the essence of the Rocky Mountain Railroad Club and all similar rail organizations that operate excursions and trips for a variety of enthusiasts.

**COURTESY OF THE COLORADO RAILROAD MUSEUM**

November 2003 – "Thunder at Hagerman Trestle" is the title of this Phil Ronfor painting that was originally commissioned by the Club for the cover of W. Morris Cafky's book, *Colorado Midland*. Christmas cards with this painting were available for sale this year. **RMRR CLUB ARCHIVES**

# Club and Foundation Publications and Memorabilia

Sources of the information for the chronology came largely from Club newsletters, books, trip handouts, information at the Club's headquarters, memorabilia at the Colorado Railroad Museum and from members' personal collections. Transcripts of interviews with early members and interviews with other members helped provide additional details. A number of secondary references (non-Club publications) were also used.

Jim Ehernberger verified many of the trips and equipment by researching the Otto Perry photograph catalogs as well as his own photographs and records to determine locomotives and train consists. Many of the locomotives used on Club excursions were identified by Otto Perry and are listed in the *Catalogue of the Otto Perry Memorial Collection of Railroad Photographs, Volume 1* (1977) and *Volume 2* (1980) published by the Western History Department of the Denver Public Library. The two volumes of this catalogue (containing over 20,800 negatives) were assembled through the efforts of members Dick Kindig, Ed Haley and Jack Thode. Dick cataloged the negatives, Ed numbered them and Jack typed filing

envelopes for storage. A few dates contained in the catalog conflict with actual excursions, but these errors are few and minor in nature.

There are many additional sources of information about Club trips. Some contain photographs of the trips themselves; others simply describe the trip or excursion. The listing of all sources would be too extensive; the following is a partial listing of publications that contain additional information and photographs of Club trips:

- Colorado Railroad Museum annuals
- Various volumes of *Trails Among the Columbine*
- *Trains* magazine
- Robert LeMassena's *Colorado Mountain Railroads*
- Individual railroad histories of the Denver & Rio Grande Western, the Rio Grande Southern, the Colorado & Southern, the Union Pacific and affiliated railroads that operated in Colorado and Wyoming
- Specific histories of Colorado places like Denver, LaVeta Pass,

## Bibliography of Books, Pamphlets and Videos and Listing of Memorabilia Produced by the Rocky Mountain Railroad Club

### Books

Cafky, Morris. *Colorado Midland*. Denver, CO. Rocky Mountain Railroad Club (World Press). 1965. Included a set of five maps, made available separately. 6,000 copies printed. Pre-publication price was $12.00 and regular price $14.00.

Cafky, Morris. *Rails Around Gold Hill*. Denver, CO. Rocky Mountain Railroad Club (World Press). Limited, numbered edition. 1955. Pre-publication price $8.50, regular price $10.00.

Griswold, P. R. *David Moffat's Denver, Northwestern and Pacific – The Moffat Road*. Denver, CO. Rocky Mountain Railroad Club (Walsworth Publishing). 1995. Price $39.95.

Griswold, P. R. *Denver and Salt Lake Railroad*. Denver, CO. Rocky Mountain Railroad Club (Walsworth Publishing), 1996. Price $39.95.

Griswold, P.R, Kindig, R. H., and Trombly, Cynthia. *Georgetown and The Loop*. Denver, CO. Rocky Mountain Railroad Club (Walsworth Publishing). 1988. (Reprinted 3 times) Pre-publication price for first edition was $24.50. Regular price $27.50. Third edition was priced at $39.95.

Haley, E. J., Kindig, R. H., and Poor, M. C. *Pictorial Supplement to Denver South Park & Pacific*. Denver, CO. Rocky Mountain Railroad Club (World Press). 1959. Pre-publication price $12.50. Regular price $15.00.

*Pictorial Supplement to Denver South Park & Pacific.* (Abridged Edition) Denver, CO. Rocky Mountain Railroad Club (Trowbridge Press). 1986. This title was not published by the Club, but was reprinted by Mr. Trowbridge using a photocopy-offset process. Since the quality of the process was not comparable to the original, the Club turned down sponsorship of this edition. None of the original authors' names appeared on the title page.

Poor, M. C. *Denver South Park & Pacific*, Denver, CO. Rocky Mountain Railroad Club (World Press). 1949. Pre-publication price $10.00. Regular price $12.50.

Poor, M. C. *Memorial Edition Denver South Park & Pacific*. Denver, CO. Rocky Mountain Railroad Club (World Press). 1976. Pre-publication price of $19.00. Regular price was $24.50, later raised to $24.95.

Thode, Jackson C. *A Century of Passenger Trains: A Study of 100 Years of Passenger Service on the Denver & Rio Grande Railway, Its Heirs, Successors and Assigns*. Denver, CO. Rocky Mountain Railroad Club. (Special printing of an article which originally appeared in the *1970 Westerners Brand Book*). 1972. Softcover. Complimentary copies for Club members who could purchase additional copies for $2.50.

Thode, Jackson C. *A Century of Passenger Trains...And Then Some*. Denver, CO. Rocky Mountain Railroad Club (Pioneer Printing). 2001. Pre-publication price $34.95. Regular price $39.95.

## Pamphlets

Boyles, Berlyn (Billy). *Denver, Longmont and Northwestern*. Denver, CO. Rocky Mountain Railroad Club. 1952. Softcover.

Cafky, Morris. *Steam Tramways of Denver*. Denver, CO. Rocky Mountain Railroad Club. June 1950. Softcover.

Ridgway, Arthur. *The Case of Train No. 3*. Denver, CO. Rocky Mountain Railroad Club. 1957. Cost $2.00.

Rocky Mountain Railroad Club. *Steam Tramways of Denver (1950), The Colorado Eastern Railroad (1951), and Denver, Longmont and Northwestern (1952, revised 1982)*. Denver, CO. Trowbridge Press reprinted these three titles as one volume. 1983. Softcover.

Rocky Mountain Railroad Club. *Denver & Rio Grande Railway, Timetable No. 19, July 23, 1882*. Reproduced by the Club in 1963.

Ryland, Charles. *The Colorado Eastern Railroad*. Denver, CO. Rocky Mountain Railroad Club. June 1951. Softcover.

Williams, Lester. *Disaster in Fountain, 1888*. Denver, CO. Rocky Mountain Railroad Club. Reprinted in 1968. Softcover.

## Maps

*Hotchkiss' Historical Railroad Map of Colorado 1913*. Hotchkiss, Inc. November 1963. The map sold for $4.74 flat and $5.00 folded.

A set of five maps pertaining to the Colorado Midland was made available to members separately in 1970. These maps were over-runs intentionally printed with the Morris Cafky book, *Colorado Midland*. Cost was $1.25 per set.

## Miscellaneous

All the maps and colored prints that were in the two Denver, South Park and Pacific books, as well as the *Colorado Midland* and *Rails Around Gold Hill* were available separately or in sets.

In addition to maps, Hotchkiss also provided the Club stationary, tickets, handouts, membership cards and other printed pieces over many years of professional relationship with the Club.

Special Annual Banquet menu for 25th Anniversary – 1963. Free to attendees.

Special commemorative stamped envelope on the 15th annual Memorial Day narrow gauge excursion – May 1966.

Special 8x10 glossy print ($1.00) and postcards ($0.10) of Club member Tom Gray's black and white rendering of the Club's locomotive 20. Printed in 1966.

The Club provided plastic wallet calendars over the years. The opposite side used a photograph taken by R. H. Kindig. The first one appeared in 1958 showing Club's engine 20 at Ridgway on the 1947 excursion;1959, C&S engine 9 was shown in 1937; 1960, C&S engine 70 was shown in 1939; 1961, RGS goose 4 was at Lizard Head on the Club's 1946 trip; and in 1966, RGS engine 20 at Durango in 1951 was featured. A similar souvenir item was the 1959 time-table for Alamosa-Silverton excursion, showing D&RGW engine 477 on Cumbres Pass. Many wallet calendars and other charts have been printed over the years. In 2003 a rainbow colored calendar with a mileage conversion table was produced.

Rosters were printed and distributed free for the years 1948 (mimeographed), 1949, 1950, 1951, 1952, 1953-54, 1955, 1956, 1957, 1958, 1959, 1960, 1961, 1962, 1963, 1964, 1965, 1966, 1967, 1968-69, 1972, 1974, 1977-78, 1979-80, 1981-82, 1983-84, 1985-86, 1998 and 2003.

Undated pocket card of *Privately Owned Unit Coal Trains Passing Through Denver, Colorado*. Probably late 1980s.

Embroidered Club patch, July 1981. Sold for $1.00.

Lined windbreaker jackets, with Club logo on the front and a rendition of locomotive 20 on the back, December 1981. Sold for $25.00.

50th Anniversary belt buckle. 1988. Cost was $10.00.

50th Anniversary commemorative plate. 1988. Cost was $24.95.

50th Anniversary calendar. 1988. Cost was $ 6.00.

50th Anniversary commemorative HO scale caboose. 1988. Given free to all attendees of the 50th Anniversary Banquet.

Dust jacket for the *Colorado Midland* by Morris Cafky. 1997. $12.00 plus shipping.

Reprint of the Santa Fe Railroad poster "Chico." 1997. $6.00 plus shipping.

60th Anniversary logo clothing items such as jackets, shirts, and baseball caps. 1998. Prices were $11.95 for baseball caps and $24.95 for polo shirts. Jackets were priced according to size.

60th Anniversary logo coffee cups. 1998. $4.00.

60th Anniversary HO commemorative boxcars. 1998. Kits were $13.95 and assembled cars were $22.95.

Special Annual Banquet menu for 60th Anniversary. 1998. Original from Colorado Railroad Museum.

Reprint of the *Denver Union Terminal Railway Timetable No. 107*, February 20, 1938. 1998.

Centennial celebration pamphlet *Engine No. 20; 1899-1999*. 1999.

Computer mouse pads with a photo of engine 20. 2000 and later. $8.00 each.

During 1962 and 1964, Mr. C. M. "Bud" Edmonds recorded the sounds of the Club's "Narrow Gauge Excursions – Journeys to Yesterday." Bud owned Colorado Springs area radio stations KCMS AM and FM. During a number of these trips, he recorded runs along the line in locations like Alamosa, Antonito, on Cumbres Pass, in and around Durango and Chama and at other points along both the Cumbres and Toltec Railroad and the D&RGW. All his recordings for Volumes I and II of his seven-record set were on Club excursions. In all, Bud produced seven records released by Train Master Records of Manitou Springs. The seven volumes set sold for $25.00. Individual volumes sold for $5.00 postpaid. Volume VI contained some "salty" recollections recorded in the cab of locomotive 483 on the Cumbres and Toltec Scenic Railroad.

## Movies

In cooperation with Sunday River Productions, the Club made available three different Super 8mm reels of Otto Perry films, 200-foot reels, ranging in price from $44.20 to $51.00. April 1982.

## Videos

"3967 Returns," The Club's 40th Anniversary excursion. Mark I Videos. 1993. $24.95.

"Around the Narrow Gauge Circle." Machines of Iron. 2003. VHS and DVD. $24.95.

"A Trip Around the Narrow Gauge Circle." Machines of Iron. 1999. VHS. $15.00.

"Colorado & Southern Narrow Gauge." Machines of Iron. 2003. VHS and DVD. $24.95.

"Gunnison Rio Grande Narrow Gauge." Machines of Iron. 2001. VHS. $24.95.

"Otto Perry's First Generation Diesels." Machines of Iron. 2001. VHS. $24.95.

"Otto Perry's Moffat Route." Machines of Iron. VHS. 2001. $24.95.

"Otto Perry's Rio Grande Southern." Sunday River Productions. VHS. 1988. $55.96.

"Otto Perry's Rio Grande Articulateds Parts I and II" Sunday River Productions. VHS. 1997. $34.00.

"Otto Perry's San Juan Express." Machines of Iron. VHS and DVD. 2003. $24.95.

"Otto Perry's Santa Fe." Machines of Iron. VHS. 2000. $24.95.

"Rio Grande of the Rockies." Irv August. WB Videos. Re-released in 2001. VHS. $39.95.

"Rio Grande Southern." Sunday River Productions. VHS. $29.95.

"Silver Rails and Golden Memories." WB Videos. 1988. VHS. Originally $54.95, but in 2001 priced at $39.95.

"Steam Over Sherman." Irv August films. WB Videos. VHS. Re-released in 2001. $39.95.

"The Fifties Express." Irv August films. WB Videos. 1988. VHS. 52 minutes. $39.95. Re-released in 2001.

"The Henderson Mine." Machines of Iron. 2001. VHS. $24.95. Members price, $18.00.

"The Uintah Railway." Machines of Iron. 2000. VHS. $20.00.

"Virginia & Truckee – Final Years." WB Videos. Revised and re-released in 2001. VHS. $29.95.

## Rocky Mountain Railroad Historical Foundation Items

A 16" x 20" color print of car 25 by Joe Priselac was sold to raise funds for the restoration of car 25. 1990. Cost was $10.00.

Computer mouse pads with a photo of car 25. 1998 and later. $7.00.

T-shirts featuring car 25. 1998 and later. $14.00.

Baseball cap with car 25. 1998 and later. $14.00.

Placemats, color photo of car 25. 1998 and later. Set of four, $14.98.

Laminated color 2002 calendar with car 25. $5.00.

# Equipment

## Rio Grande Southern Railroad Locomotive 20

### General History and Specifications

Built by Schenectady Locomotive Works, N.Y. in 1899.
Builders Plate Number 5007
Engine Class T-19, Operating Track Gauge 3 ft. "Narrow Gauge,"
Original Cost $26,000.
Wheel Configuration 4-6-0, "Ten-Wheeler."
Driver Wheel Size 42 inches, Pilot Wheel Size 24 inches,
Weight on Engine 85,000 lbs., Tractive Effort 18,650 lbs.,
Boiler Pressure 180 psi.,
Engine Height 12 ft. 2 inches.
Tender Coal Capacity 7 tons,
Tender Water Capacity 3,200 gal.,
Tender Wheel Size 26 inches,
Engine and Tender Length 49 ft. 1 inch.

Locomotive 20 operated on Florence and Cripple Creek Railroad, 1899 – 1912, on the Denver and Rio Grande Railroad, 1912 – 1916 and lastly on Rio Grande Southern Railroad, 1916 – 1951. It was placed on static display at the Narrow Gauge Motel, Alamosa County, 1952 – 1958 and was moved to Colorado Railroad Museum, Jefferson County, where it has been on display since 1958.

Engine 20 is a rare surviving example of a narrow gauge, ten-wheeler steam locomotive. It is an important example of nineteenth century engineering and the only remaining old Schenectady Locomotive Works steam engine in Colorado. Only three narrow gauge 4-6-0 engines exist in the state. They are D&RGW engine 168 displayed in Colorado Springs, D&RGW locomotive 169 on display in Alamosa, and Rio Grande Southern engine 20, the largest and most powerful, on display in Golden. It has served Colorado residents and visitors to this state for over 100 years, first hauling

passengers and freight in the central front range, then in the southwest mountains during the historic development and decline of gold and silver mining. It operated on three important railroads, each of which are no longer in existence, but which remain a significant part of Colorado's growth and prosperity. Engine 20, on display for 6 years in Alamosa County and now for 44 years in Jefferson County, remains available for public education and enjoyment due to the dedication, contributions and efforts of railroad enthusiasts from Colorado, all other states and many other nations. RGS 20 is owned and maintained by the Rocky Mountain Railroad Club and displayed at the Colorado Railroad Museum in recognition of Colorado's history and to benefit current and future generations of our citizens.

Engine 20, ordered in 1899 by the Florence and Cripple Creek

September 5, 1949 – Rio Grande Southern locomotive 20 painted and dressed up for its role as the "Emma Sweeny" in the movie, "A Ticket to Tomahawk."
**DEAN PHOTO - J. L. EHERNBERGER COLLECTION**

July 12, 1958 – Former RGS engine 20, lettered as "Portland" is seen in the C&S Rice yards with ex-D&RGW locomotives 318 and 346. **R. H. KINDIG PHOTO**

Railroad, ran between its two named towns during the Cripple Creek mining boom. The F&CC was the first railroad in the district (1894), and gathered most of the mining and passenger traffic until the Midland Terminal Railroad arrived from the north in 1895. From then, business was divided among the two roads and later others. The cheap transportation offered by the railroads, compared to freighting by animals, was one of the driving elements for prosperity of the Cripple Creek District. The F&CC was doing so well that in an effort to eliminate leased Denver and Rio Grande engines it purchased engines in 1896 and in 1899 when locomotive No. 20

July 1958 – Its boiler painted green, ex-RGS locomotive 20 is unloaded at the Colorado Railroad Museum. **E. J. HALEY PHOTO**

and six others were ordered from Schenectady Locomotive Works. These Ten-Wheelers had good horsepower and tractive effort to work the long sustained grades in Phantom Canyon, which averaged 2%, but sometimes reached stretches of 4%. Soon a third railroad was constructed from the east, the Colorado Springs and Cripple Creek District Railroad. By 1904 it was clear that there was not enough business in the district for three roads. The F&CC remained in service following the banks of Eight Mile Creek until July, 1912 when a flash flood with a thirty foot wall of water roared down Phantom Canyon and washed away most of the roadbed.

The Florence and Cripple Creek Railroad was abandoned and the equipment dispersed with engine 20 and others going to the Denver and Rio Grande. The former F&CC locomotives 20, 22 and 25 were overhauled at the D&RG shops in Alamosa. Number 20 ran from Alamosa to Antonito over Cumbres Pass to Chama and then on to Durango — the San Juan Extension — where on March 10, 1916, it was delivered to the Rio Grande Southern. When engine 20 went on RGS, the rails were the original light 30-pound rail laid when the road was constructed in 1890 and 1891. The Cripple Creek boom was tied to gold and heavy rail was put down early whereas the San Juan boom was tied to silver which value had crashed in 1893 when federal price supports were removed, so there was little money for laying heavy rail. Early on, heavy engine 20 would derail, tear up track and cause delays in passenger and freight service. Eventually money was found to add the heavier rail and from then on, the sturdy Ten-Wheeler gave reliable, long service.

The Rio Grande Southern ran from Durango west to

Dolores, then northeast over Lizard Head Pass down to Ophir, along the San Miguel River to Placerville, then east up over Dallas Divide to Ridgway, with a principal branch from Vance Junction north of Ophir uphill east to Telluride. The Rio Grande Southern was in the hands of the Denver and Rio Grande for 40 years as it was bankrupt. When the D&RGW also went into bankruptcy in 1929 the little RGS engine was cast adrift. Yet it continued to serve the area through the 1930's, World War II and the 1940's, economically assisted by the locally mined fissionable material used by the Manhattan Project. Engine 20 had adjusted to the RGS and ran faithfully except for a period during the summer of 1943 when it and another doubleheaded engine derailed and rolled over just west of Durango. During its last years of operation, locomotive 20 operated one Rocky Mountain Railroad Club summer excursion. Finally in 1951 the Rio Grande Southern Railroad was abandoned and by the end of 1952 rails and ties had been removed.

The Rocky Mountain Railroad Club bought engine 20 and business car "Rico" at a court sale in 1952. The locomotive then went to the Narrow Gauge Motel south of Alamosa. In 1958 RGS engine 20 was relocated to the new Colorado Railroad Museum, Jefferson County, founded by Bob Richardson and Cornelius Hauck. Since then, it has been a prominent display, often used in radio and TV promotions, well photographed and discussed by rail fans and enjoyed by thousands of visitors. During the autumn of 1998 it was illuminated for a night photo shoot. During April, 1999 the Rocky Mountain Railroad Club had a special 100-year anniversary commemoration party for the engine.

*Information on locomotive 20 provided by Bob Tully.*

# Denver and Rio Grande Western Caboose 0578

The Denver & Rio Grande Railroad Western Caboose 0578 entered service on the D&RG (later D&RGW) narrow gauge system in 1886. It was probably used on all portions of the narrow gauge system during its lifetime, but during its final years of service (1946 to 1951) it generally operated in the Salida/Gunnison/Montrose area.

The Rocky Mountain Railroad Club purchased the caboose in Salida from the D&RGW on November 26, 1951. It remained on railroad property until January, 1953 when it was moved ultimately to the Colorado Railroad Museum in August, 1958.

Caboose 0578 was built in a D&RG shop. It was one of 124 narrow gauge cabooses the D&RG owned. Based on a number of parameters (length, number of wheels, etc) these 124 cabooses have been divided into five separate classes. In this scheme, Caboose 0578 is a Class 2 caboose. Only 16 were built, all between 1885 and 1890. Caboose 0578 was built in June, 1886, at a cost of $685.

Of these 16 Class 2 cabooses, only nine still exist. Eight of these are in various states of repair and are on static display; seven in Colorado and one in Utah. Only caboose 0578 and 0579 are being restored and returned to the condition they were in when they were retired from the D&RGW in 1951.

When cabooses of the same class were initially built, they were all alike. But from that point on they were modified over time to increase their strength, convenience, or utility; to comply with new rules and regulations of the Interstate Commerce Commission (ICC), or simply to meet the "whim of their crews" for whom they were a home away from home.

Caboose 0578 has a 17-foot long body and two 4-wheel trucks. It is of conventional rectangular design, with a cupola in the center. A major difference between this caboose (and all Class 2 cabooses) and previous cabooses were that they were initially built with automatic air brakes. Comparable brakes were included in new freight cars and retrofitted on old ones in order to increase the safety of train operation.

Using old railroad records and photographs of caboose 0578 and the other 15 Class 2 cabooses, it is possible to identify some of the changes that took place over their lifetime.

In 1903, and again in 1911, the ICC mandated safety appli-

February 22, 1953 – Ed Haley stands beside D&RGW narrow-gauge caboose 0578 while it was temporarily stored at the Colorado School of Mines. **R. H. KINDIG PHOTO**

ances on all rail cars used in interstate commerce (the D&RG narrow gauge line crossed the Colorado/New Mexico border many times between Alamosa, Colorado, and Chama, New Mexico). These included steps on both ends of the platforms at the ends of the caboose, grab irons on the sides, and ladders to the roof at the ends of the caboose.

The 1886 erection plans for Class 2 cabooses showed three windows on each side of the caboose. However, the center windows were slowly replaced with wood panels since brakemen frequently kicked them out getting up and down from the cupola. When stoves were added to cabooses beginning in the 1880s, the windows behind the stoves were removed. This resulted in the final configuration, which caboose 0578 now has, of two windows on one side and one on the other.

There were small boxes atop the cupola roofs to house signal lanterns from about 1885 (before 0578 was built) until the early 1940s. A lantern could be placed there and used for certain night time signals such as "train in clear on siding," etc. The earliest known existing photo of caboose 0578, taken in 1937, shows the box on the cupola roof. But in a subsequent 1946 photo, the box is missing.

The original paint color scheme for cabooses was Caboose Red for the outside and Prince's Mineral Brown for the inside. The exposed ironwork was black. After about 1918 the outside was painted Boxcar Red with a pea green interior. Grab irons were painted aluminum, or white if aluminum was not available.

Initially cabooses on the D&RG were numbered 1 and up, refrigerator cars 100 and up, gondolas 300 and up, etc. But because of the growth of the railroad a revised numbering system was introduced in 1887. Cabooses in this new system were in a number block beginning with 0500. In the old numbering system caboose 0578 was number 94. When the D&RG was founded, the original lettering on the letter board was a block serif "DENVER & RIO GRANDE". From 1870 to at least 1887, the word "CABOOSE" in 6-inch Bold Roman was present in an arc above the caboose number, centered under the cupola. In 1923 the letter board was changed to "DENVER & RIO GRANDE WESTERN," reflecting a change in the corporate name of the railroad.

Beginning in 1927, a circular herald "D.&R.G.W.R.R. SCENIC LINE - ROYAL GORGE ROUTE" was added above the caboose number and centered under the cupola. In 1936, with the opening of the Moffat Tunnel, the Dotsero Cutoff, and the establishment of the new main line west of Denver, the herald was changed to "RIO GRANDE SCENIC LINE OF THE WORLD - ROYAL GORGE/MOFFAT TUN-

NEL". Caboose 0578 apparently never carried that herald. In 1939, the 'flying' "RIO GRANDE" herald was adopted as the result of a contest. This was the herald caboose 0578 carried when retired in Salida in 1951.

Since caboose 0578 arrived at the Colorado Railroad Museum in 1958, the Club has performed general maintenance to keep the caboose, which is stored outdoors, in good condition. The Club is currently completing a major restoration of the caboose which includes painting, replacing wooden parts that have rotted, repairing the roof, etc. The caboose is operational and can be used on occasional "steam ups" at the Colorado Railroad Museum.

*Frend John Miner provided the text for the description of caboose 0578. This information was used to support the application to the Colorado Historical Society for placing this caboose on the National Register of Historic Places.*

## Rio Grande Southern Business Car 021, "Rico"

In the 1890s, large portions of the Denver and Rio Grande were being converted to standard gauge. Therefore, there was a large amount of surplus narrow gauge equipment available to the Rio Grande Southern. The road ordered over 900 cars from the Denver & Rio Grande and the Rio Grande Western. In 1882, the D&RG built eight mail cars, numbered 14 to 21. In 1885, these cars were renumbered 1 through 8, and postal car 4 became the "Rico." Some sources incorrectly identify the car as being built by

Billmeyer & Small in 1880, at a cost of $1,500 plus an additional $141 for air brake fittings. This firm, located in York, Pennsylvania, built freight and passenger railroad cars for many railroads.

Postal car 4 was rebuilt in May, 1888 as excursion car 569. It was sold to the Rio Grande Southern on August 23, 1890 for $800, where it was converted to a construction dining car numbered C3. This car then became business car 21 named the

"Rico" in 1892. This Rico should not be confused with the D&RG Pullman car "Cairo" which was renamed "Rico" after extensive repairs following a derailment May 19, 1887.

On January 8, 1893, William Henry Jackson took a trip on the Rio Grande Southern to make a number of photographs of the line. This special train was initially powered by 4-4-0 locomotive 36, which subsequently broke down and was replaced by engine 9, a 2-8-0. Two business cars, the "San

May 1979 – Club members have spent many hours painting, restoring and protecting the "Rico" at the Colorado Railroad Museum. **DARRELL ARNDT PHOTO**

Juan" and the "Rico" comprised the rest of the train. A dark room was outfitted on the "Rico" so Jackson could develop his glass plates during the trip. The photographs that Jackson took on this trip have become synonymous with the Rio Grande Southern, especially the view of the locomotive 9 and the "Rico" at Lizard Head Pass. In 1895, Jackson made another trip on the RGS, this time in the "Rico" pulled by locomotive 1 and accompanied by Denver & Rio Grande car "K."

In another special trip on June 27, 1898, the "Rico" and the "San Juan" served as accommodations for Mrs. E. G. Stoiber (owner of the Silver Lake Mine & Mill north of Silverton), E. T. Jeffery (President of the D&RG), Otto Mears, William Henry Jackson and William Jennings Bryan as they traveled from Durango to Ridgway.

During the summer of 1909, RGS Superintendent Clemente Wolfinger was making his monthly trip using both the "Rico" and D&RG pay car "F." Wolfinger and the pay clerk were on board the "Rico" when it derailed, severely damaging the "Rico." The car was sent to Alamosa for repairs and was again involved in a wreck enroute to the shops. Wolfinger decided as part of the rebuild to rename the car the "Montezuma." In 1917, the car's name was changed again and simply became "Outfit Car B-21." In 1923, the car was again rebuilt and lowered with 26" diameter wheels. In 1933

it was assigned to work service as "021."

During the liquidation of the RGS in 1951, an appraisal of the line's rolling stock indicated a value of $200 for Outfit car 021, which was located at Ridgway. The Club purchased this car on June 23, 1952, for $400 at the same time as the purchase of RGS engine 20. In December, 1952, the car, now known again as the "Rico," was transported to Golden for temporary storage at the Colorado School of Mines. The "Rico" was later moved to the Colorado Railroad Museum in 1958 and was included in the lease agreement with Iron Horse Development Corporation on June 9, 1959.

Over the years, countless volunteers have worked on the preservation of this 36-foot long wooden car. As a business car, it seated eight persons and could also sleep eight people in the four berths. The interior was done in cherry and a Baker heater provided heating. Oil lamps provided lighting and the upholstery was done in crimson plush. The original exterior paint was Tuscan Red until September 1918 when it was repainted Pullman Green. When it went into non-revenue service in 1933, it was painted Freight Car Red.

*Text description of the "Rico" provided by Bob Tully.*

# Ft. Collins Municipal Railway Car 22

Early trolley cars generally rode on a single truck but as the cars grew larger, double-trucked cars appeared. Many large companies kept two sets of cars, open cars for the summer and closed cars for the winter. Soon, a "convertible" car was created where the side panels of the cars could be removed for use as an open car or reinstalled for use as a closed car. An evolution of this design was the "semi-convertible" car where the upper portion of the side panels could be slid out of the way, storing a portion of the panel above or below, while leaving the lower

May 30, 1951 – Ft. Collins Municipal Railway car 22 in service one month to the day before its last run in its namesake city. R. H. KINDIG PHOTO

portion in place. Semi-convertible cars also made boarding and leaving the car easier, which reduced injuries from falls and reduced the number of persons that evaded paying fares.

Eventually, open cars disappeared and closed cars and semi-convertibles became the most common type of car. In most cases these cars all required the use of a two-man crew, the motorman and the conductor. Just prior to the First World War, competition from automobiles, busses, and railroads

forced trolley companies to make efforts to cut costs. Most significant of these was the introduction of the Birney "Safety Car", a lightweight, single truck car that could be operated by one man, serving as both motorman and conductor. The Birney car was very popular, in cities both small and large. Small cities used Birney cars because they were economical for a system not needing large cars.

The original four Ft. Collins Municipal Railway Birneys,

numbered 20-23, cost the city about $6500. They arrived new, from the St. Louis Car Co. in May 1919. The first car to arrive, 21, was immediately used to establish a schedule on the 9-mile system that was purchased the previous year from the Denver & Interurban, which built the original Ft. Collins lines in 1907. The city operated Woeber double-truck cars until 1918. Then in January 1919, the city bought the lines, minus the cars. An additional Birney (24) was purchased from the National Car Co. for $6500. Later in the 1930s, four additional used Birneys were acquired, two from Cheyenne and two from Richmond, VA. One of the used cars was never placed into service. The others became second 24, 25 and 26.

The Club operated an excursion on the Ft. Collins Municipal Railway system on Memorial Day weekend, May 30, 1951. This was in conjunction with the Club's trip on the Colorado & Southern Railroad. Cars number 20, 21 and 25 were operated. On June 30, 1951, car 22 made its last run. This trip was reportedly the last single-truck Birney to run in regular service in the USA as well as being the last streetcar to operate in Colorado. An excellent history of the Ft. Collins Birneys is found in *Colorado Rail Annual No. 17*, published by the Colorado Railroad Museum.

The Southern California division of the Electric Railroader's Association (SCERA) in Los Angeles purchased four of the Birneys in a move to preserve them and sell them for some profit. One of the Birneys was sold to the Midwest Chapter of the NRHS, one to the Stizel family in Denver (car 26) and one to Harold Warp's Pioneer Village in Minden, NE. After completing their brokerage of the Birneys, the SCERA netted only $80 total profit on the sale of the four cars.

The Club purchased car 22 from the SCERA in 1953 for $115, which was paid for in three installments. The car was moved from Ft. Collins to Denver at a cost of $133.90 and stored at the Golden waterworks west of town until it was moved to the Colorado Railroad Museum in 1958. In 1963, members constructed approximately 600 feet of track at the Museum under electric wires and poles to operate the Birney. The cost of the construction of this track was approximately $2,400 and the work was overseen by the Club's Equipment Committee. Some of the work was performed by trained D&RGW laborers hired by the Club.

In 1994, The Club leased the Birney to the Pikes Peak Historic Street Railway Foundation (PPHSRF). This fifteen-year lease included giving the PPHSRF the rights to restore the car and

November 6, 1964 – Former Ft. Collins Municipal Railway car 22 on display at the Colorado Railroad Museum. **R. H. KINDIG PHOTO**

operate it in the future on their lines in Colorado Springs. The car was taken to Colorado Springs on November 23, 1994.

Since that date, volunteers of the Colorado Springs and Interurban Railway, as they have become known, have spent countless hours rebuilding the car from the trucks up. The car was disassembled in 1995 and 1996. Serious restoration activities began in 1999, with grants of funds from the International Brotherhood of Electrical Workers Local 113 and others, which permitted rebuilding of the original 600-volt DC motors. The Uhrich Locomotive Works in Strasburg, Colorado has repaired the wheels and included new bearings, repaired hairline cracks in the wheels, reground the flanges and turned the wheels and axles. Steel frame members of the original body have been cleaned, repaired or replaced.

In 2000, the PPHRSF volunteers reassembled the truck (motors, wheels and suspension system). The car ends were reframed with new hardwood posts and beams and the original slat roof removed to allow access to the roof rib sections. The car steel body was reassembled, including new and refurbished steel floor channels and angles. Work was planned to install the compressed air system. In 2003, the PPHRSF approached the Club will proposals to extend the lease to permit that organization some certainty in their planned restoration and operating activities. As of the close of the year, the discussions were still underway.

*A concise history of the Birney cars operated in Ft. Collins is found in the pamphlet "Trolley Cars of Ft. Collins," by E. S. Peyton, R. A. Mooreman and K. Jessen available from the Ft. Collins Municipal Railway Society, Inc.*

## Former Public Service Company of Colorado Motor Car

Obtained through the efforts of Club member Eldon "Olie" Larsen, this motor car was unknown for many years, until May 1993 when it was identified as Club equipment. The

Fairmont motor car is a model M-9-G built in the late 1940s. Club member Gus Mocilac has spent many hours restoring it to operating condition.

# Los Angeles Railway PCC Car 3101

With the growing popularity of the automobile, and improvements to roads and highways across the nation, American trolley lines were in steep decline. As losses mounted, operating companies reduced maintenance on cars and lines themselves. Trolleys became less reliable and street systems uncomfortable to ride on. As early as 1921, the American Electric Railway Engineering Association began urging the idea of a standardized car. In 1929, the Electric Railways Presidents' Conference Committee (PCC) developed a standard design. In 1932, the first PCC was tested and in 1934, the type B PCC was assembled using an entirely new design car body from Pullman Co. The St. Louis Car Company finished the development work and started production of the PCC car. The new streamlined design, with fast starting and stopping, improved braking, and quiet, smooth riding, made the PCC car very popular with the riding public. Production peaked in 1946, with 800 cars being manufactured, and continued until 1951. By then almost 5000 had been produced in the U.S. and Canada.

The Los Angeles Railway ordered 30 cars from the St. Louis Car Company on May 8, 1942. The cars were numbered 3096 through 3125 and were the only PCC cars built during 1943. The cars operated on 42-inch gauge track (as did the streetcars in Denver). In 1945, Los Angeles Transit Lines (a National City Lines property) took over operation. The PCC cars were repainted from a two-tone yellow scheme to the "fruit salad" scheme of yellow and green, with white roofs. This is the color of the Club's car. By 1963, the Los Angeles Metropolitan Transit Authority abandoned the remaining streetcar lines in Los Angeles. Most of the cars went to Cairo Egypt with a few going to Chile. Car 3101 was sold to the Gold Camp Railway and Museum in Cripple Creek. A sister car, 3100, is on display at the Orange Empire Railway Museum in Perris, CA.

The Club acquired car 3101 in June, 1969, and paid only $200 for it. In October of that year, the Club moved the car at a cost

August 22, 1964 – Gold Camp Railway car .01 (formerly Los Angeles Railway car 3101) seen at Cripple Creek (top) and at the Colorado Railroad Museum (lower) in an undated photo. **R. H. KINDIG PHOTOS**

of $1,032.75 to the Colorado Railroad Museum. Most of the Club's work related to this car was cosmetic. In 1994, the Club entered into an agreement loaning the PCC car to the Pikes Peak Historical Street Railway Foundation (PPHSRF) in Colorado Springs. The PPHSRF has added this car to their collection of PCC cars in hopes of street operations in the city in the future.

*Most of this information was provided courtesy of Charles Brown and the Electric Railway Historical Association of Southern California (ERHA-SC). The book "Yellow Cars of LA," edited by ERHA-CA member Jim Walker, has more detail on the PCC cars from Los Angeles, including photos of 3101 in service.*

# Former Colorado & Southern Box Car

The Club's tool car was donated by Colorado & Southern RR in 1959, and moved, less trucks, brake gear and couplers, to the Colorado Railroad Museum by Duffy Moving and Storage Co. for $116.25 in July, 1959. The car is a Colorado and Southern standard gauge, old time wood sided, steel ends and Murphy roof boxcar. It was probably a maintenance of way unit before converted to an oil storage trackside car with interior steel lining, which sat near the C&S roundhouse. It was painted red and stenciled with the old round C&S black and white emblem before being moved. A new wood floor was installed and it was wired for lights and wall plugs.

There are six 23" by 33" windows, one on each end and two on each side, about 6 ft. from the ends. The entrance is by a 36" door on the south side. Inside the car, the Club has built 15 ft. 10 inch long shelves on each side west of the door. The north shelves are 32" deep and the south shelves are 27" deep, each 6-foot high with 3 shelves. The east side has a bench across the full width as well as along the north wall for over 16 feet. These are

May 1979 – It is break time for Club members resting in front of the former C&S tool car on a weekend workday at the Colorado Railroad Museum.
**DARRELL ARNDT PHOTO**

June 26, 1959 – Crews begin the move of the donated C&S boxcar to the Colorado Railroad Museum where the Club would store equipment, tools and supplies. **IRV AUGUST PHOTO**

35" deep, 37" high and fitted with drawers and shelves. This is an excellent tool and storage unit for the Club, but as with all old equipment, it needs regular maintenance, now a bit over due. We have not found any original number or markings. It was probably a 13000 or 14000 series car. Photographs of similar cars sitting by the C&S roundhouse have been located but we have no history of the Club's car.

## Live Steam Locomotive 999

In November, 1963, the Club acquired 55 year-old nine-inch gauge 4-4-0-steam locomotive 999 from Mrs. George Lindsay. Locomotive 999 and its tender, a 9-inch gauge 4-4-0 engine, were built by George W. Lindsay while training at Manual High School in 1907. It was supposedly patterned after the famous New York Central engine with the same number. George ran his locomotive at Denver's Manhattan Beach at Sloans Lake until 1910. Manhattan Beach opened in 1891 and became an immediate success, but it rapidly deteriorated after the fire of December 27, 1908. The park's main attraction was a 3,000 seat castle-like theater, which was destroyed in the fire. Number 999 survived the fire at that amusement park in 1908. The park reopened in 1909 as Luna Park, but it was not the same as its predecessor and soon failed.

More than fifty years after the locomotive stopped running at the park, Susan Lindsay, George's widow, donated it to the Rocky Mountain Railroad Club. It was in considerable disrepair and in numerous parts and pieces. Club members restored the engine and tender. It was placed on display at the Colorado Railroad Museum, along with seven wooden patterns that Mr. Lindsay used for casting truck pedestals, journal boxes, wheels and other components.

The locomotive is primarily cast iron, with a sheet metal jacket and all wood cab and pilot. The steam and sand domes, bell and rear supports to the cab are cast brass. Cylinder ends, trim and some piping are made of copper. The frame is made of cast parts, bar stock and heavy sheet steel. The four leading wheels, 3 1/2 inch diameter, are solid cast while the four drivers, 8 1/2 inch diameter, are spoked wheels. There is no number plate on the center front of the smoke box and it does not have a headlight, although there are places to fasten both, and both are shown in early photographs.

The entire engine as well as the tender is black with the smoke box, all wheel tires and several operating water valve wheels painted silver. The bell, both domes and several trim strips are polished brass.

The cylinders are 3 3/8 inches in diameter by 5 1/4 inches long. The boiler and smoke box are both 9 1/2 inches in diameter. The locomotive is 60 1/2 inches long with a maximum width of 15 1/2 inches at the cab roof. The combined engine and tender is 89 inches long. The height from the top of the steam done (its highest point) to the top of the rails is 23 5/8 inches. The tender frame is made of wood a with shaped steel water tank and coal bin. The tender's eight wheels are the same size and shape as the leading wheels on the locomotive. On the rear of the tender is a small link and pin coupler.

When the Club accepted the gift of this locomotive Mrs. Lindsay stipulated that should the Club dissolve, the locomotive would be given to an historical society or a museum. It was her wish that it would never be destroyed. By unanimous action of the Board of Directors on January 31, 1964, Mrs. Lindsay's stipulation was accepted and the locomotive preserved, as she desired.

This locomotive was on display at the Colorado Railroad Museum but in March, 2002, it was moved from the museum to the City of Edgewater Historical Museum. The Club and city officials arranged for a 10-year loan for this locomotive to be displayed on the second floor of City Hall.

May 2002 – The Club's live steam locomotive 999 in its display case at the Colorado Railroad Museum before its relocation to Edgewater. **CONNIE FOX PHOTO**

*Description of live steam locomotive 999 provided by Bob Tully.*

## Live Steam Locomotive 210

On April 17, 1965, the Club received a 9-inch gauge 4-4-0 live steam locomotive from Mrs. Joan Humphrey, owner of this rather famous machine and daughter of A. W. Ainsworth, a Charter Member of the Club. This locomotive was lettered for the Denver, Northwestern & Pacific and numbered 210. It operated at Elitch Gardens from 1893 to approximately 1935. The locomotive is now displayed at the Colorado Railroad Museum. It should be noted that that the 4-4-0 locomotives of the Denver, Northwestern and Pacific were actually numbered 390 and 391. Locomotive 210 would have been, in real life, a 2-6-6-0 mallet.

The engine carries the number 210 on the front plate and is a nine-inch gauge, coal burning, live steamer which was built for service at Elitch's Zoological Gardens in north Denver. Frank H. Root of Denver installed the miniature railroad, which had about a mile of 8 pound rail, at Elitch's in 1893, one year after the Gardens were opened by Mary and John Elitch. Mr. Root owned and operated this small railroad until his death in 1935. He constructed and worked on locomotives and rolling stock in a small shop on West 38th Avenue next to the Denver Tramway's West End Car House across the avenue from Elitch's. In addition to our Denver Northwestern and Pacific No. 210, he built and operated No. 1201, another 4-4-0. He also operated a 4-6-0, numbered 1600 which was lettered Denver and Rio Grande Western. A third, gasoline powered locomotive (No. 348) that looked like a steam engine was maintained for standby service on his railroad.

It is believed that engine 210 was built before 1895 and was operated until 1935. We have photos showing it running at Elitch's between 1902 and 1906 and during 1928 when it was photographed double heading with No. 1600. This 4-4-0, as well as

No. 1601, pulled up to eight cars with no sign of being overloaded. The passenger cars were 42 inches long, 14 inches wide and designed to carry three or four children or two adults. Following Frank Root's death his nephew inherited the railroad which was sold to Virgil C. Hardy on April 21, 1936. The tracks at Elitch's were taken up shortly thereafter. Number 210 was stored for many years at the shops of Wm. Ainsworth and Sons, Inc. It was cleaned and refurbished at the Club's tool car at the Colorado Railroad Museum before being put on display.

The locomotive is primarily of well-riveted and welded cast iron and steel. It has a very nicely shaped sheet steel boiler jacket. The entire pilot is made of brass and copper. The bell and top cap of the straight smokestack are bronze. There are four bands of polished silver steel around the boiler jacket as well as some strips of the same material around the fancy steam and sand domes. The four leading wheels are solid and 2 7/8 inch diameter, while the four drivers are spoked and measure 8 1/4 inch in diameter. It is missing the builder's plates once located on each side of the smoke box. There are small holes where the plates, approximately 1 1/4 inch high and 3 inches long, were present as shown by marks in the paint.

The engine and tender are painted black. The cab roof, window trim, rails around the coalbunker and covers of two toolboxes on the tender are painted red. The bell is polished bronze or brass. Both the bands on the domes and the boiler jacket bands are polished steel. The cylinders are 3-inch diameter and 4 inches long. The smoke box is 8 inches in diameter while the boiler is 9 1/2 inches in diameter. The locomotive alone is 54 inches long. The combined engine and tender measure 7 foot 1 inch in length. The height to the top of the steam dome, which is slightly higher than the smokestack, is 23 inches from the top of the rails. The tender, which measures 31 inches over the wood frame, is made of shaped light steel. It sits on two four-wheel trucks, which have 3 3/4-inch diameter wheels. The tender and engine are both fitted with a link and pin type coupler.

This locomotive is on display in the basement of the Colorado Railroad Museum in Golden. It is on its own aluminum track, but shown in one closed-in display along with the Club's five inch gauge steam engine, Colorado and Southern engine 4, and the 1 1/2 inch scale model of Central Pacific 173 owned by the Museum.

*Description of steam locomotive 999 provided by Bob Tully.*

## Live Steam Locomotive 4

The Club acquired a five-inch gauge 2-6-0 live model narrow gauge Colorado & Southern steam locomotive from the widow of Bill Soper in July, 1969. The model is on display at the Colorado Railroad Museum.

Locomotive 4 and its tender were built by Bill Soper in his home machine shop. All parts were carefully manufactured and assembled commencing in 1960 and completed 3 years later. He operated his engine on a circle of track in his back yard. This extremely well detailed live steam engine was modeled after Colorado and Southern narrow gauge engine 4, which was Bill's favorite when he worked as a crane and wrecker operator on the South Park line as a young man. He left the railroad in 1924.

The prototype for this 2-6-0 passenger locomotive was built by Cooke Locomotive works of Paterson, New Jersey in 1884 as Denver, South Park and Pacific engine 39. It was renumbered 109 in 1885 and then Denver Leadville and Gunnison 109 in 1889. It was rebuilt and became Colorado and Southern locomotive in 1900. A photo taken as it operated in 1927, showed it with a "bear trap" cinder catcher.

Locomotive 4 is primarily cast iron and steel, welded and bolted together along with well made bar, formed and cut steel plates. The center front numberplate, bell and some operating valves are brass and bronze. Unpainted copper pipe is present in several locations. The two leading wheels are 2 inches in diameter and the six driving wheels are 4 1/2 inches in diameter.

The engine and tender are black. The smoke box, driving rods, wheel tires and journal boxes are painted silver. The numberplate, bell and a couple of valves are polished bronze or brass. The steel cylinders are 2 3/4-inch diameter and 4 1/8 inches long. The smoke box measures 6 inches across whereas the boiler is 7 inches in diameter. The engine is 38 inches long with a maximum width of 12 1/2 inches. The top of the smokestack is 16 3/8 inches from the top of the rails. The combined length of the engine and tender is 4 feet, 10 inches. The tender has a steel frame and the water tank and coal bin body is made of shaped light steel plate. Its 8 wheels are 2 1/2 inches in diameter and mounted on nicely made frames with coil springs. Small, well-constructed knuckle couplers are on the tender and the front of the engine.

This locomotive is on display in the basement show room of the Colorado Railroad Museum in Golden where it has been since it was acquired. After being in its own case for 32 years it is now shown in one display, but on separate aluminum track along with two other small live steam engines.

*This description of live steam locomotive 4 was provided by Bob Tully.*

## Denver & Intermountain Railroad Car 25

The Woeber Car Company of Denver built car 25 in 1910, one of 317 cars built by the company during its years of production. The car entered service on February 11, 1911, for the Denver & Intermountain Railroad Company (D&IM). The car is an interurban type, self-propelled electric passenger car that was used primarily on Route 84 of the D&IM. This 13-mile route connected Denver with Lakewood and Golden. The fifty-two-passenger standard gauge car measures 48' 6" long with a height of 14' 2" and weighs 29 tons. Four 50-hp electric motors power the car.

Car 25 was an early example of commuter rail in the Denver area. Denver's light rail system operation by the Regional Transportation District in the 1990s and into the next century, can identify Route 84 of the D&IM as a commuter line.

Over the years of its operations, many people traveled daily back and forth to Denver and Golden via this route. Students bound for the Colorado School of Mines rode the cars along with soldiers going to and from Camp George West. Governor John C. Vivian commuted between his home in Golden and the state capital on Route 84 during his terms of office from 1943 to 1947. Trains ran daily from 6:00 a.m. until midnight and could reach speeds of 60 miles per hour on track west of Kipling Street. The average trip from Denver to Golden, one way, took forty minutes. The D&IM was part of the Denver Tramway Company after 1910 and the DTC assigned its own equipment to service on Route 84. Besides car 25, four other large cars, numbers 21, 22, 23 and 24 and DTC cars 818 and 819 regularly operated along the D&IM lines, including Route 84.

Shortly after the Denver Tramway Company discontinued passenger operations on the former D&IM lines in June, 1950, the Club made plans to purchase car 25. The transaction was completed on October 12, when the car body (not including motors was purchased for $150. Since electric freight operations continued to Golden until March 16, 1953, the Club was able to operate excursions using car 25 to Golden and Morrison. Local newspapers covered several "Last Runs," but by March, 1953, the overhead electric lines were taken down and the track removed between Lakewood and Golden. In April, the Club purchased the four motors in car 25 for $160.

During 1953, the car was stored at the Denver & Intermountain car barn located at Myrtle Avenue and Zuni Street (2055 Myrtle Avenue). The Club paid for the insurance on the car. In 1956, according to insurance records, the car was located in the yard of the Duvall Davison Lumber Company at 1313 Ford Street, in Golden. By 1958, the car had been moved to the Colorado Railroad Museum and was covered under the agreement with the Iron Horse Development Corporation.

The car was displayed at the Colorado Railroad Museum for many years painted in yellow that adorned the car when it was removed from service. On December 12, 1988, it was moved to the Denver Federal Center. In 1990, the Club formed the Rocky Mountain Historical Foundation, a 501(c)(3) corporation, to enable tax deductible donations to be made for the restoration of car 25. This project was established to preserve, restore and eventually operate car 25, the last fully intact survivor of Denver's once vast 300-mile electric railway system.

Most of the work is being performed by volunteers with donations of funds and materials from members and local businesses. More than 11,000 volunteer hours have been performed on this project so far with many more needed to complete the restoration

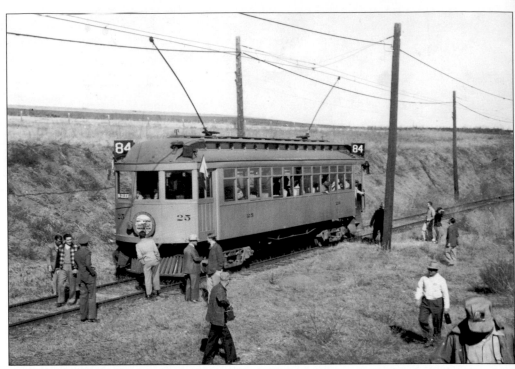

May 18, 1952 – Club excursion using D&IM car 25 from Denver to Golden and return.
**N. R. MILLER PHOTO – KLINGER COLLECTION**

March 15, 1953 – D&IM car 25 is shown in the Duvall Davison Lumber yard at Golden after its final movement and prior to its relocation to the Colorado Railroad Museum. **R. H. KINDIG PHOTO**

work. The work performed to date include, but is not limited to, repairing wood rot on the exterior of the car, new wood siding, a new canvas, roof, replacement of rattan seats and all windows, refabrication of window shades and interior lights and much electrical work. A new roof walk was constructed, the pilots rebuilt on the front and rear as well as removal, stripping and revarnishing of all interior oak woodwork. The exterior was stripped and repainted the original dark green color that was on the car when delivered in 1911.

# Index

It would not be possible to index all the persons, places and events contained in this history. However, the following lists major excursions, locomotives used by the Club, persons who had a significant role or influence and other activities that the author believes are important to identify. In some cases, the page referenced for a person may be that person's first appearance in the history, but subsequent pages not listed in the index will also contain other information about that person.

This index was prepared by Roger Sherman, whose meticulous attention to detail has resulted in a thorough cross-reference of information.

**(Bold** type indicates a **photo.)**

Marlboro Train: 121, 123.
Mason, Steve: 135, 136, 139, 141, 142, **146**.
Matthews, C. L.: 36, **49**.
Max, Charles: 42, 80, 81, 82, 83, 124.
Maxwell, John: 8, 13, 14, **17**, 19, **23**, 35, 36, 37, 42, 58, 123.
McAllister, Ralph: 117; 3-inch scale railroad: 84, 86, **92**, 94.
McClure, Ralph: 18.
McCormick, Steve: 95.
McFadden, Bryant: 93, 97.
McKee, Faye: 63.
McKee, Ted: 63, 64, 66, 67, 69, 79.
McKinney, Alexis: 88.
McSpadden, R. W. "Mac": 120, 121.
Melcher, Newell: 140.
Mid-Continent Chapter, National Railway Historical Society: 59, 137, 138.
Midland Terminal Railway: 71, 127, **149**, 161; Steam Locomotive: 2-8-0: #59: **18**, 22, **26**.
Miller, Neal: 8, 35, **49**, 86, 126, 141.
Miner, Frend John: 136, 139, 141, 163.
Minnich, Fran: 135, 136, 139.
Minnich, Joe: 104, 139.
*Model Railroader*: 139.
*Moffat Road, The*: 60.
Mocilac, Gus: 165.
Morgan, David P.: 63, 66.
Morgan, Stan: 114.
Moriarty, Jerre: 139.
Morison, Emma: 101, 104, 114.
Morison, Jack: 7, 40, 59, 65, 95, 101, 103, 105, 107, 114, 119.
Mt. Blanca and Western Railroad: 36, **37**.
"Mr. Nut": 29.
"Mudhens and Sport Models": 58.
Nall, Bruce: 124, 127, 135, 136, 138, 139, 141.
Narrow Gauge Circle: 118, 159.
Narrow Gauge Motel: 17, **51**, 160, 161.
Narrow Gauge Museum: 36.
*Narrow Gauge News*: 37.
National Model Railroad Association: 60, 87.
National Railway Historical Society: 9, 35.
National Register of Historic Places: 9, 135, 136, 138, 139, 163.
Ness, Howard: 13.
Nevada State Railroad Museum: 97.
*New Ways to Run Railroads* (Alco Products): 70.
*New York Times*: 69.
Noel, Dr. Tom: 140.
North Jersey Recording Associates: 43.
O'Hanlon, Herb: 19, 29, 31, 34, 36, 63, 64, 88.
Orange Empire Railway Museum: 166.
Overton, Richard: 9, 60.
Parkhurst, Ron: 71.
Patrick, Mel: 85.
PCC: see Electric Railways Presidents' Conference Committee.
Perry, Otto C.: 8, 11, 12, 13, 14, 15, 18, **23**, 29, 35, 36, 69, 79; Films: 6, 34, 36, 80, 87, 93, 95, 96, 97, 116, 118, 157, 159.
Peterson, Dan: 18, 37, 40, 44, 45, 58, 89, 98, 116.
Pfeifer, Jack: 9, 20, 127.
"Photo Stop 1947": **156** .
*Pictorial Supplement to Denver South Park & Pacific*: 8, 40, 42, 44, 45, 46, 57, 59, 60, 93, 123, 157. Abridged: 103, 157.
Pikes Peak Historical Street Railway Foundation: 9, 120, 138, 165, 166.
Platte Valley Trolley: 113, **114**, 115.
Pool, G. W.: 127.

Poor, M. C. "Mac": 6, 8, 9, **17**, 20, 37, 39, 40, 42, 43, 44, 45, 58, 65, 82, 93, 116.
Powder River Coal Basin: 128, **133**.
Powell, Chuck: 118, 127.
"Preserved Rail Heritage Tour" 1987: 105.
Princess Cruise Lines: 121.
Priselac, Joe: 113, 114, 115, 117, 159.
Public Service Company of Colorado: Fairmont Model M-9-G Track Motor Car: 165.
Rader Rail Car: 121, 123.
*Railfan's Refrain*: 61.
*Rails Around Gold Hill*: 39, 40, 41, 51, 157, 158.
Railway and Locomotive Historical Society: 113.
Ranniger, Jim: 87, 88, **94**, 95, 97, 99, 103, 119, 129.
Ranniger, Lil: 88, **94**, 119, 129.
Ranninger's Roadbed Commissary: 88, 89, 93, **94**, 95, 96, 98, 99, 100, 101, 102, 103, 104, 105, 108, 110, **111**, 115, 118, 119; "Silver Commissary": **111**.
Regional Transportation District (RTD): Light Rail: 83, 118, 119, 122, 125, 135; Light Rail Car: #113: **146**.
Reich, Neal: 7, 93, 94, 95, 97.
Richardson, Robert W.: 6, 9, 17, 37, 39, 44, 45, 86, 88, 115, 127, 161.
Ridgway Museum, The: 9.
Riley, Bob: 57.
Riley, Jack: **17**, 58, 88, 116.
Rio Grande Southern Railroad: Bankruptcy: 33, 35; Equipment: Business Cars: #B20 "Edna": 18, 19, **27**, 33, 35; #021 "Rico": 9, 35, 96, 161, **163**; "Montezuma": 164; Cabooses: #0400: 19; #0403: 14; Coach: #311: 19; Goose #3: **13**, 14; #4: **13**, 14, 19, **26**; #5: 14; #6: 19, 93; #7: 93; Steam Locomotives: 4-6-0: #20: 9, 14, **15**, 16, **23**, 33, 35, **37**, 107, **160**, **161**; 2-8-0: #74 19, **26**, **27**, **33**, **49**; Trips: **14**, **15**, 16, 19, **23**, **24**, **26**, **33**, **49**, 108; Videos: 159.
"Rivers of Silver, Ribbons of Steel": 85.
Rizzari, Francis: 36, 37, 125.
*Rocky Mountain Rail Fan*: 13.
*Rocky Mountain Rail Report*: See Rocky Mountain Railroad Club Newsletter.
*Rocky Mountain Railroader*: 11.
Rocky Mountain Railroad Club: Annual Dinner: 16, 22, 29, 34, 36, 37, 38, 39, 40, 41, 42, 43, 45, 57, 58, 59, 61, 65, 68, 70, 71, 82, 84, 85, 86, 87, 89, 90, 93, 95, 97, 99, 101, 102, 104, 106, 107, 110, 114, 115, 116, 118, 120, 121, 122, 124, 126, 129, 136, 137, 140, 143, 159; Picnic: 30, 31, 34, 35, 44, 59, 66, 84, 89, 114, 115, 116, 137, **139**, 142; Bylaws: 31, 39, 144; Drumhead: 14, **41**, **155**; Eastern Division: 31, 32, 33, 36, 37, 38, 39, 40, 42, **50**; Equipment: Track Motor Car: 117, 165; D&IM #25: 9, 10, **31**, **33**, 34, 35, 36, 37, 41, 44, 45, **49**, 90, 108, **109**, 113, 114, 116, 117, 122, 124, 125, 126, 127, 128, **133**, **134**, 135, 136, 137, 141, **143**, **146**, 169, **170**; Ft. Collins Birney #22: 9, 36, 45, 46, 62, 90, 100, 120, 122, 124, 138, 143, **165**; D&RGW Narrow Gauge Caboose #0578: 9, 33, 37, 41, 44, 45, 90, 137, 138, 139, **162**; PCC Car #3101: 9, 71, 72, 90, 122, **166**; RGS Business Car #021 "Rico": 9, 35, 36, 37, 41, 44, 45, 82, 84, 90, 96, 118, 127, 142, 144, **163**; Locomotives: Live Steam: 4-4-0 #999: **168**; 4-4-0 #210: 168; 2-6-0 #4: 71, 169; Narrow Gauge RGS 4-6-0 #20: 35, 36, **37**, 40, 45, 66, 67, 90, 98, 107, 108, 127, 128, **133**, 135, 136, 138, 142, **144**, **149**, **150**, **155**, **160**, **161**; Equipment Committee: 10, 55, 129, 136, 138, 141; Equipment Restoration Fund: 43, 64, 115; Film and Video Library: 69, 80, 96, 116, 139; Logotype: 14, **21**; Mission Statement: 10; Paralleling with Foundation: 137, 138, 144; Newsletter: 9, 11, 13, 18, 40, 42, 44, 59, 64, 66, 67, **71**, 97, 98, 99, 106, 123, 125, 127, 136, 137, 140; Annual Book Drawing: 86; Policy Book: 136; Roster: 18, 22, 62, 90, 142; "Video Potpouri": 120; Strategic Planning: 135; Website: 123; WHQ (World Headquarters): 122, 139.

Publications / Memorabilia

Equipment

Index

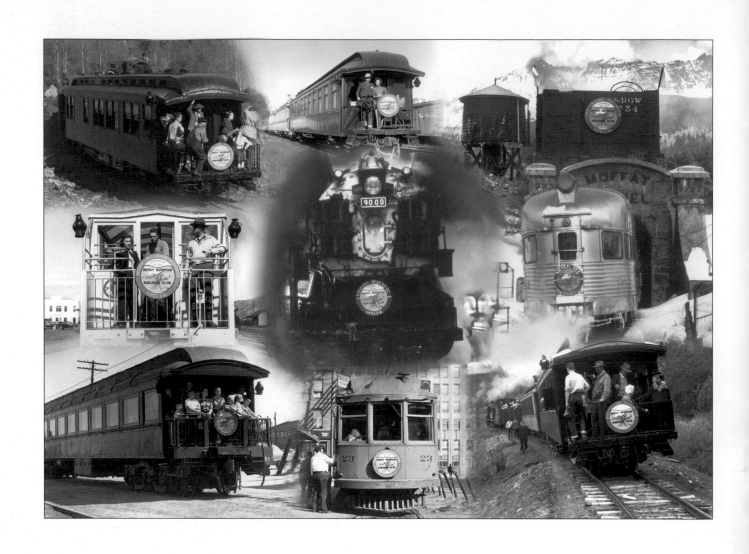

# The End